M000279315

The Big O

The Big O

An empowering guide to loving, dating and f*cking

Oloni

HarperCollins*Publishers*

A note on language: I have used the preferred language and terminology of all communities discussed within the book at the time of writing.

In order to protect people's privacy, pseudonyms have been used throughout the book when describing personal anecdotes and stories, both of my own and those of my contributors. Other personal details have also been changed.

This book contains sexual content that may not be suitable for younger readers.

HarperCollins*Publishers*
1 London Bridge Street
London SE1 9GF
www.harpercollins.co.uk

HarperCollins*Publishers*
1st Floor, Watermarque Building, Ringsend Road
Dublin 4, Ireland

First published by HarperCollins*Publishers* 2022
10 9 8 7 6 5 4 3 2 1

The author of this work is not a registered sex or relationships therapist but has made every effort to ensure that the information contained in this book is as accurate and up-to-date as possible at the time of publication. Medical and pharmaceutical knowledge is constantly changing and the application of it to particular circumstances depends on many factors, therefore it is recommended that readers always consult a qualified specialist for individual advice. This book should not be used as an alternative to seeking specialist medical advice which should be sought before any action is taken. The author and publishers cannot be held responsible for any errors and omissions that may be found in the text, or any actions that may be taken by a reader as a result of any reliance on the information contained in the text which is taken entirely at the reader's own risk.

While every effort has been made to trace the owners of copyright material reproduced herein and secure permissions, the publishers would like to apologise for any omissions and will be pleased to incorporate missing acknowledgements in any future edition of this book.

A catalogue record of this book is available from the British Library

ISBN 978-0-00-852413-5

TPB ISBN 978-0-00-852414-2

Printed and bound in the UK using 100% renewable electricity at CPI Group (UK) Ltd

This book is produced from independently certified FSC™ paper to ensure responsible forest management.

For more information visit: www.harpercollins.co.uk/green

To the women who refuse to let society dictate what they should and shouldn't do with their bodies.

Contents

Introduction: Let's Talk About Sex

The career that I have today talking about sex was an accident. A fortunate accident, but an accident nonetheless.

I was in my early twenties, had just graduated from studying journalism and was struggling to get some work experience. Month after month, I met with what were quite clearly copied-and-pasted rejection emails from magazines. But the one that stood out to me was from *Cosmopolitan.*

As someone who was always talking, thinking and writing about relationships, love and dating, it just made sense for me to want to be at *Cosmopolitan.* When you think of sex and you think of magazines, *Cosmo* comes to mind, right? You see, I too had '355 Ways to Sexually Satisfy Your Man in the Bedroom' (sometimes without him even being there!). I could absolutely identify '55 Ways of Telling Whether That Guy You Swiped Right on Will Be Good in Bed'. I had all of my headlines planned, so why wouldn't *Cosmo* want me? I was perfect for them!

My boyfriend had just broken up with me and, well, to be honest this just left me *more* inspired in my search for something that would empower me and make me happy. In some ways I miss being in my early twenties. I wasn't afraid to make crazy decisions for my career. So one afternoon I decided to go and squat in the offices of Hearst Magazines and not leave until I got what I wanted.

I took my portfolio and résumé with me down to Oxford Street in Central London where I ran to a food store and bought a hamper full of biscuits, cakes and other treats. I then circled my way back to the Hearst buildings, the home of all your favourite magazine publications. As soon as I arrived I told the person behind the desk that I wanted to see someone from *Cosmopolitan.* He asked if I had a meeting scheduled, to which I replied no but I'd sit and wait till someone came down to see me. He tried to convince me to leave, explaining that no one was available and that I should try coming back with an appointment. Poor guy didn't realise who he was dealing with!

Oh, they're not coming down, you say? Well, they're not going to sleep inside there, right? I held firm. After hours and hours of waiting, a drained battery and a frazzled security guard who was getting more and more suspicious of my intentions, the editor's assistant at *Cosmopolitan* came down. Impressed with how committed I was, she gave me work experience on the spot.

I was in! I was going to write for *Cosmopolitan*! My self-belief had paid off. It felt like a huge success. But then something happened that I didn't anticipate. As I spent more time in the magazine world, it became clear to me that my sexual experiences weren't the ones that I was reading about online or in print. Much as I had grown up loving these publications, I realised that I just didn't see much of myself there. So I continued to consistently blog about my journey.

Almost immediately, I started getting women emailing me for relationship advice and I realised I must be on to something. After a while, I even got a spare SIM card so women could speak to me on the phone (and some men too!). The dilemmas they sent me weren't always that different from each other either. Patterns started to emerge: cheating partners, unhappy sex lives, culture clashes, being afraid to come out. Over the years I've spoken to many of you about these subjects and more. There's no sex dilemma that shocks me today – I've genuinely heard it all.

- 'When do I introduce my boyfriend to my kinks and fetishes?'
- 'How do I tell my sexual partner I have herpes?'
- 'I don't know if I'll ever be able to orgasm.'

What dawned on me was how few places people had to go to actually talk about these issues. And the opportunities to hear people speak about them openly and honestly were few and far between. I realised I wanted to do more than write articles of tips for readers; I wanted to really *speak* to people. I wanted to connect with them, empathise with them, tell my own relatable stories, give direct advice.

I was going to build myself a career talking and educating people about sexual pleasure.

Sex, sex, sex

Why do we need to talk about sex? The truth is we do talk about it. A LOT. As a society it's clear that sex will always be a subject that grabs our attention, whether we like it or not. It's why they say, 'Sex sells,' because it does. Think about the jokes we hear, the content we watch or even the gossip that makes that tea extra hot. Music artists have long understood that a music video is not a music video unless some ass is being thrown around in a circle as a video vixen twerks on a handstand. I grew up listening to the lyrics of 'Doin' It' by LL Cool J (which, might I add, also promotes safe sex), and I stayed up to watch MTV's uncensored version of raunchy music videos, singing along to Jodeci's 'Freek'n You'. These Nineties classics are great for your sex playlists, but they also make you believe that cisgender, heterosexual women (i.e. women whose gender identity matches their birth sex and who are attracted to the opposite sex) are benefiting from sex all the time. Don't get me wrong, the music was and is amazing. And what straight or bisexual woman doesn't enjoy watching LL lick his lips repeatedly? What I'm getting at, though, is that sex in our culture and society is a huge thing, but real-life conversations about pleasure are still not.

Sex is part of all of our lives, whether we're having it regularly or not. Really, the question shouldn't be 'Why do we need to talk about sex?' but 'Why *aren't* we talking about sex more openly?'

We have serious conversations about other aspects of our lives, such as our career, our health, our family – you name it. But as soon as the topic of sex comes up, we get awkward, embarrassed or start sniggering. As a result, we're nowhere near as educated as a society as we should be. Sex is a very important topic, yet we've allowed myths, religion and culture to push us away from talking about a subject that quite literally shapes our future and brings us pleasure.

And guess what? It hasn't worked! We're still obsessed by sex. Instead of quelling our fascination, the attempt to shut down conversations about sex have only whetted our appetites. Only now, we're going in armed with misinformation, shame, ignorance and misogyny.

The conversation that we end up with isn't around sexual health or happiness. It's male-centred and heteronormative (i.e. it presents heterosexuality as the norm). We all know how sperm travels to an egg, we understand that if blood rushes to a penis it becomes erect, we even understand what male ejaculation looks like. But how many people could even point out the clitoris on a diagram (let alone find it in real life)?!

Our odd relationship with sex is part of the reason why some women are afraid to leave an unfulfilling relationship, out of fear that the number of men she has slept with will increase and make her look 'used'. We're still being taught that body count over-rides happiness. In some cases we've even used abstinence as a replacement for sex education, when studies have shown that abstinence-only education not only doesn't stop teenagers from getting pregnant, it actually leads to more teen pregnancies.

And what about a sex education that includes the LGBTQ+ community and their pleasure? Imagine that! You probably can't. For most of us, our sex education was so fixated on heterosexual reproductive sex that it barely left room for people with diverse experiences or gave us the opportunity to learn about what different sexualities look like. But one-sided education on a topic isn't education, it's exclusion and erasure.

While having the internet has made it easier than ever to access information, it hasn't always provided the tools for us to know how to sift through that information and sort out fact from fiction. Why else do you have people out there believing you can't get an STI from oral sex or that pornography emulates real-life sex?!

Talking about sex on a biological, emotional and physical level are all vital. It helps us not only to understand how our bodies work, but also to become comfortable with them. We become empowered when we make what feel like the right sexual decisions in our life. When we're properly educated, we recognise what feels and looks normal in relationships, romantic or casual. And we start to recognise what feels and looks good to us as well.

Growing up, I saw women (I am women, btw) use sex as a form of validation from men, or as a tool to make him stay in a relationship. While some of us have unlearned that, there are elements of those messages that still linger and I notice it in the conversations I have with women, day in, day out.

On the flip side, I can't tell you the number of times I've been stopped at social functions, in restaurant bathrooms or just randomly out and about by women wanting to express how grateful they are for my work. I know from the feedback I get that I have helped many women take charge of their sexuality and empowered them to have better sex and the much-needed conversations with their sexual partner that they were once too scared or shy to have. Those encounters show me that women are redefining what sex means to them, and that is powerful.

The birds and the bees

I was never given the 'talk' from my parents. I barely understood what was going on with my body during puberty. I'm going to tell you about my own background and talk to other people about their upbringings later in this book. But while I think it's important to acknowledge the damage that secrecy and misinformation about sex can do, I don't want to dwell too much on what the generation before us did wrong. Better to focus on what this generation can do right.

I really believe the attitude is there, and the appetite. I know too well from my followers that women are ready to shake off this negativity and shame and to start claiming their sexuality fully and proudly.

But we are up against it here. For all that WE might be ready, there are still hurdles to get over. There are still people who believe we shouldn't be talking about it. Sex education isn't nearly comprehensive enough and there are plenty who would rather keep it hush-hush altogether.

It's time to change that. And in order to change it, we have to talk about it! And that's precisely what I want to do with this book. *The Big O* answers all your mind-boggling sex questions and helps women have better sex — the type of sex that makes you want to be a co-host on my podcast *Laid Bare* so you get to answer our very first question (if you know, you know!). This book is here to give you the sexual-pleasure education you deserve and which you have been denied for so long. It shares never-before-told stories of mine, unseen 'hoe' and sugar-baby entries from other women and important sexual-history facts that have shaped our relationship with, and understanding of, sex.

If you thought you were having bad, OK or good sex before, *The Big O* will show you how to have amazing sex. We'll discuss different styles of self-pleasure, how to gain confidence in the bedroom, how to express how you want to be touched and how to increase your chances of orgasm with a partner, and take a look at different cultures and their sex secrets.

Not only that, this book will show you just how much of a sexual babe you are! It will remind you over and over how deserving you are of pleasure, sexual intimacy and desire, and never to settle for less in the bedroom. The pages in this book will give you the tips that you need to help enhance both you and your partner's sex lives. It'll debunk myths, challenge societal norms and show you what good sex and consent looks like.

How do I know I'm going to do all this? Because I have the unique privilege of knowing what women *really* want to know about. It's not conjecture, it's not based on some anonymous market-research survey; it comes directly from you. The insight I have into the reality of other people's sex lives is something I can confidently say companies would pay big bucks to have access to!

As a result, I've helped thousands of women improve their sex and dating lives, become the ambassador and spokesperson of a top retail adult store, and have continuously created content around sex, love and dating for over ten years, which has repeatedly gone viral and created wider conversations between intimate partners and friends.

I have been the beginner of trends, the curator of wild sexcapade stories and an agony aunt. I'm the big sister you turn to when wanting to get over a guy and the friend you ask for sex advice when you're trying to get under one. I've been the reason behind people getting married and finding the love of their lives and also the cheerleader for someone trying their first ever sex toy. It's fair to say I know my shit and have done for a very long time.

With *The Big O* I'm finally able to put it all in one place and give you something you can keep, share and refer back to whenever you need to. I genuinely feel so grateful for everything you have shared with me over the years, for the relationship I've been able to build with my readers and listeners, and it's been an absolute pleasure to write this book for you.

The first time I ever created a thread on Twitter about women's real-life sexual experiences, I just knew I was on the verge of something big. As I sat there typing out the word 'Ladies' for the very first time, I felt a swell of excitement. Somehow I just knew how much noise it'd make.

Now what you're holding, my dear reader, is bigger than any thread I have ever shared, any dating challenge I have ever orchestrated or any podcast episode I have ever released. I am so excited to finally introduce you to ... *The Big O*!

A note on language

The title of this book, *The Big O*, alludes, as you have probably guessed, to orgasms. In particular, it refers to the pleasure gap between cisgender women and men in opposite-sex couples. This disparity in the amount of sexual pleasure — and especially the number of orgasms — experienced between these two groups of people is a large part of what inspires my work. It is also one of the key themes of this book. Because of this, the majority of the language I use throughout this book will be describing their experiences.

That is not to say that my content isn't also useful to those who are LGBTQ+, it's just that, for the most part, the research I'm citing has predominantly been done on straight cis folks. And this also reflects the majority of my audience. While it is certainly possible to extrapolate on some LGBTQ+ aspects, I don't think it would be fair or indeed accurate to claim that this book speaks equally to those experiences. There are key differences in the ways LGBTQ+ people experience sex and relationships and, while it was important to me to include discussions of some of these, I won't be addressing them in depth.

However, I have endeavoured to differentiate when I am talking about gender, and when I am talking about anatomy. So when I say 'women' I am, for the most part, talking about all women, regardless of what sex they were assigned at birth. When I'm talking about people with vulvas, I try to make that clear too.

My main aim with this book, though, was to connect with my audience, just as I do on social media and on my podcast. Let's be real, I was not about to turn this into a textbook. So while I am always about challenging assumptions and breaking down toxic ideas about sex, gender and relationships, it was also important to me to write in a way that readers would recognise, understand and relate to.

CHAPTER 1

My Sex Education

My mum took them away from me at 14. She didn't believe I needed them. Condoms, I mean. They were given to me in secondary school by a sexual health company, which made regular visits to local schools in the borough.

They were cheap branded condoms, which had an expiry date you could barely make out on the back of them. We got three varieties: ribbed, regular and flavoured.

Their aim was to educate teenagers about sex, but they were no better than Coach Carr from *Mean Girls*. You know, that infamous scene where he says: 'Don't have sex, because you will get pregnant and die! Don't have sex in the missionary position, don't have sex standing up, just don't do it, OK. Promise?'

The school's aim was clearly to scare the shit out of us with all the possible STIs we could be at risk of getting, and for some it worked, but for others it just made us more inquisitive about the subject of sex. I mean, let's be real: you tell a bunch of teenagers not to do something and are they really going to listen?

I also signed up to look after a lifelike baby doll over one weekend. My secondary school used it as a project to help deter young girls from falling pregnant. We had a dummy that was attached to our wrist and we would have to tend to the doll for 10–15 minutes whenever it would randomly cry during the day or in the middle of the night. The teachers who assigned the task were able to see how often the doll was left to cry and how well it was looked after. I only did it because it seemed fun and an excuse to get out of doing other homework, but after the first night of no sleep I was ready to rip the mouthpiece off my wrist and remove the batteries from the 'baby's' back! I'd had enough! What's interesting is that there are studies which show that the baby doll schemes don't lower the rates of teen pregnancies.[1,2] Either way, I was so glad when I returned it back to my teacher the following Monday morning.

There was no sex education between my mum and me. I don't think she ever had one growing up either, aside from the biology. The topic didn't need to be touched on in my household as we were children of God and sex before marriage was simply a sin. No ifs, no buts. It was a sin.

'But, Oloni, what do your parents think about what you do?' – one of the most common questions I'm asked as a Nigerian woman from a strict Christian background.

It's not a bad question either. After all, even though Nigerians have a tremendous amount of sex, it's never spoken about in our community. We're taught that sex is not for pleasure **unless you're a man** but for procreation between married couples only. Clearly, in reality Nigerians are having a lot of sex and like to fuck, just like everybody else. People are just pretenders.

When I was a kid, I asked my mum where babies came from; she explained that they came from God.

... God.

OK, yeah, sure, Mum.

I knew there was more to it, but how could I argue? She was a very Nigerian mother. Whatever she said was gospel, whether I wanted to believe it or not. If children never spoke in school playgrounds about sex, I'd probably still believe her.

It's not my mum's fault. She wasn't taught about this stuff and she definitely wasn't taught how to talk about it. But I intend to break that cycle. Even if we weren't brought up talking about this stuff, we can learn. And we can make sure that our friends and siblings and younger cousins and even children grow up with a healthier attitude towards their bodies and towards sexual pleasure.

I don't believe anyone raising kids wants to put them at risk. I believe most people want their children to be healthy, happy and to be able to make good choices for themselves. But unfortunately, so many of our parents and teachers were raised in sex-negative societies, communities and families themselves – what else can they do but pass it on?

'So how have you got away with talking about sex, Oloni?' – I know, right? And I don't just talk about sex on social media either; I also put on consent workshops for school kids, guest speak at sex events, talk on TV and on my podcast and now you're reading a book by me about orgasms!

Look, I'll be honest, my very Nigerian parents had to warm up to the idea of me writing about sexuality. I think a turning point was after they saw me win an award for my blog in 2015. They saw how happy I was doing what I loved, and they could see that I was good at it. One thing I love about my mum, even in all her Nigerianness, is that she has always supported me doing what makes me happy and celebrated all my wins. Oh, and also, I have a younger sister who's a doctor so that kind of got me off the hook a bit. So one out of two daughters on the straight and narrow — that's not too bad, is it? (She read this bit and told me to stop with the self-deprecating jokes, but would I be from London without them?)

I will say my mother genuinely enjoys hearing about the dating stories and romance aspects of what I do. I can't see myself sitting down with her anytime soon to discuss the female orgasm gap, but then again, who knows? When it comes to openness around sex, I've come a long way from my upbringing.

When I was growing up there were three things my mother did want for me: to learn to cook, to go to university and to find a husband. If I managed all three, the message seemed to be, I would have fully graduated as a functional adult.

Even though I grew up with Christian beliefs, I always knew I wasn't going to wait till marriage before having sex. I did purposely wait to be in a committed relationship, though, because I saw that as a safety net. I believed it would keep me from being hurt, because whoever had chosen to be with me would be incapable of hurting me. How silly, right? Monogamy, or any sort of relationship for that matter, is never a guarantee that you won't get hurt by someone. It's also way too much responsibility to put onto another human being. It was in that short-term relationship that I learned my first lesson on love – never to allow your happiness to depend on a man.

Back in 1998 when I was still in primary school I'd already had a warning for misbehaving from my favourite teacher. I couldn't tell you what I'd done prior, I just know I was walking on thin ice if I didn't stay out of trouble. My parents eventually got another phone call and were told to pick me up from school. They were also told I'd not be going to the class group trip to the beach. What was my offence, you ask? Saying the word 'lesbian'. I laugh today, because I realise just how ridiculous it was, but at seven or eight years old I was shitting myself that I'd be disciplined for saying a word to a classmate. Now, I don't know if I asked if someone was a lesbian or whether I was just excited about a new word I'd just learned, but either way, my classmate quickly ratted me out. I kissed that beach trip goodbye and my mum picked me up from school early that afternoon. My bed was the first thing I ran to, and I remember sleeping the whole day after, fearing that I'd be punished by my dad for saying this word that was clearly forbidden.

I don't blame my mum for not sticking up for me (she doesn't even remember this story when I bring it up). She was so used to me being told off, and remember, she never had the best sex education growing up, especially as she was raised in a strict Muslim household. And until I was 13, talking about LGBTQ+ experiences and issues in school was illegal under Section 28 in England. But I still think this was a pretty shocking way to handle it. It really gives you a sense of the restrictive attitudes many of us grew up with, and that are still indoctrinated in most societies.

Listen, sex and relationship education is complicated. If I'm really honest, I'm not sure it's even possible to deliver all the information and all the nuance that comes with it in the limited time slots that teachers have to do so. But the fact that I and so many other people left school without properly understanding our own anatomy – that I find unforgivable. Science teachers had us dissecting frogs in class, but they let boys leave school not knowing that women pee and menstruate from different holes.

I'm not saying we need to swallow a medical textbook before having sex for the first time, but a little bit of knowledge wouldn't hurt. We might learn the words 'penis' and 'vagina' at school, but beyond that, forget it. I lose count of the number of people I hear confusing their vulva with their vagina and not knowing the correct name for their labia. We talk about men not knowing where the clitoris is, but to be completely fair, how would they? Most of us aren't taught the first thing about what our genitals look like or how they work, and we're going into our intimate encounters just sort of hoping we'll magically figure it out. As a sex educator, I really believe that accurate information about how our bodies work is the foundation of good sex. But few of us actually get that. So let me take the opportunity to change that right here and now.

Anatomy lesson

Vulva, not vagina

This is a mistake people make all the time. The word 'vagina' actually just refers to the muscular canal inside your body that leads up to the cervix. The vulva is the name for the area outside your body, which includes the labia majora and labia minora (aka your inner and outer pussy lips), the opening to the urethra, where you pee out of, as well as the clitoral hood (the layer of skin that covers the clit) and the glans clitoris itself. This is the little 'nub' at the top of your vulva that most people think of when they think of the clit, but actually what you see or feel on the outside is really only the head of a much larger organ.

Your clitoris is like an iceberg

For a long time, our understanding of the clitoris was pretty limited. Until very recently, many medical textbooks didn't show the clitoris on diagrams at all, or, if they did, there was no information about the nerves or internal structure.[3] I guess because the clit isn't involved in reproduction it just wasn't considered relevant?! But seriously, can you imagine a world in which such ignorance about the penis was considered OK?

Anyway, things started to change in 2005 when Australian urologist Helen O'Connell published her extensive research, revealing the full anatomy of the clit. It turned out it was about ten times the size that people had previously believed and most of it was *inside* the body.

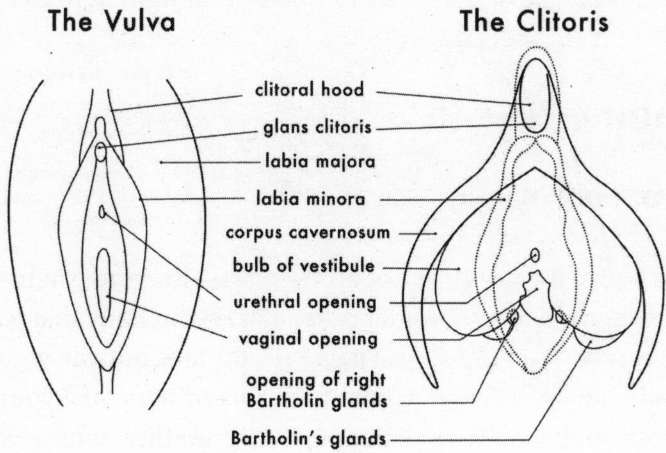

Shaped something like a wishbone, the internal clitoris extends back into the body and actually straddles both the urethra and the vagina. The bulbs of erectile tissue on either side become engorged during arousal. Meanwhile the glans itself has an extremely high density of nerve endings, making it one of the most sensitive organs in the body.[4]

The multi-tasking penis

Usually when we refer to the penis we're just talking about the shaft and the head. But the penis has internal parts too, erectile tissue that extends back into the body. Hanging below the penis is the scrotum, which contains the testicles, aka the balls.

The head of the penis is called the glans (like the clit!) and if the guy hasn't been circumcised he will have a foreskin covering it (just like the clitoral hood covers the clit!). At the very tip of the penis is the urethral opening.

The penis has various jobs. It receives sensation, it penetrates during sex, it ejaculates and it urinates.

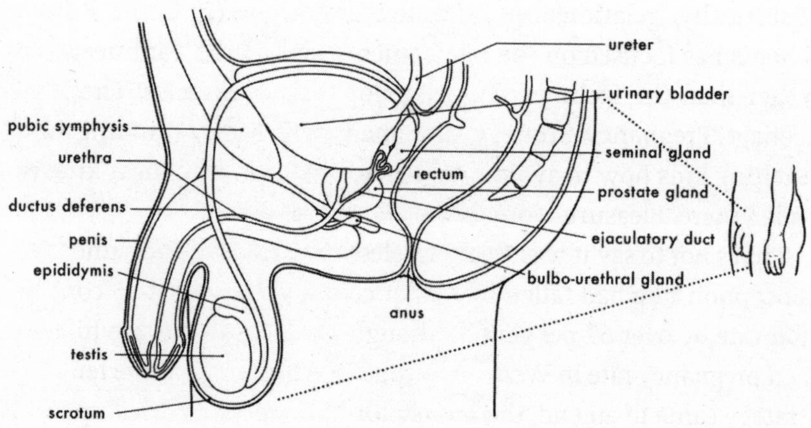

Same origins but different levels of importance

Did you know that, to begin with, all foetuses' genitals look the same? That's right, we all start out with the same parts and it's not until about six or seven weeks in that they start to organise themselves into different configurations. So even though the final result looks very different, they actually have quite a lot of similarities. There's also a small section of the population who are born with primary sex characteristics that don't neatly fit into social assumptions of what constitutes male or female.

Both male and female genitalia have a highly sensitive organ to which blood flows during sexual arousal – the clitoris and the penis. In fact, they develop out of the same genital tissue. So it's kind of mad that so much of our sex education and culture is dick-centred. Now, I already told you that the penis has multiple functions and of course it makes sense to teach people about those. By contrast, the clit is built *entirely* for pleasure. Literally its only job is to receive and transmit sensation. Honestly, how are we teaching sex education and not mentioning that??

I'm confident that my experience at school was pretty typical. Historically, relationships and sex education (RSE) in British schools has focused on the mechanics of sex and on contraception rather than the feelings, sensations or social dynamics. The 1999 Teenage Pregnancy Strategy ploughed government funding into teaching kids how to avoid pregnancy, but for most of us it kind of ended there. Pleasure? Forget it.

That's not to say it was totally useless. By 2018 England's under-18 conception rate had fallen by 62 per cent and the under-16 conception rate by over 65 per cent,[5] although the UK still has the highest teen pregnancy rate in Western Europe.[6] Furthermore, as the ten-year strategy came to an end, the money for RSE provision dried up. And successive cuts to local governments caused it to drop down the list of priorities, which means that, despite the availability of some fantastic independent sex educators and training providers, many schools remain stuck in the condoms-on-cucumbers rut of the late Nineties.

A 2018 poll of 16- and 17-year-olds by the Sex Education Forum and the National Education Union showed that 52 per cent of pupils thought more time should be spent on RSE and 34 per cent wanted the subject to be treated more seriously. Socially and legally, a lot has changed since I was at school. We now have same-sex marriage, and sexual orientation and gender identity (under the language of 'gender reassignment') are protected characteristics under the 2010 Equality Act, yet 22 per cent of teenagers surveyed said they did not learn anything about LGBTQ+ issues in RSE, 27 per cent said they did not learn about pornography and 30 per cent said there was little information on sexual pleasure.[7]

In September 2020, RSE became mandatory in all secondary schools in England. Sounds like progress, right? Hmmm ... not entirely. The new guidelines do mention subjects like consent and identifying healthy relationships, and touches on the fact that porn is not representative of real-world sex. The curriculum highlights the importance of including LGBTQ+ people and says that 'there should be an equal opportunity to explore the features of stable and healthy same-sex relationships'. It also pays lip service to the idea that physical, emotional, mental, sexual and reproductive health and wellbeing are interconnected.[8] But how these lessons will manifest will depend on the available resources. And, if you ask me, it still leaves a lot of room for interpretation and the glossing-over of important aspects of sex – notably, pleasure.

In addition to all of this, my sex education never came from people who looked like me, so I often found it difficult to relate. This might not sound like a big deal and I'm sure there are people for whom it wasn't an issue, but for me the white-washing of standardised sex education made it really difficult to connect with it. It's not just me, either. Much has been written on how kids from Black, Asian and minority ethnic (BAME) backgrounds frequently feel excluded from

RSE and unable to identify with the information given, and we know well that systemic inequalities can often lead to unequal sexual health outcomes even if and when they *do* access the services on offer.[9]

Nowadays, there are organisations working to address this, including the NAZ Project, South London's Love Sex Life project and the team at Decolonising Contraception. But when I was a kid it often just felt like this information wasn't *for* me.

The effects of porn on sex education

When I look back to some of my first sexual experiences, it's so clear to me that I didn't really have a clue. I was just imitating what I'd seen in the media and porn. I remember a time when my first proper boyfriend, Liam (you'll hear more about him in later chapters!), and I wanted some privacy, so he booked a hotel near my home. This was perfect as I always felt like I had to be careful with all the noises we were making. What happened next was important, because it showed me another reason why sex education is vital.

As we started to have sex I decided this was the time I would start imitating what I saw in porn. I screamed, like something out of xspunkyvideos.com. I thought that was what sex was meant to sound like. I made those theatrical noises sex workers are paid to make to add to a male-gaze fantasy. Liam couldn't help himself – he burst out laughing. If I was white, I would have turned red. He hugged me and we both laughed as we lay down. I want to say it was the last time I ever faked my moans, but it wasn't. For so long I believed that in order to enjoy intimacy, I had to put on a show.

It was also during my teenage years that streaming porn services really took off. In the early days of the internet, porn was something that loaded slowly, pixel by pixel, onto your screen, but by the mid 2000s you could access all kinds of videos in seconds. By 2005 internet porn was making around $2.5 billion (about £1.3 billion) annually.[10] The best-known of these streaming sites is arguably Pornhub, which launched in May 2007, just a month before the very first iPhone and the same year that Kim Kardashian's sex tape was leaked, garnering more than 93 million views worldwide.

My curiosity about sex and my almost total lack of education around it is what led to me hastily reducing the volume on the TV so no one could hear as I watched *Eurotrash*, or to my mum nearly catching me watching late-night Channel 4 'blue films' that I had no business watching as a kid in my bedroom. As soon as I heard my bedroom door open, I'd quickly pretend to be asleep, but I knew she knew. By 16 I was watching porn through LimeWire and other peer-to-peer file-sharing sites and then pretending I had no idea why the family computer had a virus. I saw it all, before truly understanding any of it: anal, orgies, interracial, gang bangs, viral videos that would make you throw up. I discovered a world I didn't know existed and, honestly, not all of it was good. But it did open my eyes to the possibilities sex offered.

I'm obviously not anti-porn, but I can't pretend it didn't have an impact on me growing up. The fake sex noises I made with Liam makes that clear. I cringe when I remember it now.

These days there's a lot more choice in what porn you watch. There are ethical production companies where the worker's rights are respected, they're properly paid and you can be sure nobody has been pressured into doing a scene they don't feel comfortable with. But we need more awareness and education around what porn is (a performance deliberately designed to get viewers off!) and what it isn't (a step-by-step guide to what real-life sex should look like!).

Racial sexualisation

As a Black woman it would be a huge oversight for me not to mention that Black girls and women are being routinely hypersexualised, fetishised and adultified from a really early age.

Even as kids, we are seen as 'grown up' due to how we look, and it is a really common experience. I remember when I was ten years old I was gifted this very pretty dark-blue top and trouser set for my birthday. I loved it so much. It came embellished with black feathers around the wrists and at the bottom of the trousers. Let me tell you, I felt like a real groovy chick when I put it on!

My parents had no issue with it but when my aunt came over from Nigeria for a holiday it was clear she felt differently. One day during her stay she said she wanted to go for a walk so I quickly got dressed and wore the matching set. I remember her giving me this deeply unimpressed look, the kind that Patience Ozokwor would save for her daughter-in-law. She said my clothes were meant for adults and that it was basically inappropriate. I remember feeling so insecure but not understanding why. What I saw as a fun and dramatic outfit, she clearly saw as sexual. That was the last time I wore it.

Unfortunately, this is very far from being a one-off. Black girls are constantly having their bodies policed and treated like adults, when they are very far from being so. This reminds me of a story that hit the headlines in March 2022 about a 15-year-old girl, named in the press as Child Q, who was strip-searched by police after the school falsely accused her of cannabis possession. No one contacted her parents and there were no other adults present when the two police officers searched her, including exposing her intimate body parts and forcing her to remove the sanitary towel she was wearing at the time.[11] Can you imagine this happening to a white 15-year-old?

Alongside this tendency to view Black girls as older than their years, society has also been taught that Black women have a greater appetite for sex, in comparison to white women who are seen as pure and demure (and more likely to be believed if they experience sexual violence).[12]

The hypersexualisation of Black women started way back when Europeans first travelled to Africa and saw how they lived. The lack of clothing, which was worn due to living in a very hot place (duh), their non-monogamous relationships and style of dancing made the Europeans believe that the women were sexually driven and were trying to seduce them.

Colonisers used dehumanising tropes to put Black people into reductive categories so as to bolster the idea that they were 'less civilised' and to somehow justify the slave trade. By the time of the Jim Crow segregation era in post-civil-war America, which lasted from the late nineteenth century into the mid twentieth century, there had emerged three racist 'characters' assigned to Black women. The first was the 'Mammy', a dark-skinned, usually larger-sized maid who was loyal to the white family she served. She cooked, she raised their kids, and (her captors told themselves) she was happy to do so. She was mostly seen as asexual, not needing any pleasures beyond the 'joy' of service.

Next there was the 'Sapphire' who was portrayed as the sharp-mouthed Black woman, known to be 'sassy' or 'feisty'. Finally, there was the 'Jezebel', a woman who uses her sexuality to lure in white men. This racist and sexist trope was particularly dangerous because it helped prop up the idea that Black women 'couldn't' be raped. It was used to push an agenda that justified sexual violence against Black women – 'She was asking for it.'

These tropes still follow Black women today and have been seen throughout every part of the media. Think about the majority of Black female characters on TV. Do they not embody the tropes I name above? Our stories are *still* constantly being told through the lens of white people, leaving no room for us to be our best multi-faceted selves.

And when we're not having our bodies policed and disrespected, we often find ourselves being fetishised. You might know the story of Saartjie (Sarah) Baartman, who was born in 1789 and became famous after she was forcibly exhibited as a freak show attraction. Baartman had steatopygia, which is an accumulation of a large amount of fat on the buttocks, resulting in her having a larger-than-average bottom half. She was brought over from Cape Town,

South Africa, to London in 1810 when she was 21 years old. As an 'exhibit' Sarah would wear next to nothing and walk around on stage and sing. For extra money, people could even touch her.[13]

It's fair to say not everyone thought this was entertaining. Baartman's shows attracted the attention of abolitionists, who found her treatment appalling and attempted to have her captors prosecuted. Her captors denied she was working against her will and Baartman herself actually testified that she was there out of choice. It's hard to know the truth. She herself was illiterate, her so-called 'employers' would have had a lot of power over her and it's doubtful she felt like she had many other choices.

In any case, she moved to Paris in 1815 where she continued to be displayed as a freak of nature before apparently being sold to an 'animal trainer'. Scientific racism abounded in France at the time and Baartman was pressured into being studied, observed and painted naked. Historians believe that she was almost certainly sold for sex during this time, with one biographer writing that she was 'literally treated like an animal'.[14]

In 1815, at the age of just 26, Baartman died from an inflammatory disease. But her degradation didn't end there. Her brain, skeleton and sexual organs remained on display in a Paris museum until 1974. Even after death, she was still fetishised and demeaned.

In the mid Nineties South Africa began its campaign to repatriate Baartman's remains, with newly elected president Nelson Mandela leading the request in 1994. It took another eight years but eventually, in 2002, Saartjie Baartman was returned to her home country, where she was finally laid to rest.

Her story seems like an extreme example but echoes of it still play out in the lives of Black women today. Black women are frequently seen as conquests, temptations and exotic delicacies by non-Black men. I've lost count of the number of times I've had a guy refer to me as a chocolate bar of some sort or been told 'I only have sex with Black women'. Why? As far as I'm concerned there's no answer to this that doesn't have undertones of fetishisation.

And for me it's never anything except a very uncomfortable moment that I wish would just stop.

If it's not our skin that's being fetishised, it's other aspects of our Blackness, from our bums to being told, unprovoked, that we have dick-sucking lips (DSLs).

Today we see women in hip-hop and pop celebrating their sexuality like never before – something men have been allowed to do for years with no objection because I guess they've been told it's their world and we're only here to add to the fantasy. Well, that narrative has indeed changed; the Nickis, Megs, Cardis and City Girls of the world are owning and celebrating being sexual as well as being the star of their own show, instead of just being fancy props for the male gaze. There's nothing wrong with either, if this is how you enjoy expressing your sexuality and as long as the woman has autonomy over the situation, but Black women should be able to own their narrative and have full say over when their bodies should be celebrated and desired.

I feel as though female rap has played a huge part in pushing female sexuality. It's getting the conservatives mad, but it's starting necessary conversations that we have been told to be quiet about – challenging the same attitudes that kept us from discussing our pleasure, discovering clitoral stimulation and being straight up in the bedroom. Their music is often criticised, but female artists talking about sex isn't new, there's just a politics of 'respectability' around it when it isn't said in cute and merely suggestive (rather than explicit) ways. It's not as if that music no longer exists, it does, but as someone who grew up listening to less sexual female artists in the Nineties, I believe it's the new rap ladies of today who have encouraged me to tap into my sexuality for my own enjoyment and not just when a man wants it.

CHAPTER 2

Society, Stigma and Slut-shaming

Alongside our family and community upbringing, the thing that has the most impact on how we understand sex is the society in which we live. Depending on your upbringing, you might be able to relate to the attitudes, experiences and childhood memories I described in Chapter 1, or you might not. But if you grew up in the UK, particularly in the Nineties and Noughties, you will almost certainly have been exposed to a lot of the same social norms as me, and the same broader cultural attitudes to sex.

Some accepted norms around sex in British culture include the expectation that most people want and have sex but that, in general, people's sex lives are private. We love a bit of sexual innuendo and making euphemistic jokes, but being open about the details of our sex lives is not considered appropriate. A lot of things are considered socially acceptable on a surface level, but you don't have to dig too far to find the stereotypical British prudishness. Obviously most of my followers and the people who interact with me on social media are women who *want* to talk about sex and *want* to hear other people's stories and escapades. But don't think for a minute that I don't also come under fire for 'oversharing'. I've lost count of the number of times people have told me the stuff I talk about is TMI or asked me why I feel the need to discuss it at all (you'd think my bio reading 'sex and relationships expert' would give it away!).

This is because, for all that we are starting to move towards a more sex-positive society, a lot of us are still held back by taboos and stigma.

Research shows that our sexual lifestyles in Britain have changed substantially in the past 60 years, and we are more liberated than we used to be,[1] but there are definitely still some bad attitudes hanging around. Plus, let's not forget that we are brought up by parents or carers whose own upbringing took place in a previous generation, so they may well be passing on old-fashioned or outdated views. And once we've internalised them, it's not always easy to just let go of those views, even if we think of ourselves as progressive and sex-positive.

What counts as a taboo?

A taboo is any behaviour, practice or even *topic of conversation* that is avoided, prohibited or restricted. Often taboos arise out of religious beliefs, but they can also be social and cultural. For example, eating pork is taboo in religions such as Judaism and Islam. In some countries, touching someone on the head or displaying the soles of your feet can be considered taboo. When it comes to sex, though, it's kind of the other way around – it's actually hard to think of examples of things that *aren't* considered somewhat taboo. We're making progress. Magazines and the media are filled with conversations and tips and honest discussions of sex. The very fact that I'm writing this book shows that sex is a lot less culturally taboo than it once was. But that doesn't mean it's not still a big taboo for lots of people in this country and around the world.

Taboos and stigma overlap in the sense that anyone who decides to ignore the taboo, to behave in a sexual way or talk about sexual subjects is likely to find themselves subject to social stigma (shout out to all my Twitter haters!).

Stigma is when we attach a negative value to a certain quality, circumstance or behaviour. Usually, the things we attach stigma to are things that are considered *outside of the norm*, or things that are seen as being disruptive or antisocial. There's a lot of stigma attached to being unemployed, for example, to needing to claim benefits, to immigration, to having served time, to mental health problems or addiction. Let me be clear: I don't think people should be judging others for the circumstances in which they find themselves, especially when a lot of the time people don't know the whole story. But people do judge. People make assumptions about what those circumstances say about that person. It's prejudice, plain and simple, and sadly it's all too common in everyday life.

When it comes to sex, we also attach stigma to things we don't consider normal, or which challenge our expectations of how people should behave. There are some attitudes that apply across society, but of course what we think of as 'normal' is also influenced by the sort of culture or background we grew up with. In many communities, there is stigma around even *talking* about sex.

In the UK in 2022 sexual relationships may be considered pretty normal, but that doesn't mean none of us experiences stigma. The stigma around sex kind of operates by degrees. Vanilla, heterosexual sex in committed relationships probably has the least amount of stigma attached to it. Add in a bit of kink and the stigma goes up a notch. Casual sex is generally more stigmatised than relationship sex. And even though we have same-sex marriage now, LGBTQ+ sex remains far more stigmatised than straight sex.

Probably the clearest example of sexual stigma many of us have witnessed in our lifetimes was during the peak of the HIV/AIDS epidemic. If you grew up in the late Eighties or early Nineties you might even remember the terrifying 'Don't Die of Ignorance' adverts, which featured a black marble tombstone etched with the word AIDS. The campaign certainly raised awareness about HIV/AIDS but in an era where the only real treatment was prevention, it also fuelled a lot of fear, prejudice and, with it, stigma, which still exists today.

A common assumption back then was that if you identified as a gay person you were likely to have HIV. The homophobic headlines that took over newspapers during that period included 'Britain threatened by gay virus plague' and 'AIDS is the wrath of God, says vicar'.[2]

In November 1984 a lead article in *The Times* declared that 'many members of the public are tempted to see in AIDS some sort of retribution for a questionable style of life'.[3] This violent stigma around HIV/AIDS meant that people from the LGBTQ+ community faced abuse and were sometimes too scared to get tested out of fear of it being positive.

We've come a long way in terms of the research that is now put into HIV treatment and the information that is available online. HIV is now treatable to the point where many people who are on effective medication can't pass it on (see page 281). But we still have a very long way to go in terms of social attitudes, due to people not having the right sex education or just choosing to be ignorant. And stigma still plays a part. For some people, the stigma associated with HIV remains so overwhelming that they don't want to get tested. Given that we have effective treatments now, it's heartbreaking to see how social attitudes can *still* stand in the way of people doing what's right for themselves and their health.

Such is the power of stigma, and this is why we need to fight it.

Stigma allows little room for us to have an honest conversation surrounding sex and sexuality. When we live in fear of being seen as transgressive, of being judged and maybe rejected by our families, friendship groups and communities, we can't be totally honest about who we are and what we need. Stigma leaves no space for us to develop our understanding and instead forces us to stay in boxes we didn't ask to be put in. In the worst-case scenarios, it can put us in physical danger. Or we can find ourselves completely alone in dangerous or unhealthy situations, with no one to turn to for support.

In her memoir, Egyptian-born British journalist Alya Mooro describes growing up in an Arab family and the ways that taboos around the subject of sex shaped her experiences of it. As a woman, she writes, the idea of having a sexuality, or being sexual, or even *thinking* about sex was considered *3aib* (pronounced '*ahhyb*'), an Arabic word meaning 'shameful'.

In the only conversation she ever recalls having with her mother about sex, she was simply told, 'Don't have sex until you're married or he'll think you're a whore and never love you.'

But prohibition rarely works. Just as abstinence-only sex education in the US does little to stop teenagers having sex,[4] neither does a culture of silence and stigma around sex. 'Shaming girls into avoiding sex doesn't work,' writes Mooro. '[All it does] is ensure that they won't be able to talk about those things.'

She recalls an occasion, in her teens, when a condom came off during sex with her then-boyfriend. She knew she needed to get the morning-after pill but her local pharmacy refused to sell it to her because she was underage. Desperate, she was forced to beg a random woman in the street for help. The woman finally agreed to go and buy it for her, but it did little to ease Alya's humiliation. '[The woman] returned, handing it over to me – in my school uniform – with a look of half-pity, half-disgust,' she writes. 'I remember wishing then that I could have spoken to my mum and asked for *her* help rather than this stranger in the street, but it just wasn't a conversation I could even begin to have with her.' Her boyfriend, meanwhile, couldn't care less. 'I freaked out. He made jokes about baby names,' she remembers bitterly.

Given how taboo sex was in her culture, Alya's entire relationship had to be conducted in secret. Even as the relationship went sour and she began to realise her boyfriend was lying to her and sleeping with other girls, confiding in a friend simply wasn't an option. From sexual health scares to heartbreak, she was completely alone. 'That I couldn't speak to anyone meant I existed in a world that only included me and him ... It ultimately meant that I had no one I could turn to when I needed help,' she writes.[5]

Taboos and stigma impact straight cis men as well. Interestingly, it's much easier for a woman to be flexible and creative about how she expresses her gender than it is for a man to defy convention around what counts as 'manliness'. Think about it. A woman can go without make-up, choose trackies and trainers instead of heels and a dress, she can wear jewellery or not, it's up to her. But if a guy exercises anything close to the same freedom, he's at risk of judgement and ridicule. I was scrolling on Twitter some time ago and came across a famous male ex-*Love Island*-er. He was wearing a pink striped turtleneck, with pink lace gloves and a pearl bracelet. Can I add that he also looked amazing? But his photos were purposely thrown onto social media to spark outrage by users who clearly wanted to provoke laughter and abuse towards a man because he wasn't following the script. His masculinity was being called into question simply because of a colour and fabric choice.

When it's allowed to run unchecked, stigma can define a person's entire existence. It reinforces that there is only one way to live and that we all need to adhere to it, or else we'll be shunned.

Slut-shaming (*or*, why are some men intimidated by female sexuality?)

One topic that comes up repeatedly for me in my conversations with women is slut-shaming. Slut-shaming is when people (and let's be honest, we're mainly talking about women) are judged, shamed or otherwise socially rejected because of their sexual identity or sex life. For some people, being sexually promiscuous – having and enjoying casual sex with multiple partners – will lead to them getting slut-shamed. For others, even just having sex before marriage, even if in a relationship, can be seen as a big enough taboo to lead to slut-shaming.

One of the first times I was ever slut-shamed was at university. I'd seen some girls I had mutuals with calling me all sorts of names on social media – 'Hoe-loni' being one that springs to mind. I actually find that quite funny looking back now, but at the time I definitely didn't. When I saw it I swear my heart stopped for a moment. What had they heard? Why was I even the subject of their conversation? Back then I wasn't even all that sexually experienced, but I also knew you didn't need to be; you could still become the object of someone's judgement.

Those girls knew exactly what being branded a 'hoe' could do to a woman's reputation, especially somewhere like university where you're only a few degrees of separation from everyone else and word gets around fast. You might think I'm being dramatic, but I was absolutely mortified. I was so scared of being seen this way, I made sure I didn't have sex with any other guys who went to my university for a while! It was a clear evil move – by slut-shaming me, those girls had succeeded in partially policing my sexuality. Don't worry, I still had sex. I just made sure it was with guys from London who didn't know anybody on campus (because one thing guys at that age will do is talk!).

These days, I get slut-shamed on social media every other day (usually by cishet men), and it doesn't always bother me because I know they're still getting their heads around a woman who takes pride in educating others about their sexuality and celebrating her own. Call me a slut all you like, it does nothing.

On other days I brush it off because I know that no matter what they may believe about me, they don't actually know me. The assumptions they make about me bear little resemblance to the reality, so their words hold no weight. When you know something isn't true, sometimes it doesn't really bother you. This is something I've told myself many times. Because for some people hearing a woman *talk* about sex is enough for them to judge her.

But I'd be lying if I said it never got to me. I think this is because a part of me knows that deep down I'm not half as sexually explorative as many would like to believe. And I'm not 100 per cent sure that's completely out of choice. I love the work I do and I'm so proud of the platform I've built up, but the reality is that I'm hyper-visible now and so I still choose to be very careful with how and who I fuck. Maybe my 19-year-old self is still in there, mortified and forced to fuck around by stealth because actually that kind of judgement *does* hurt. Maybe deep down I know that I still operate in survival mode. So, yeah, while I'd love to sit here and tell you it's possible to shrug off slut-shaming entirely, I have to be honest and say it does still occasionally hold power over me.

When people brand you as 'easy' they do it in order to control you and to let others know that you don't have agency over yourself. And this can have scary and dangerous consequences, both in terms of the risk of being ostracised socially, or in the way that sexual partners treat you.

It won't have escaped your notice that men's sexuality is not subject to this same level of stigma. That men want, enjoy and seek sex is accepted as totally normal. There might be some individuals who would view a guy as a fuckboy or a player if he'd slept with a lot of people (and I do mean a lot – we're talking upwards of 100 people), but for the most part society pretty much lets them get away with whatever they want because 'boys will be boys', right?

The same is not true for women. We get judged. Our body count matters. People believe it says something about us, and honestly, many of us believe this too. I get women messaging me all the time stressing because their new partner has asked about their body count and they're worried he's going to think less of them. Why? It makes no sense. When I look at a man I don't think about what's between his legs. I wonder what he does for a living, I wonder if he smells good, if he's single or married, if there's an ex still claiming him. I don't obsess about what's gone on between his legs. However, that's what women have to put up with. Society is obsessed with what we do with our bodies and who we share them with to the point where men will literally use your body count as a deciding factor when it comes to how much respect they want to give you.

I've observed in online social spaces men having these silly body-count conversations and I hear women trying to counter their arguments by pointing out that a woman might have made poor sexual decisions or been lied to about the future of the relationship just so a guy can sleep with her. Now, that definitely happens, but why do we need to take this line of argument at all? Why do we have to make out like our body count is some sort of accident or pretend that the way in which we enjoy our sexuality is down to 'poor decisions'? It's almost as if we're infantilising ourselves to convince cishet men that we're still worthy of being respected. And why do we want to imply that we're incapable of making sexual decisions? 'Oh, I'm sure she didn't *mean* to sleep with that many people, poor thing was probably tricked into it' ... ?? No. We should be able to confidently say we enjoy sex just as much as men and leave it at that.

We also have the 'Madonna–whore complex' to contend with, a term coined by Sigmund Freud (don't worry, we'll get to him and some of his wacky theories later on in the book). Although Freud had some questionable takes, a broken clock can still be right twice a day. The Madonna–whore complex is described as 'the inability to maintain sexual arousal within a committed, loving relationship' and 'is said to develop in men who see women as either saintly Madonnas or debased prostitutes'. The theory points out that some men put their wives, whom they love and respect, on a pedestal (otherwise known as the Madonnas), in the same boat as their own mothers, making it hard to desire them sexually. On the other hand, these very same men have no issue lusting after and sleeping with women they have no regard for (aka the whores).

The Madonna–whore dichotomy labels women either as 'good girls' – pure, sexually inexperienced and showing little or no interest in sex, their 'reward' to be paired with a man as his personal trophy – or as the 'bad girls' seen as whores who have a huge thirst for sex, enjoy being degraded and aren't worthy of a serious relationship or marriage.

It's important to keep in mind that the Madonna might have sex, but she won't be the one who's initiating it, because she's not meant to have a sexual appetite. Anything that screams 'I like sex' becomes questioned and might even tiptoe along the line of having the characteristics of the whore archetype. We can enjoy sex, but only when men call the shots.

Freud put it like this: 'Where such men love, they have no desire and where they desire, they cannot love.'

We see this play out a lot in films and TV shows. Remember when Charlotte marries Trey in *Sex and the City*? He is unable to have sex with her due to erectile problems. They wait until just before they get married to finally be intimate, but it soon transpires that Charlotte is his Madonna. She even catches him fapping away to porn in the bathroom!

Samantha tells her during brunch: 'Trey sees you as his virginal wife, not his sexual plaything.'

This trope, which has been so prevalent in the media and in pop culture, is the result of a society based on the different Abrahamic faiths, which equate sex to sinning and the Madonna in this theory to the Virgin Mary.

Today, some men are not only unable to be sexual with their partner, they also find it difficult to enjoy sexual acts they deem as inappropriate when it involves their wife. Cumming on her face? Anal? Forget it! That's saved for the women they're only sexually interested in.

They see wives, mothers and even girlfriends as not being able to enjoy the kind of sex they want. These Madonnas are more worthy of their respect, and if they enjoy sex it might possibly make these men think less of them.

Even some mothers struggle to see themselves as sexual beings, as the stigma society places on mums prevents them from being able to celebrate their sexuality how they want. In fact, a 2012 study found that 'despite its essential role in motherhood and life, and the health benefits known to be associated with sexual activity, public expression of sexuality is still primarily associated with being young, childless, and unmarried'.[6]

This isn't shocking. I have spoken to several new mums who have found it difficult to tap back into their sexuality, because they're worried about how they'll be perceived and judged. But here's the thing: being a mother is just a new side to you and does not erase the sensual part you were gifted with. We should not have to limit who we are to make men or society feel comfortable.

The slut or saint theory plays a role in why some women have a tough time dating and figuring out when the right time to sleep with a guy is. They're concerned they'll be put into one of two binary categories, and that he'll lose interest immediately after sex. I'm sure many of us have worried that we might have slept with a guy too soon, thereby losing any chance of the relationship progressing and wondering what box we've now been put into.

A lot of the Black women I grew up with were scared to be sexual due to the stigma of being seen as a slut. We weren't able to admit that we enjoyed sex and were forced to play the 'wifey material' role, even if we had no interest in it. I still remember when I told a friend that I had slept with three guys (no, seriously, it was genuinely three at the time; I've quadrupled that number, plus some, since then); she was in shock and told me to 'take it easy', encouraging me to be seen as the sexually inexperienced girl, which, now looking back, I still was. I may have slept with three men, but if I'm honest I didn't know what the hell I was doing. She wasn't the only one who had that attitude either. I grew up with a lot of Nigerian girlfriends who went down the celibacy route, tailoring themselves to be everything they believed a man would desire if it meant being chosen to be his girlfriend or wife. Yes, a 'Pick Me' strategy. Some of them regret it, because it meant they spent a huge chunk of their time pretending, when they could have been discovering themselves in and out of sex.

We've heard many lyrics telling us that 'you can't turn a hoe into a housewife' because many still believe women who have sexual urges and agency are not deserving of love and romance, but plenty of women who enjoy sex are finding love, happiness and more.

Trying to squeeze women into two boxes pits them against each other and leaves little room for us explore the different sides we all have. We shouldn't have to be seen either as sluts who men make love to secretly and seek out only for sexual gratification, or as saints who pretend they don't have a sex drive.

And if you think that penalising women for having multiple sexual partners is a universal thing, think again. There are many cultures in the world where it's considered completely normal, even accepted and encouraged. Among the Aché people of Paraguay it's not unusual for people to claim to have several fathers on account of the various men their mother slept with during her pregnancy.[7] Himba people, who live in northern Namibia and Angola, have the highest rates of children born from extramarital relationships ever reported – 70 per cent of couples have at least one child who was fathered by someone else. Not only that, it's all completely open and above board. In this community, having multiple partners outside of your marriage is not just tolerated, it's expected.[8]

So how did we get to a place where our sexuality became so stigmatised? In Western culture the sexual double standard stretches back thousands of years, but historians reckon that, in the UK at least, it got progressively worse during the nineteenth century, particularly around the time that the government began to try to regulate the sex industry. Under the Contagious Diseases Acts of the 1860s, police were essentially allowed to detain any woman suspected of carrying an STI and to force her to undergo a medical examination. The supposed intention was to help prevent the spread of disease among women working as prostitutes and their clients. However, since the authorities didn't need to provide any evidence as to why they believed the woman to be infected, you can imagine how that power got abused pretty quickly.[9]

'Women's sexuality was to be defined by fear and immorality,' writes historian Fern Riddell. 'The Acts helped create a rhetoric that saw the free enjoyment of sex — one that was not restricted to seeing it merely as a form of procreation — as something bad, associated with disease and sexual immorality.'[10]

⚠ **Content Warning: Sexual violence.**

Laws such as these only encouraged society to see sexually liberated women as unworthy of respect. More and more women's sexual past was being brought up in rape trials and used as a measure of how 'respectable' she was and therefore how reliable a witness.

Honestly, there are so many examples of women having their sexual history dragged up and described before the court in order to somehow 'prove' they couldn't have been raped. The assumption that's being made is that a woman who has previously sought out and enjoyed sex can't be a victim of sexual assault. In fact, often the implication is that as an openly sexually active woman she practically *invited* the interaction. In other words, she 'brought it on herself'.

Technically, lawyers in the UK are not allowed to bring up a complainant's sexual history during a rape case anymore, except in strict circumstances.[11] But that doesn't mean it never happens.

In 2012 footballer Ched Evans was convicted of raping a 19-year-old woman and sentenced to five years in prison. But in 2016, having served just half of this sentence, he mounted an appeal and the case was brought to retrial. This time the conviction was overturned and Evans was acquitted. It then emerged that a large part of the appeal was based around 'fresh evidence' about the complainant's sexual history. Not only did Evans's legal team put forward statements from two different men who claimed to have had consensual sex with the woman in question, she was also questioned in detail and at length by lawyers about her previous sexual partners, the positions she favoured and the language she used during sex.[12]

As women's rights groups pointed out at the time, cases like this make it very hard for other women to come forward about sexual assault. Who wants to have their sex life dragged through the mud and be told that their previous preferences and activities make them less reliable witnesses? On an everyday level, too, the fear of being slut-shamed can lead to women holding back when it comes to advocating for their sexual needs. It can stop them exploring their own pleasure, and it can even limit who they date. Even now, I hesitate to tell guys I'm dating that I talk about sex or that I'm a sexual content creator because I feel like the first word they hear is sex and the last word they hear is sex! And I know that inevitably that's going to colour their opinion of me.

The threads of sexual experiences I receive from anonymous women on Twitter have shown me time and time again that some – no, fuck it, *many* – men do not like seeing women enjoy their sexuality. Whenever a woman writes in about how she felt fulfilled, had fun experimenting with different men or how she used her sexuality, it's met with comments such as 'fear women' or 'these women are for the streets'. When we take control and enjoy sex, it threatens the patriarchy because it exemplifies our independence. And when has the independence of women ever benefited from the very same system that was built to hold us back?

It's probably part of the reason why the myths surrounding our sexuality have been around for so long and, quite frankly, why there's so much work that still needs to be done.

Fortunately, women are more sexually liberated today than they used to be. Research shows that we are definitely levelling up when it comes to our behaviour and our sense of freedom to choose how we want to have sex, and with whom (and how many!) we want to have it.[13] But we do still face challenges, as I'll be discussing throughout this book.

As do men! We often think of men as being allowed to be more sexual than women, but at the same time rigid expectations around masculinity often means they're denied the opportunity to be sexually fluid. You only have to look at football to see this. In 2022 it's plain mad that there are only two gay players in the upper echelons of men's professional football that we know of. Twenty-one-year-old Australian footballer Josh Cavallo came out publicly in October 2021, which made him the world's only openly gay male top-flight pro footballer,[14] followed by Blackpool player Jake Daniels in May 2022, the first UK player to come out since 1990.[15] By contrast, there are five lesbian or bi women in the Lionesses, England's national women's team, *alone.*[16]

This brings me on to an important point: that some sexual identities are more stigmatised than others.

LGBTQ+ identities

Sex *as a whole* is still a reasonably taboo subject. But as I mentioned at the start of this chapter, some types of sex are more taboo than others. There's a lot less stigma around having sex in a monogamous hetero marriage than there is around having casual sex with multiple partners. And there's definitely more stigma associated with LGBTQ+ sex.

It's like there's a hierarchy of what kind of sex is considered acceptable. There's actually a diagram about this called the 'Charmed Circle'. At the centre of the circle are the types of sex seen as 'good, normal, natural' and around the outer edge of the circle are the types seen as 'bad, abnormal, or unnatural'.[17] Anthropologist Gayle Rubin came up with it in the Eighties but, honestly, not all that much has changed. We might have same-sex marriage now, but society still stigmatises queer identities.

Things are improving but not fast enough. The Stonewall School Report 2017 shows that anti-LGBTQ+ bullying and language has decreased across Britain's schools since 2012. But almost half of all LGBTQ+ pupils still face bullying at school, and more than two in five trans young people have tried to take their own life.[18]

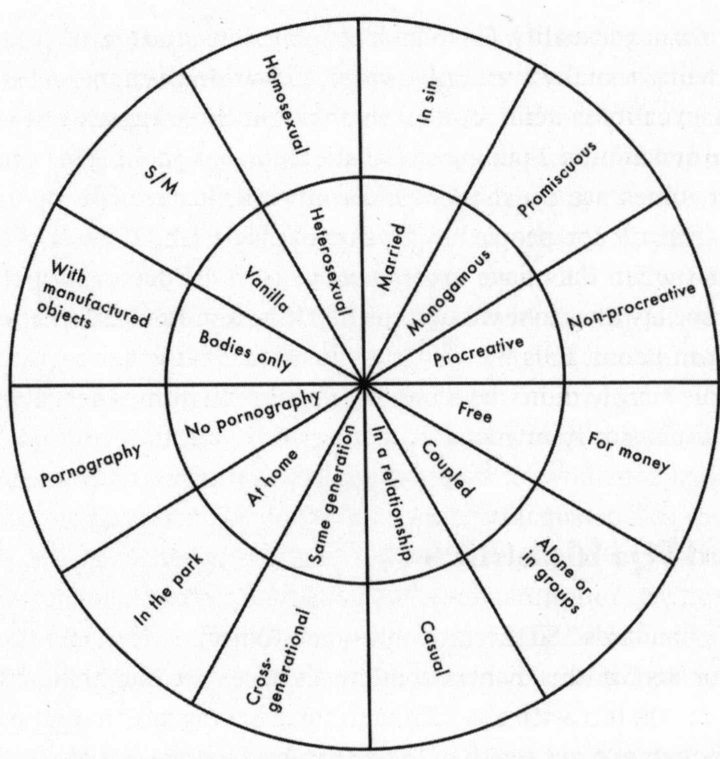

When we allow ourselves to believe or buy into stigma, we allow ourselves to make false judgements about people. We assume that by knowing someone's sexual orientation or gender identity, we also know their preferences, personality and behaviour. This couldn't be further from the truth. Challenging stigma is so important if we want to be truly sexually liberated and to allow all people the same rights and freedoms.

People of all sexual orientations can feel stigmatised, even when that orientation means they are not sexually active. One of the weirdest contradictions about sexual stigma is that, while you can be shamed for being what society deems 'too' sexual, you can also be judged for not being sexual enough. There is a huge stigma around admitting that you're not that interested in sex, for example. For women this lands us right at the crux of the patriarchal desire to control our sexuality. The patriarchy doesn't want us to be sluts, but not being sexually available *at all* is not considered an option either.

Asexuality is defined as experiencing little or no sexual attraction, and around 2 per cent of people in the UK identify as asexual (sometimes 'ace' for short).[19] In the abstract, this idea doesn't seem too difficult for people to get their heads round. The challenge comes when they have to apply it to an actual person, especially one society likes to sexually objectify. Model and asexuality activist Yasmin Benoit tells me that, when she first came out as asexual, people simply didn't believe her. 'They just assume there's something physically or mentally wrong with you, that you must be stunted somehow, or traumatised. Or you have a hormone deficiency or a personality problem that you can just kind of counsel yourself out of. [I also get told] "you just haven't met the right person yet. You think you're too good for everybody, no one meets your standards." So there's a quite a lot of stuff.'

For Yasmin this disbelief had multiple layers. The first is society's discomfort with the idea that a woman might use her sexual agency to opt out of sex. The second is around society's expectations of Black sexuality. As I mentioned in Chapter 1, the fetishisation of Black bodies dates back to slavery. Under colonial rule, Black people were dehumanised and compared to animals, with heightened, unrestrained sexuality being a key part of that caricature.[20] Black female bodies were also frequently appraised based on their reproductive value. White people like to think that racism has gone away, but even now in 2022 we are still suffering from the hangover of those views.

'People just don't think that Black women would be asexual,' Yasmin explains. 'I mean, we are probably the most hyper-sexualised demographic in the world. So we are sexualised and expected to behave in a particularly sexual way from a much younger age. And if you don't meet those expectations, or those milestones, people are a lot more likely to think that there's something wrong with you, more so than they would with a young white girl that wasn't expressing her sexuality in a particular way. And it's just hard for people to compute that you might be asexual and Black (and, in my case, sexually unavailable and uninterested). They see your body as being sexual, and they see [sex] as being something that drives you.'

Much of Yasmin's activism revolves around challenging these views, as well as providing much-needed representation to other young ace people. As we've already discussed, stigma around sex can force us into boxes that don't fit us and that we never asked to be in, but asexuality (like all types of sexuality) is a spectrum, and Yasmin says there's no right or wrong way to behave or identify within that. 'You don't have to actually use the terminology. You don't have to try to fit yourself into a label or micro-label unless you feel like it's helpful in articulating your experience.'

She's also keen to stress that, despite the stigma, it is perfectly possible to live a life that's true to yourself and to be happy. 'There is nothing wrong with you – being asexual isn't a problem,' she says. 'And you can live a happy, fulfilling life with great relationships while being asexual. It's not a deal-breaker for the right kind of people.'

As well as sexual orientation, there's also stigma around being kinky, being non-monogamous and being promiscuous, all of which we'll discuss in later chapters. Depending on what kind of community you come from, even being an openly sexual person can be taboo – this puts people in danger, both physically (for example, from homophobic bullying and misogynistic violence) and emotionally, through shame and lack of support. It's vitally important to challenge all these stigmas both for ourselves and to stick up for people whose sexual identity is different to our own.

Increasingly, there is a visible and accessible community for everyone, but it can still be hard to figure out who you are sexually and what you want out of your sexual relationships. Over the next few chapters I'll be exploring how we do that and giving you advice on how to let go of taboos and stigmas, and how we can start to rise above slut-shaming and own our sexuality.

CHAPTER 3

Virginity

'I gave him everything! I was half a virgin when I met him.'

Regina George, *Mean Girls*

I was 18 when I had my first penetrative sexual experience with a man. We worked at the same local supermarket. I remember spotting him before I actually had a job there and literally tilting my head. You know that little tilt you do when you're checking someone out? Yes, that!

It was a weekend job and they had me in the bakery section making the sandwiches. I honestly had no clue what I was doing. At the end of one of my shifts I decided to shoot my shot and ask him where a can of tomatoes belonged. Yes, I do consider this shooting my shot! What else would it be? We both knew it was my way of starting a conversation.

Liam was French and he had recently moved to London. Although he'd lived in France all his life, he fell in love with London and decided not to move back but instead to learn English and continue his studies here. He refused to date me at first because he didn't want to be in a relationship with someone he worked with, but soon we were spending pretty much all of our breaks at work together. After some time it became clear we had feelings for each other. Then one day I was told by my boss that I was being moved to a different store to work. Later that same day, Liam asked me to be his girlfriend. I remember him being glad that I was moving stores, because it meant we could be in a relationship.

He would always take me home after every shift of mine since we worked different times. There was a particular day when I realised that my sister and mum wouldn't be home. Back then we called this having a 'free yard' and it was perfect for what I had in mind. After getting Liam to take me home, I kept dropping hints that no one was home, as an indication of wanting to do the do. I was ready to become a woman! I was ready to have my cherry popped, be deflowered, lose my V card! I was going to be the second girl in my friendship circle to lose her virginity and I could not wait!

Once inside my bedroom, I pulled out a condom and told my boyfriend I was ready to have sex. He laughed and asked if I was sure, to which I screamed 'YES!' and quickly stripped off my work uniform (you would have thought I was a cartoon character given how quick I was!).

When the big moment came, I will be honest, it was an uncomfortable experience for both of us. We were awkward and I had no clue what I was doing. There was no blood, just an awkward discomfort and one position throughout: missionary. I mean, I wasn't exactly going to start riding him like a cow girl, now, was I? Not in this economy! But I was so happy. I'd finally done it!

I told my girls immediately when I saw them next. It felt like something out of *Grease* when Sandy's friends plead with her to 'Tell me more, tell me more!' except rather than asking me whether it was love at first sight, their bursting questions included 'Did it hurt?' 'Did you feel comfortable getting naked?' 'Were the lights on or off?' 'Did he go down on you?'

I was happy to spill the tea on all of it. Truth is, it did hurt a bit, but this was probably because we didn't use any lube, which is really important and is discussed later on in this book. There was also a real lack of foreplay. I wasn't sure how long we'd have before my house wasn't so free. I didn't feel uncomfortable getting naked, from what I remember, because we'd been dating a bit and he made me feel safe and relaxed. The lights were on as I wanted to see and remember everything we did. And I'm pleased to say Liam *did* go down on me. I can't tell you how long it lasted, but it felt nice. At the time I didn't know you could cum from oral sex, so when he did it I was usually the impatient one to move on – but from the start I have to say he was always invested in my pleasure, which I loved about him.

Once we'd had sex that first time, Liam and I couldn't keep our hands off each other. No, seriously, we had sex just about everywhere, and I mean everywhere: his brother's spare bedroom, the park, his house, hotels, behind bike sheds, his auntie's living room when everyone was asleep! We explored, we laughed and we fucked. Yeah, we fucked a lot.

Our relationship eventually came to an end, which I'll tell you about shortly, but that was how I lost my virginity. Or, at least, that was when I had my first experience of vaginal penetration, which is what society deems as 'losing your virginity' – my sexual debut. We'll come back to why that's problematic later in the chapter, but what strikes me now, when I look back on it, is the idea that I was 'losing' something in that interaction. Exactly what is lost? What has been taken? And why have we placed such a huge significance on this thing, this moment. Having sex for the first time was exciting, sure, but it was very far from being the groundbreaking, life-changing event I'd been led to believe it would be.

What even is virginity and why does it matter so much?

Most of us understand virginity as the state of not having had sex. Before you have sex you're a virgin. After you have sex? Not a virgin anymore. Sounds straightforward until you start asking questions. Questions like: *Well, what counts as 'sex'?* and *Why is it so important that we've given it a whole name of its own?* and *Why do we even care?*

The first and most important thing to say is that virginity is a social construct. That basically means it's a thing humans invented, like the need to say bless you after someone sneezes and giving someone the evils if they start coughing. It is not actually a biological reality. Your body and mind do not experience any significant changes and there is no way to physically tell if someone has had sex or not – although a lot of people still believe there is (at least on women).

I remember a conversation that took place in the break room with my colleagues from the job I mentioned earlier. It was before Liam and I started dating but he was there and so were some of my friends from college who also worked at the store. In total there were around eight of us. As always for a group of horny teenagers, the subject of sex came up and we all had a conversation about who we thought was and wasn't a virgin. And how did we do this? By looking at each other! Yes, all we did was look at each other's faces to try and decipher whether that person had had sex. It felt like being in Year 9 again, where boys would look girls up and down to decide if she was 'frigid' or not. It sounds ridiculous and that's because it is. When I shared that I'd never had penetrative sex, they all gasped in the room. Even Liam thought I was lying. 'I don't believe you. Really?' he said. Well, he soon found out!

One of the many myths we've been taught is that, for people with vaginas, first-time sex will be a blood bath. This is based on false ideas about the female anatomy, in particular the hymen, which is imagined to be a sort of special seal over the vagina that breaks in glorious ceremony on first contact with a penis. This, ladies, is what I like to call total bullshit.

See, the idea of an 'intact' hymen is completely scientifically inaccurate. It's also a dangerous tale, which harms a lot of cis women in different cultures all over the world who are expected to hold up a white bedsheet with blood on it as proof that she has waited till her wedding night to have sex. But the reality is that all vaginas are different and while some women can bleed during penis-in-vagina (PIV) sex, due to irritation or minor tearing to the membrane, it isn't something that happens for all.

Many people still imagine the hymen as this tissue that completely covers the entrance of the vagina, which isn't true as the appearance varies hugely from person to person. It can go all the way around the edge, it can have a half-moon shape, it could have holes in it and on very rare occasions it can stretch all the way across. It is actually extremely rare to have a hymen that covers the entire opening to the vagina. This is called an 'imperforate' hymen and is actually considered a medical issue, since it can stop menstrual blood from passing. Luckily, it can be corrected through minor surgery.[1]

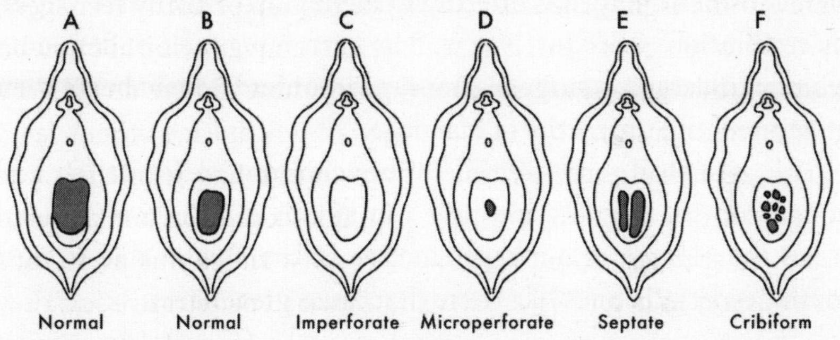

For most vagina-owners, the hymen does not 'break' during sex, it merely changes. Any sort of vaginal penetration can change the shape of the hymen, including fingers, tampons, a rabbit dildo or even riding a bike. It can also change naturally with age. Your hymen stretching or changing shape is not proof of your sexual experiences, it's just a part of your body and not everyone is even born with one.

Why do we have hymens in the first place, then? Good question. One theory is that it helps to keep bacteria out of the vagina during childhood (if you've ever changed a baby girl's nappy you'll agree this seems like a legit use for it!). Canadian gynaecologist Dr Jennifer

Gunter once compared the hymen to baby teeth, saying: 'It exists for a narrow developmental stage, and then once it has served its purpose, it takes on a variety of shapes and flexibility. Because at that point it's not needed. So you should think about the hymen as something covering a narrow developmental phase. And once it's taken on, once we've done with it biologically, we don't need it anymore.'[2]

Once again, there is no way to physically tell if someone has had sex or not, but the idea that the hymen can prove it either way is still harming young girls and women around the world, so much so that in some places young women are subjected to humiliating vaginal examinations known as 'virginity testing'. Both the World Health Organization and the American College of Obstetricians and Gynecologists (ACOG) have stated that such tests have no scientific merit or medical validity, with the former describing the practice as 'a violation of human rights'.[3] Yet we still hear stories about cosmetic surgeons offering hymenoplasty billed as a 'virginity restoration' procedure,[4] as well as harrowing tales of desperate women undergoing surgery after rape in order to avoid being seen as 'tainted' and unworthy of marriage.[5]

This is such a good example of how accurate information and education can tangibly improve our sex lives. When we understand the biology of our reproductive system, we're able to bust myths, especially ones like these that cause great harm.

Another concept we've bought into is the notion of 'tightness'. I recently asked my followers to send me their sex problems anonymously and one woman sent me the following: 'My vagina is really tight, it's always a shock to men. Sex isn't painful though, thoughts?'

I admit at first I was tickled by this because this wasn't really a dilemma. If you aren't feeling any sort of pain and you're comfortable, then there really isn't a problem. But it struck me that being told 'Oh, baby, you're so tight' is a standard 'compliment' that a lot of men give women during PIV sex. I put the word compliment in inverted commas because ... is it a compliment? What is it actually saying? Because a tight vagina is associated with virginity, it's kind of drawing on the idea that the woman is sexually inexperienced and that this is somehow a good thing. In fact, tightness can mean many things. It could be down to feeling uncomfortable, needing more foreplay to feel relaxed, needing more lubrication. It could be down to a psychosexual condition such as vaginismus. It could even be a trauma response. But still, some women use it as a way to measure how amazing their vagina is – how well it grips and hugs his penis, the effort that the guy will have to go through to put it in (when really he should be concentrating on foreplay and lubrication). And all this is painted as a badge of honour and virtue. (This isn't to say you can't take control and do your Kegels during penetration to help add to the pleasure.)

By the same token, there are still some people who believe the more partners a woman has sex with, the wider her vagina will be, even though this is simply untrue. It's just another myth told to scare women out of having sex. After all, we don't tell men that the more women they have sex with, the tinier and more shrivelled their dick will become. The muscles in the vaginal walls are just like any other muscle in your body. And, like other muscles, they stretch and contract. How do you think they give birth to babies? They stretch, but then they snap back again. If you don't end up with massively elongated thighs from doing quad stretches, why would you imagine this happening to the vagina? If you smile extremely hard a hundred times, will the shape of your mouth also permanently change?

Once again, having sex for the first time (or indeed any number of times) does not have a tangible impact on our physical body. But I still want to know how this one moment in our lives became so important. We really romanticise virginity, and the idea of losing it, to the point that it can blind us to the reality of our situation.

I receive hundreds of dilemmas every month and within them there's always a young woman struggling with the fact that the person she's having sexual or relationship problems with was her 'first'. Despite her clear unhappiness, she'll tell me about how her boyfriend has been her only love and the one she 'gave it up to', as if this somehow makes a difference. She's usually between the ages of 18–25 and what seems clear to me is that she's finding it harder to let go because of the narrative she's been taught about the significance of her first time.

Having sex for the first time with someone is *not* an excuse to hold on to a love interest when the relationship is going terribly. There is life, love and lots of sex with other people if you allow yourself to believe there is.

As I say this, please understand that I'm shading my 19-year-old self who cried her eyes out after she was dumped by Liam. Yep, he dumped me because I caught him flirting with other women via text. When I confronted him he just said the words, 'I don't want to do this anymore' – the guy kicked me to the curb when he should have been grovelling for forgiveness!

Of course, part of the reason I found that break-up so difficult was because I was just inexperienced, so this was a new type of pain. He also moved on pretty quickly and plastered his new girlfriend all over Facebook. However, I know that part of it was also that he was my first. I wanted more from the relationship because I'd been led to believe that him having 'taken' my virginity mattered, that it made the relationship special somehow. White men behind the cameras in Hollywood had told me that you skip off into the sunset and live happily ever after. But there was no sunset, there was no skipping, just me walking down Hertford Road on a grey London day with tears streaming down my face.

You'll remember at the start of the chapter that I ran through some of the slang ways we talk about losing virginity: popping your cherry, being deflowered, getting rid of my V card, giving it up. Boy, these are some interesting and outdated ways to simply say having penetrative sex for the first time. The choice of words we've adopted, and sadly normalised, attach a false narrative to women's first PIV experience with a man.

Whether we want to admit it or not, language sometimes subconsciously plays a deciding factor in how we feel about and see things. That's why I think virginity needs a rebrand! I think it's fine that the concept of having sex for the first time feels important to us, but why does it always have to be about 'giving away' or 'losing' part of ourselves? It makes it seem like something that diminishes us, that we have no control over. Wouldn't we feel like we had more agency if we talked about our 'sexual debut' rather than 'losing our virginity'? To ditch the outdated views we carry about sex, we can start by finding new words to talk about our experiences.

Purity culture

It's 1997 and a 21-year-old home-schooled Christian virgin has just released a book called *I Kissed Dating Goodbye.* In it, he advocates getting rid of the idea of dating so you can work on your relationship with God. The book's publication is the latest in a series of events that bolster the so-called 'purity movement' across America.

The purity movement is often said to have formally begun as a response to the HIV/AIDS epidemic during the Eighties and Nineties, but, let's be real, it was also a way to police sexuality, especially women's. And it was extraordinarily effective. Four years earlier, the Southern Baptist Convention in the US launched its 'True Love Waits' campaign, encouraging Christian teens to take a pledge to stay sexually abstinent until marriage. But it was with the help of young voices like *IKDG* author Joshua Harris that the idea really started to take off. The book sold more than a million copies and was the reason many Christian teens adopted purity culture. Passed around through many youth groups, it promoted extremely toxic and misogynistic messages. It slut-shamed women and framed them as damaged if they had sex outside of marriage. In short, it saw women as property and valued them based on their virginity.

Harris has since said he regrets writing the book and has apologised to his readers.[6] But the damage was already done. Writing in the *Washington Post*, American author Lyz Lenz said, 'Purity culture taught me that I ought to be passed down from father to husband, more an inheritance than a human ... I was taught that my holy calling was to open my legs for one and only one and bear him children. Barring that, I was to keep them closed and never express desire or lust or fear or longing.' She added: 'The insidious message of purity culture still clings fast in my marriage, and I often put it at the root of some of my deepest anxieties and fears.'[7]

Why am I telling you this story? Well, to share part of where a lot of sexual trauma for young women and men today may have started.

Purity culture was something I certainly saw growing up: young Christian girls who made a vow to their fathers that they'd 'save themselves' for marriage in what was clearly just another way to police their bodies and restrict their sexuality. I saw it in the media, too. Remember when Britney Spears was the unofficial face of it? Then later on we had the Jonas Brothers showing off their purity rings and speaking about how they were going to wait till marriage. We saw it with Jessica Simpson, too! Basically, any American popstar in the late Nineties and early Noughties seemed to have to toe the line of being squeaky clean.

But back to Britney for a second. As someone in the limelight who was constantly questioned about the state of her virginity, forced to reiterate over and over that she had never had sex, wasn't it weird that she was also so sexualised? A 16-year-old pop singer whose virginity was fawned over by the media and constantly interrogated – doesn't that sound like a subsection in unethical porn? They knew that fetishising her innocence would appeal to creepy men and also made other young girls idolise her, encouraging them to act like she did on screen in music videos, presumably to please the boys and men around them.

Purity culture taught women to relinquish all ownership or even awareness of their sexuality, and to dress conservatively, in a way that would not distract men (because, of course, they can't control themselves!), but at the same time, it promotes the idea that they *are* sex objects, that all they have to offer is their untouched vagina. It's disgusting.

It also asks us to believe simultaneously that men are the rightful caretakers of our sexuality, that we should cater to their sexual needs willingly and joyfully, but also that men are horrible people who can taint you. It doesn't make sense. And why do men want to promote this idea anyway? I've asked this question before, but it bears repeating: *Why would any guy want someone to think that their touch is inherently dirty or damaging?*

It would take a book much longer than mine to try to explain exactly why the patriarchy comes up with this stuff, but what I can observe is that men can tell how powerful our sexuality is and some of them want to do all they can to cap how we choose to explore it.

When we put all this negative pressure on sexuality, it comes as no surprise that many people have a hard time responding in an open and understanding way to sex, particularly when we're just starting to be sexually active. I used to run a phone-call dilemma service for my followers, and I remember one time a young woman who'd booked a session to speak to me explained how she lived in London but had gone to university in Manchester and, although she had graduated two years before, she still found herself in Manchester every weekend because her church was there and she was too afraid to leave. This caller told me she wanted to start dating but found it hard to do so because she was scared to form connections with other men.

In what sounded to me like clear brainwashing, her pastor and other members of her church had made her feel like she was doing something wrong if she tried to pursue a relationship with a man. Her friends in London all had pretty average dating lives, but she didn't because she couldn't escape the grip of purity culture. Her reason for calling me was to get help unlearning the shame and guilt she felt. Now, I didn't have the answers, because this was obviously something that went deep, but I listened, shared my perspective and suggested she get some sexual therapy sessions.

I can't tell you how often I've heard of similar scenarios, and I'm not saying that you shouldn't wait till marriage to have sex if that's what feels right for you. I understand why someone would want to and there's nothing wrong with that – do what makes you feel empowered and happy. My issue is with the branding of purity culture and the way it does not allow women to have agency. You are not impure because you have sex. Sex isn't dirty; people who create harmful rules about how we enjoy consensual sex are the dirty ones.

More than anything, we need to stop giving people who clearly don't understand sexuality so much power. Instead of letting people who clearly fear and avoid sex make the rules, let's start listening to the people who actually enjoy it. Aren't they better placed to tell us how to get the most out of it?

Some 'first times' matter more than others

Not everyone has the same first sexual experience, but we only use one to define what we call 'real sex' and that's penetrative, penis-in-vagina sex (PIV). In fact, some women place so much emphasis on having vaginal sex for the first time, that they intentionally become what I call 'the everything-but girl'. The everything-but girl will indulge in a hand job, maybe a cheeky blowjob, even anal sex, but she'll save vaginal penetration for when she says 'I do'. Sorry, but how does this make sense? As *Sex and the City*'s Samantha Jones rightly says, 'Front, back, who cares? A hole is a hole.'

If your first sexual experience includes oral sex, anal sex or any other act used to help you reach an orgasm, have you still lost your virginity? A lot of people would say no. Because society only values the heteronormative experience and a lot of us don't view those other activities as 'real sex'. Now, I've spent a lot of time here arguing that virginity itself is bullshit and we don't need to regard the 'first time' as any more significant or valuable than any other time, but the fact remains that a lot of us do. And when we define 'losing your virginity' as being the first time you have a penis in your vagina, we are not only excluding other kinds of heterosexual activities, we are also leaving out a lot of LGBTQ+ people who don't have PIV sex at all.

The restricted way we conceive of virginity has left out the reality of other stories, which are equally as important and deserve to be told. When we only centre penetration and penises in sexual experiences we're telling bi and lesbian women that their experiences only hold relevance when a man is involved.

I spoke to my friends Ro and Nana (you'll hear more from them in the next chapter) whose podcast *Two Twos* is about being Black lesbians living in London today. I was interested to hear that, even for these two confident grown women who use their platform to talk candidly about their experiences and dispel myths about lesbian culture, the concept of virginity is a bit muddy.

'I had sex with a woman before I did with a man and I didn't think I was losing my virginity. I don't think I even thought it was sex. I just thought I was "doing things" with a girl,' Ro admitted to me. 'I always said I was a virgin, even though I'd had sexual relationships with women. And I guess now as an adult, looking back, I just cancelled out all of that. It's almost like I'm saying that those relations with women [weren't] sex when [they were] sex. And I've centred my virginity around experiences with men.'

This is crazy when you think about it. Here's someone for whom the experience of sleeping with a woman felt far more pleasurable and meaningful, safer and more fulfilling than the experience of sleeping with a man, yet because of the way we've defined virginity, and with it 'proper sex', she didn't think it counted. She cancelled it out in her mind! Do you see how disheartening that is? And what about lesbians who've never had experiences with men?

Does that mean they've never had sex? Even if they've had multiple orgasms and got head, and had fingers and dildos inside them? Are they just virgins forever? It's hard to imagine anyone would honestly think so, but Nana told me that the power of the myths around virginity mean that they know queer women who have internalised this idea.

'It's weird that they still call themselves virgins,' she agreed. 'They definitely do *everything* with women, like receiving the strap and stuff, but they're still calling themselves virgins! And they're never going to be with a man so why is it still viewed and centred around that? I think it's just so heavily ingrained in our minds and just in our whole system that virginity is centred around a man's penis.'

When we change how we recognise what virginity is – and our attitude to what sex is – we open ourselves up to a better understanding of the different ways we can enjoy pleasure. Sexual gratification looks and feels like so many things that it makes very little sense to just shape it around heteronormative ideals. There's a reason why bi and lesbian women are having better sex than women in opposite-sex couples.[8] We shouldn't be shaping intimacy around one type of sex. And when that type of sex has created the orgasm gap, maybe it's time to explore further ...

Oloni's tips for your sexual debut

As I've said all the way through, the concept of virginity needs serious questioning. But I do also know that the first time you have penetrative sex is a big deal for a lot of us and obviously I want to help you get as much pleasure out of it as possible.* So here are a few of my tips for making your first time a fun and empowering experience ... at the very least I hope it will be better than mine was!

* Please remember that the age of consent in England and Wales is 16 years old.

1. Have a conversation about boundaries beforehand (see page 129).
2. Use lubrication and condoms (see page 133).
3. Engage in lots and lots of foreplay (see page 130).
4. More foreplay!
5. Include a small vibrator (see page 105).
6. Check in with each other afterwards (see page 156).
7. Aftercare (see page 155).

CHAPTER 4

Sexual Identity

Given how many messages we receive around sex, how many taboos we encounter and how much stigma there is around being open about your sexuality, it's no surprise that a lot of us get to our twenties or even thirties without really understanding our sexual identity. And in many cases, we've never even questioned it.

Instead, we take what our families and communities tell us, and what we see on TV and in the media, to be the norm (usually cisgender heterosexual). The assumption a lot of us make is that if that's what everyone else is doing, that must be what we want, too. It makes me laugh, really, when you think about it. We don't assume we'll have the same taste in food or clothes as everyone else around us, so why would we assume that about sex? I love Supermalt, for example, and sadly I have friends with bad taste who hate it and really enjoy Ginger Beer.

These ideas around how sex should go down and what sorts of relationships and activities are and aren't OK are what sex educators and therapists call 'scripts'. It's that voice in your head that says you 'should' want a relationship or that you 'shouldn't' be turned on by rough sex. Scripts can be a little bit different for everyone, depending on family background, culture and religion, but for those of us who grew up in the UK between 1990 and today, there will also be a lot of similarities.

I told you already that my mum's key ambitions for me were that I would learn to cook, go to university and find a husband. There was absolutely no question of whether I *wanted* a husband, or whether I was even attracted to men! It was just assumed. In a context like that, how on earth do you start to work out what you *really* want and discover the extent and complexity of your sexuality?

The answer, for a lot of people, is that you don't. And sad to say, an awful lot of people still go through life doing what's expected of them, staying away from anything that feels 'taboo', following the script they've been handed and having pretty miserable sex lives as a result.

I don't want that life. And I don't want it for you either. My mission is to empower women to discover, explore and own their sexuality and sexual identity.

So where do we start?

Well, first of all, it's important to say that people have always had sexual identities and orientation that fall outside of the hetero-normative, strictly reproductive model. Yes, it's true that in the UK straight, cisgendered sex, ideally within marriage, has long been considered the morally 'correct' sort of sex to have, but *that doesn't mean people haven't always been having other kinds.* As historian Fern Riddell points out in her book, *Sex: Lessons from History*, it would be a great mistake to assume that until now everyone was just obediently getting married to someone of the opposite sex and having sensible, procreative PIV sex with that person for their entire lives. In fact, there has long been a queer culture in the UK; LGBTQ+ people have always existed, same-sex wedding-like ceremonies have happened in history and people of all genders have enjoyed a variety of sexual activities in and outside of committed relationships.[1]

We often hear, for example, that more people are having anal sex because of porn. There's absolutely no way of knowing if this is really true because we can't go back in time and survey people from earlier centuries about their butt play, but we know for sure that modern-day porn did not invent anal sex. Although the term 'bum-fucking' first appeared in print in 1879[2] (in an erotic magazine, no less), the act existed a long time before then.

So next time you're worrying that your fantasies are too nasty, or that you're straying too far from what's 'normal', remember that it's nothing new. People have been doing this stuff for a long time!

One thing that did happen during the nineteenth and twentieth centuries, though, is that scientists started to study human sexuality and treat it as something that could be researched and understood objectively. Not all of this has been helpful. Early attempts to categorise sexual behaviour in a scientific way often ended up furthering sexist ideas and turning some preferences and behaviours into 'disorders'. I talk a lot about how Freud said clitoral orgasms were 'immature' and that the proper way for a woman to orgasm was vaginally, through PIV.[3] Let's be real: this was just one guy's shitty opinion in 1905, but the idea stuck around for decades, and it is still a problem for people now!

Another example is the *Diagnostic and Statistical Manual of Mental Disorders* (*DSM*), a text first published by the American Psychiatric Association in 1952, which helped to scientifically classify mental health disorders in order to help with diagnosis and treatment. It was a really groundbreaking moment for mental health and the manual is still used today, although it's been updated five times since the original publication. But what if I told you that the first edition listed homosexuality as a mental disorder? For real. It wasn't until 1974 that it was taken out and even then they still kept in a section about 'sexual orientation disturbance', which meant that anyone who felt confused about their sexuality could still be classed as mentally ill.[4] This was finally removed as well, but not until 2013.

With attitudes like this around, no wonder it's taking such a long time to ban conversion therapy in this country. In fact, the arguments around that were playing out even as I was writing this book! In February 2022, the government closed their consultation on the proposed new law that would have banned the practice. Everyone assumed the outcome would be positive and that the law would be put into place later in the year. After all, they'd been promising to do it for years.[5] But the following month a document was leaked revealing that it wasn't going to go ahead after all.

After a huge public outcry, the government U-turned and agreed to go ahead with the law but will still exclude trans people from it. Even though all of the UK's leading medical bodies have condemned the exclusion of trans people, the Prime Minister continues to insist that banning trans conversion therapy is 'complex'.[6]

When it comes to trans people, one in five have been pressured to access services to suppress their gender identity. And unsurprisingly, those numbers are even higher for Black, Asian and minority ethnic queer people as well as disabled LGBTQ+ people.[7]

In some ways, science has stood in the way of our sexual freedom just as much as religion and cultural tradition. The scripts we get are influenced just as much by faulty 'facts' as by moral beliefs and social conventions.

In the 1960s sexologists Virginia Johnson and William Masters did studies where they brought couples into their laboratory, observed them having sex (yes, literally!) and collected data about how human bodies and brains respond. They came up with the 'human sexual response cycle', which stated that our experience of sex went as follows: desire, arousal, orgasm, resolution.[8]

At first this sounds pretty accurate, right? We feel horny, initiate sex (or masturbation), get wet and turned on before building up to cumming and feeling satisfied afterwards. But actually there are still some gaps here. What about women who are multi-orgasmic, for example? Although Masters and Johnson's work was useful, unfortunately they were still operating within a very patriarchal world and so their model is based mostly on the man's experience of sex.

These days, the research shows that women don't necessarily experience a set beginning and end but can move back and forth, going from arousal to desire, to orgasm and back to arousal again.[9] We don't have a 'fallow' period in the same way that men do, so for us orgasm doesn't have to signal the 'end' of sex.

Basically, if your experience of sex has always felt a little out of line with your male partner's, this is why! If you find you need another orgasm after you guys are done having sex, that's not necessarily a sign that he's done anything wrong, that's just how your sexual responses work. Similarly, if you notice that you sometimes don't really get turned on until a bit later in the session, that's normal too. Just because your man gets hard doesn't mean your body has to get wet at the same time. We're all different.

There have been some really useful discoveries to come out of sex science, though, which I think we can definitely use to help us figure out what we want and what works for us. Have you heard of Alfred Kinsey? He's known as the 'father of sexology' because he was one of the first people to study sex neutrally, to view it not in moral terms but just as a pleasurable activity that humans do for fun.

Based at the University of Indiana in the US, his research in the 1940s and 50s showed that people of all genders enjoyed sex (not just men!), and that we like having it in lots of different ways, including outside of marriage. Oh, and he also found that the vast majority of people masturbate. But as you can imagine, these revelations were pretty controversial in post-war America, and he actually had his funding pulled as a result.[10] Once again, though, this is evidence that just because the social norms at the time dictated one thing, it does *not* mean everyone was behaving that way.

One of Kinsey's most famous discoveries is that sexual orientation isn't either/or. People don't have to be all-straight or all-gay and, actually, most people are somewhere in between. He also observed that sexual behaviour, thoughts and feelings were not always consistent over time. In other words, who we're attracted to can change. Sometimes, all you can think about is getting that D.

At other times you might notice you're more attracted to women or having more lesbian fantasies. This is totally normal.

Kinsey came up with the idea of a scale from zero to six where zero meant exclusively heterosexual and six meant exclusively homosexual. Instead of assigning people to a category, this allowed researchers to place them somewhere on this spectrum. They also understood and accepted the idea that people could move up and down it at different points in their lives.[11]

It's important to note that more contemporary academics have pointed out some flaws in Kinsey's theories, one being that the scale implies that if you are 'more' attracted to one sex, you are 'less' attracted to the other. It also does not distinguish between sexual attraction and sexual behaviour, which don't always align. However, even if this framework is now somewhat outdated, it was useful in the way it challenged people to think more openly about sex and sexuality at the time.

0	Exclusively heterosexual
1	Predominantly heterosexual, only incidentally homosexual
2	Predominantly heterosexual, but more than incidentally homosexual
3	Equally heterosexual and homosexual
4	Predominantly homosexual, but more than incidentally heterosexual
5	Predominantly homosexual, only incidentally heterosexual
6	Exclusively homosexual
X	No socio-sexual contacts or reactions

Did you notice that there's also an X category for people who don't experience sexual attraction at all? Yeah, Kinsey and his team also acknowledged the existence of asexuality, something we're *still* struggling to accept today, as you heard about in Chapter 2: Society, Stigma and Slut-shaming when I shared my interview with asexual activist Yasmin Benoit (see page 41).

When I first heard of the Kinsey Scale in my mid-twenties it made total sense to me. Back then I was socialised into believing my sexual attraction could only be towards men. I'd always kind of known I was attracted to women, but since I'd only dated men I didn't really know how to define myself at that time. So was I bicurious? Or was I bi?

My first TV crush as a teenager was Sugar, star of the hit TV show *Sugar Rush*, played by Lenora Crichlow. Interestingly enough, Sugar was also the secret crush of her best friend, Kim. This was my first real introduction to questioning my sexuality, because Kim and I had something in common: we both fancied Sugar. It was such an amazing coming-of-age show, so you can imagine how my heart broke after it got cancelled.

Looking back, I had many girl crushes, but I didn't act on them because I was too afraid to explore that side of my sexuality. So I struggled to know what to call myself. Today, I understand that I'm definitely sexually fluid, regardless of who I've actually dated.

Knowing that my sexual orientation didn't have to be one or the other, it didn't have to be perfectly 50/50 (and it was totally OK that I'd only dated guys) and that it could change was a really useful way to start to think about it. There's no official test you can do to find out where you fall on the spectrum, but there are plenty of unofficial ones you can do. Just google 'Kinsey Scale test' and have fun! If you like that sort of thing, there's also a BDSM test.

Another scientific discovery that's really helped me understand *my* sexuality is the dual control model of sexual response. I first read about this in Emily Nagoski's book *Come As You Are* and it blew my mind. The model itself was developed by sexologists John Bancroft and Erick Janssen in the 1990s and basically it explains that how we respond sexually is dependent on the balance between 'sexual excitation' (being turned on) and 'sexual inhibition' (being turned off).[12]

Nagoski describes this as like having an accelerator and a brake.[13] The accelerator scans your surroundings for sexually relevant information and sends a 'Time to get horny!' message to your brain. This 'sexually relevant information' could be anything from a hot guy you see in the street to a tweet you read on your phone, a picture, a fragrance that reminds you of an ex, a memory of a hook-up, the feeling of tight jeans pressing on your vulva when you sit down or just a fleeting fantasy in your imagination. All of these things will send 'turn on' messages to your brain and have the potential to get you in the mood.

But not always! See, you also have a brake. And it's the brake's job to scan your surroundings for potential threats – reasons why now is not a good time to get aroused – and send a 'Calm it down, sis!' message to your brain. These could be things like being at work, being on the bus, knowing your mum is in the next room, worrying about getting pregnant, feeling unconfident about your body. They don't have to be real situations. Even just the memory of something slut-shamey a church aunt once said to you can be enough to slam on the brakes. That's why, as I said in Chapter 2: Society, Stigma and Slut-shaming, it's so important for us to try to rally against taboos and stigma, because they can really get in our heads and stop us having fun.

The reason I think this is so useful for understanding sexuality is that it helps explain why some people are really easily turned on and up for sex and some people need a little bit more time and attention. It also explains why we might sometimes find it really easy to get in the mood and other times it feels like an effort. If you've got a lot of things pressing your brakes, whether it's shame about sex, insecurities about your body or concerns about sexual health, it's gonna be hard to get aroused. It doesn't mean you're not a sex-positive person with a strong sex drive, it just means you need to take the time to address those things. I'm going to talk about body confidence and sexual health later in the book and I hope what we've covered already is helping you start to let go of any shame you might feel about your sexuality.

The dual control model can also help us figure out which partners are right for us. If you have an ex who you used to have amazing sex with, but your current partner is not quite lifting you to those same heights, it might be because something about this relationship is hitting your brakes. Have a think about what it might be. Same goes for those of you who always fantasise about that amazing hook-up you had one time but for some reason you've never been able to recreate that experience with anyone else. What do you think it was about that time that was really revving your accelerator? What was special about that situation that meant it didn't hit your brakes? Taking the time to think about this stuff and identify your 'ons' and your 'offs' will help you take that knowledge and understanding into your next sexual interaction.

I've definitely noticed that I feel more turned on and free during intimacy when the person I'm with is comfortable (and makes me feel comfortable) having flirty conversations about sex. Talking about sex with my partner is an accelerator for me, for sure! And looking back at some of my previous sexual experiences, the ones that have left me feeling self-conscious have been the ones where the foreplay wasn't enough to get me stimulated. So for me, lots of foreplay is definitely a key part of removing the brakes!

There's a questionnaire you can do to figure out what your excitors (accelerators) and inhibitors (brakes) are. It includes things like 'I *have* to trust my partner to become fully aroused' and you rate yourself on a scale of one to five depending on how much you relate to that statement. It's available on Emily Nagoski's website. I'll include the link in the resources section at the end, along with some of the other tests and surveys I talk about in this chapter.[14]

Forgetting the science and 'official' advice now, there are actually so many ways to start exploring your sexuality and identifying what you're interested in and who you're attracted to. It might sound obvious but one of the best places to start is social media – I mean, that's where I have a lot of my conversations and it's where I see people raising really interesting points. If you've been surrounded by a single narrative or 'script' your whole life, you can guarantee that's going to get blown out of the water the minute you go on TikTok. And that's a good thing! You don't have to agree with everything you read on Twitter or see on Instagram and YouTube, but just putting yourself into these online spaces where people are having open conversations about sex can really help break down our assumptions about it and expose us to new ideas.

I wouldn't have known what pansexuality was if it wasn't for these very same mediums. It helped put a word to a sexuality that I felt like I could identify with. It's the same with a lot of the kinks I'm into; I felt that I might be a bit weird for being into some sexual activities, but with Facebook communities and discussions on YouTube there's so much out there that allows you to understand yourself and realise there are other people who can relate.

If you don't already follow them, I definitely recommend you check out Shannon Boodram, Angelica Lindsey-Ali, Yeside Olayinka-Agboola, Dalychia Saah and Rafaella Fiallo, Weezy and Mandii B from the *WHOREible Decisions* podcast, Angela Yee from *Lip Service*, Rukiat Ashawe and Yoni M.

And I'm sure I don't need to tell you that listening to podcasts and reading books and articles about sex is a very good starting point. If you are a regular listener to *Laid Bare* you will already know that we love to break down what our sexuality means to us and how we identify, and I honestly do believe that hearing other people having conversations about this stuff will encourage you to ask *yourself* those kinds of questions.

Also, it can make it much easier to have conversations with people IRL. Instead of just awkwardly trying to raise the subject, you can say to them, 'I was listening to a podcast the other day and they were talking about this thing ...'

And of course I have to mention porn! Now, porn is no replacement for sex education – definitely don't watch porn and think it's a how-to guide – however, it was my sexual performance education. It was where I learned how to give head, where I saw anal sex for the first time and witnessed what it looked like to have an orgy, and it acquainted me with BDSM and dirty talk.

I think we should acknowledge that you *can* learn stuff from ethical porn, (I'll talk more about the importance of the distinction between ethical and unethical porn in chapter 5) particularly about your likes and dislikes and what turns you on. I remember the first time I saw Cherokee D'ass suck dick when I put it on for me and my friends to watch as teens and was like, 'I wanna try that!' I saw how she gripped the dick, used two hands and didn't stop to breathe for a long period. (Please breathe!) Now, obviously a lot of the porn we probably watch is made with the male viewer in mind so it might not be quite to your taste, but if there's a particular scenario or dynamic or pairing you keep finding yourself going back to, it's worth stopping to think about how you might like that to play out if you were to do it for real.

If visual porn is not your thing, there's also audio porn. I've recently got really into audio porn and I've been so impressed. You can definitely tell it's aimed more at women: the scenes have more context, there's more build-up and the dirty talk is a lot more authentic. There are literally hundreds of different stories and fantasies so you can easily dip in and out and see what turns you on. It's also totally private – nobody's ever going to know the filth that's going into your headphones!

If you haven't heard of sex menus, I also recommend googling them and having a look at a few online. It's basically a list of possible sexual activities, kinks and partner configurations and you can rate each one based on how appealing it is to you.

Some sex educators recommend using them with your partner so you can discuss what you're into and find out your compatibility, and I'll come back to that in Chapter 10, but actually I think it can be just as useful to do it on your own. Pour yourself a drink, sit down, let go of any pressure you might feel to adhere to certain expectations or appear a certain way to other people, and be truly honest with yourself about how each item on the list makes you feel. You never know, you might surprise yourself. Then again, you might find out you're not into any of that stuff and that's fine as well.

Knowing you're totally straight and totally vanilla is also really empowering. If what you're really, really horny for is missionary sex in a long-term relationship then I'm happy for you! Because now you can go out and enjoy your best nut without wondering if you're missing out or whether you 'should' be trying different things.

LGBTQ+ identities

There are some people who know from childhood that they're gay or trans, but I also think it's a very common experience to realise it slowly as you grow up. But what if you've been brought up in a culture that tells you there's only one way to be? Because, let's be honest, that's most of us. We live in a society that assumes we are cis and heterosexual unless we present evidence to the contrary. So many of the stories we hear and the cartoons we watch as children are based around heterosexual love and relationships, and the assumption is that we are straight until proven otherwise. There's a term you sometimes hear to describe this, which is 'compulsory heterosexuality'.

Even in 2022 there are people living closeted lives because the pressure to conform to heterosexuality is so great. Many people can also face real danger from their family and/or communities if they are open about their sexuality. Remember Liam, my boyfriend who I first experienced sex with? Well, two years later, when I was at university, I'd regularly travel back down to London and one time he asked to meet up. I'll be honest, at one point I was convinced he'd seen the light and wanted to get back together. He dragged me out to this student union club night, where we got tipsy and danced the night away.

I remember him screaming something in my ear on the dance floor but not being able to make out what he was saying, so we went and stood outside the toilets where it was a bit quieter. Then he said it: 'I'm gay.' I just remember hugging him and screaming 'OMG!!' He explained that I was the first person he had told and it felt beautiful. We carried on dancing the night away to the Kooks' 'Naïve' till we were ready to go home.

It was a blurry night, but my overall recollection is just being happy for him. He might have broken my 19-year-old heart, but I couldn't feel bitter about it. There I was, trying to get back a boyfriend who had realised he wasn't actually *into* women! He'd had to pretend because he wasn't sure. Now, away from school and all the pressures and expectations that come with being a teenage boy, he'd found the freedom to finally figure out his sexual identity.

Liam and I still speak (in fact, he hates the alias I've given him in this book!). We still check in with each other and he's a big fan of my podcast. He's also in a very loving relationship and likes to give me unsolicited business advice.

The National Survey of Sexual Attitudes and Lifestyles (Natsal) is a big nationwide research project carried out every ten years. It's actually one of the biggest surveys of sexual behaviour in the world. Back in 1990, when they did the very first one, just 6 per cent of men and 4 per cent of women reported ever having had a sexual experience with someone of the same sex.[15] Ten years later, at the turn of the millennium, those numbers had risen to 7 per cent for men and 10 per cent for women.

This isn't because there were more LGBTQ+ people, it's because attitudes towards sexuality were changing so people felt more comfortable talking about their attraction and experiences with people of the same sex. The researchers who carried out the survey said the rise in people reporting same-sex experiences was partly down to 'more tolerant social attitudes'.[16]

This might be true, but for those of us growing up in the late Nineties, it didn't feel that tolerant. Don't forget that until 2003 it was literally illegal for teachers to talk about being LGBTQ+ (in England and Wales). Section 28 was brought in by Conservative Prime Minister Margaret Thatcher in 1988 and it banned the 'promotion of homosexuality'. If you were a queer kid growing up back then, the only mention of your sexual identity you ever heard at school was most likely in the playground and I'm gonna bet it probably wasn't all that nice.

Do you remember the story I told you in Chapter 1 about being suspended from school for saying the word lesbian? (See page 13.) Looking back, it's so easy for me to chuckle at that, but it clearly displays the negative attitude society had towards children discovering a non-heteronormative world. Would I have been sent home if I'd said, 'Why do men and women kiss?' or commented that 'Sarah has a boyfriend'? It quickly made me feel as though there was something wrong with being queer.

Today, I can't imagine having a child and being called in to remove them from school for the whole day or missing out on a school experience because of a random word they'd learned and yelled out in class. (News flash: that's what kids do!) That teacher would be met with a stare-off by me or at least an argument defending my child.

Sometimes I wonder what motivated my school teacher to send me home that day and if it was due to the laws, or the fact that my school was filled with other kids whose parents also had an extremely negative attitude towards the LGBTQ+ community.

It's still tough to be an LGBTQ+ kid growing up in the UK, but more recent surveys show that one in five Gen-Z people identifies as somewhere on the LGBTQ+ rainbow.[17] But that doesn't mean I don't get people in my mentions who are still clearly displaying a form of homophobia; they're just not as obvious about it as they once were.

Figuring out your sexual identity in a world where many people still think it's OK to make jokes or comments about it (I still regularly hear the claim that bisexuality doesn't exist!) is not easy. I identify as pansexual, which means I feel attraction to all kinds of people, regardless of gender, but I'll be honest and say that as someone who has mostly dated cis men, I don't think I am the right person to speak on the queer experience. I wanted to talk to women who actually know what it's like to grow up feeling at odds with the messages and assumptions around them, so I called up my friends Ro and Nana from the *Two Twos* podcast, which they describe as 'two Black lesbians living in London speaking their unapologetic truth'. You might have heard them already and if you haven't listened to their show, you should! They have such incredible, funny and honest conversations, featuring guests who come to talk about everything from starting a family as a same-sex couple to being gay and Muslim, grappling with trans and non-binary identities and, of course, the reality of living, loving and fucking as an LGBTQ+ person!

Like me, Ro (short for Rosie) grew up in a religious household. Her family were Mormon and she went to a Catholic school so the messages she got her whole childhood were very heteronormative and very sex-negative. 'Everything was just around no sex, no sex, no sex,' she says. 'The only conversation I had with my mum at home, she just said to me, "If you come home pregnant, then I have to disown you." That is what the conversation was.'

They both told me that lack of representation in their community but also in the media made it hard for them to figure out their sexual identity until later on. 'I remember seeing [the early 2000s ITV show] *Bad Girls*,' recalls Nana. 'There's so many lesbian storylines in *Bad Girls*, but it still never clicked for me! It never clicked and I feel like it's because they weren't Black. They didn't look like me! So I thought, "Oh, I can't ... this is not ... I can never be gay."'

While Ro knew she liked women from a really young age, there was nothing in her life at that time that gave her any kind of language or framework for what that meant. 'I definitely knew that I liked women,' she says. 'I knew from primary school, but it was never, ever something that I really had the language for. And it's only now, looking back, that I can say ... I was queer or I was a lesbian. But at the time I thought it was gender confusion. I thought that maybe I was a boy because as far as I knew, only boys fancied girls. It wasn't until I became a teenager that I saw Jessica Betts on

Missy Elliott's [reality TV show] *Road to Stardom* and that's the first time I saw a Black masculine-presenting woman. I was like, "OK, this is what can be, I can be this person." It was just about being comfortable within myself to be able to present like that, but it didn't even come until my early twenties.'

As I mentioned, sex education for those of us growing up in the Nineties left a lot to be desired. And if you were LGBTQ+ you were basically invisible. 'It was very hetero,' says Ro. 'But because it was so religious at my school, they tried to avoid talking about contraception and things like that as well. But because I didn't feel like I was included, or I couldn't relate, I just used to switch off.'

Having gone to a less conservative school, Nana has vivid memories of being taught how to put a condom on a banana in citizenship class but agrees that there was absolutely nothing to help a young queer person figure out their sexual identity. Instead, like a lot of young people, she turned to porn. Now, I've already said I don't think this is a good way to get your sex education, but is it any surprise that kids do just that if their sexuality is simply not being reflected in the information they're getting at school or from their parents?

'"If you have sex, you'll get pregnant." That was the beginning and end of my sex education by my parents,' Nana says. 'In school it was just about having a family. It was very heteronormative. There was nothing on two women being together or two men being together. There was nothing even about gender expression, nothing like that.'

Ro and Nana both describe themselves as 'masculine-presenting', which means they tend to dress in a more typically masculine way – you're more likely to see them in hoodies and shirts than in a dress. But they tell me the term is more open-ended than other labels. Masculine-presenting people might still wear make-up sometimes, for example, and have long hair.

'When you initially come out on the Black [queer] scene, it's normally about "studs" and "femmes",' explains Ro. 'If somebody's a stud you're on the masculine spectrum in terms of how you present and your mannerisms are a bit more masculine as well. Whereas femme would be the opposite. You're more what society deems to be feminine – feminine features and the way you present to the world in that way. And if you're "stem", you're somewhere in the middle of all that. They might be someone who wears boys' clothing, but they wear a wig and make-up and lashes and stuff like that.

'So when we say "masculine-presenting" it's to give room to express your masculinity in a less rigid way. This is something that I feel quite strongly about. I don't say that I'm a stud. People might look at me and say that I'm a stud, but when I open my mouth, I'm still very feminine. I have all these feminine mannerisms and stuff like that. And I feel like it's unfair for me to take away from stud identities and say I'm a stud when I'm not.'

'There's definitely a spectrum,' agrees Nana. 'Me and Rosie are both masculine-presenting, but we're not the *same* masculine-presenting. In terms of outwardly how we look, I think people would look at Rosie and think she's more masc than me. But we're both definitely on the spectrum somewhere.'

Of course, when you're going through the world not looking the way people expect women to look, that can add another level of stigma. Ro has a child from a sexual relationship she had with a man when she was 20 (as discussed, the pressure to conform to heterosexuality is so strong that many queer people end up having relationships with people of a different gender even though they know that's not really what they want) and she says that navigating NHS maternity care while looking the way she does meant dealing with a lot of ignorance.

'I remember I was in labour and [wearing] my basketball shorts and my big T-shirt. And everyone kind of looked at me like, "Why is this person pregnant?" Then after I had my daughter and we used to go to get her injections and stuff like that, I just saw the lack of knowledge and education throughout the NHS staff every single step of the way. They'd just be looking at me like, "Is this your niece?" and [telling me], "The mum has to bring the child to the doctor appointment." And I'm like, "I *am* the mum."'

Both of them found coming out to their families and friends difficult. Like me, Nana's family's expectations were very much that she'd get married to a man and have children.

'When I came out, my family's response was basically just like, "Why? Why?" I remember my mum asking me why I couldn't do this after I'd had a child or why couldn't I get married to a man and just do my thing on the side! It's just like, it doesn't need to be that way! Everybody should be able to live a fulfilling life and live their truth authentically.'

This is so upsetting to me. I'm not stupid, I know it happens. I know there are people out there living their true identities on the DL. There are men and women with families who are sleeping with other people on the side, but honestly, nobody should have to live that way. For a start it's deceitful and dangerous, and if you're not practising safe sex (which cheaters are less likely to do, as we'll discover in our sexual health chapter later on) then you're also putting your family's health at risk. I can't really imagine how distressing it must have been for Nana to hear that suggestion from her mum but, like me, she's working to break down the stigma and both she and Ro hope that through having open conversations about this stuff on their podcast they can help change attitudes.

But they didn't just encounter homophobia from their families. Even close friends found it tricky to deal with their sexual identity and many have dropped away over time. They also both realised they were having to stifle their true selves around their old friends.

'I'm not friends with the same people I was friends with in school just because we've grown apart, but I remember going on holiday with two of my friends at the time and one of them was like, "Um, can you leave your lesbian clothes at home, please?"' remembers Nana.

Ro agrees. 'I realised that I was holding back about who I was when I was in those friendship circles. I didn't realise how much I was until they weren't my friends anymore, but I've seen how in different areas of my life I flourished just because I'm unapologetic about who I am now. I'm not pretending to be somebody else, and it just gives you room to grow, which wasn't happening before.'

And all that's before they even get out into the world and have to deal with the ignorance there. Ro tells me about a time she went to give blood and the male nurse took one look at her and asked, 'Why are you a lesbian?' and Nana still gets nervous any time she has to go to a sexual health clinic.

'I get scared!' she says. 'When I first started going I was scared to tick the box of either bisexual or lesbian, because most of the nurses are African and so I was scared about what their attitudes might be and what they'll be thinking or even what they say. Because they will just say what's on their mind. So that makes somebody uncomfortable to go and get a sexual health test, which everybody needs to be responsible and to stay safe.'

Even when they're not dealing with outright ignorance, LGBTQ+ people also have to contend with stereotypes and fetishisation from people who see their sexuality as fantasy fodder. Lesbian identities in particular get fetishised by straight men. As any queer woman can tell you, tell people you're gay (or bi) and it's not going to be long before you get asked if you want to have a threesome or some dickhead offers himself and his unwanted penis to you, thinking he's being generous.

'I think men really, really think the world revolves around them,' says Nana. 'They're always inviting themselves! If you say you're in a relationship with a woman or you like women, it's all, "Can I join?" And it's like, "No, sir, you cannot join." A year or two ago I went to a party with a partner and she introduced me to her male friend who she had been friends with for years. He was just like, "Oh, yeah, let's all have sex." And he was serious! We just looked at him like, "WHAT?"'

A big part of what I want to do in writing this book is to show women that things can be different. Just because we were brought up a certain way and exposed to certain attitudes doesn't mean we have to adhere to those attitudes and continue to uphold them in our lives. You deserve to have the kind of sex and relationships *you* want, and to be able to identify in the way that feels right for *you.* I asked Ro and Nana what they'd like today's queer youth to have that they didn't have growing up.

'I want them to have choices and to know that those choices are very much attainable for them,' says Ro. 'And for them to know that it's OK to express yourself in whichever way you want and that they can switch and they can change. And they can have the patience to figure themselves out without any judgement. I just want my platform to highlight lots of different, especially Black queer, experiences so that people can see themselves as at least one of those. And also know that it's interchangeable; you can see yourself in this person one day, and the next day this person. You don't have to be so rigid with your life.

'We're also trying to bridge the gap between the cishet community and the queer community. So it's not just about being visible, it's also about trying to teach people outside of the community that we're actually just human and to respect us in other spaces. Because we want to exist in spaces that are not just queer, without the fear of being judged or [the] fear of being misunderstood.'

I also asked what they thought about the concept of 'coming out', because it always occurs to me that straight people don't have to come out because they are just assumed to be straight. But society puts this pressure on LGBTQ+ people to constantly explain themselves.

'I feel like coming out is bullshit,' says Ro. 'The reason why we have to come out is because society has really suppressed us so much that we have to first come out to ourselves. And then coming out to other people, we have to explain ourselves. I just hope that society can move on to the point where you can just be whatever you want to be, with no one having to explain anything to anybody.'

'I think with coming out, you often have to explain your identity with it,' agrees Nana. 'Because people will have questions. People always feel like there must have been something that happened to you for you to be queer. And no, that's not the case, babes. I just like what I like, and I shouldn't have to explain that. Say, if you're in a workplace, I should just be able to talk about my partner, who happens to be a woman. I shouldn't have to make an announcement [saying], "Oh, I'm gay." So I definitely feel that it's something that we should be moving away from. And I think that's happening with Gen Z; they're kind of just like, "I am what I am."'

All of us are really passionate about making sure things are different for women and LGBTQ+ folks coming up now. Like me, Ro and Nana want to offer a voice and provide a platform for accurate information, education and (sometimes brutal!) honesty about sexuality and relationships. And we want to showcase the diversity of Black love, too! I asked Ro and Nana about their thoughts on the representation around what Black love is and told them how I feel that queer stories are sometimes left out.

'Often when we think about Black love, we just think about hetero couples, because it makes everyone more comfortable,' says Ro. 'At the end of the day, people don't really want to look outside of themselves and look at other experiences. But when you take away queer Black love, you are kind of saying that their love is not valued as well. But I don't think "queer Black love" [should be separate from] "Black love"; it's all under the same umbrella that is Black love. And so when shows don't feature queer people, even if there are queer people involved, if they're not showing them in the promos, it's almost like we're not good enough, we're just there to tick a box. And there's so many more examples. What about the trans experience? What about the Black disabled experience? It's all a very much valued Black experience and we need to be included because we also have joy as well, you know?'

Speaking of joy, you know I had to ask them some filthy questions, too. It was important to me to showcase the difficulties and challenges of identifying as LGBTQ+, but this is *The Big O* after all; it's a book about pleasure and living your best sex life, so I wanted to end this chapter on a positive note. Studies show that lesbians have more orgasms than straight women,[18] so *of course* I wanted to know their secrets! Here's how that conversation went down:

Oloni: I'm sure you already know that when it comes to women having sex with women, they receive the most orgasms in comparison to heterosexual women. Why do you think that is in general?
Nana: I would think it's men thinking about themselves and their nut before actually thinking about pleasure in the woman. And also, women not being vocal and not saying what they like. But a lot of [heterosexual] sex is really focused around men's satisfaction and I think when it comes to women who have sex with other women, the reason it's so pleasurable is because they're really looking to satisfy *each other.* It's not always about cumming either. And I think when you approach it like that, you're more likely to cum, basically.

O: What are your favourite sexual positions?
N: Leg 'pon shoulder! Yeah, I would say missionary, leg 'pon shoulder, staring into the eyes. We love a bit of romance!
Ro: We love a trib as well!
N: Oh, tribbing is fantastic.
N: It's basically just rubbing vulvas together – that stimulation is very, very good.
R: It doesn't even have to be vagina and vagina, it could be a body part and vagina.
N: It could be like a thigh.

O: I was listening to this podcast the other day where they were talking about when women are discovering themselves and want to start having sex with women, so they want to get intimate, they're ready to explore, but when it comes down to eating vagina, they're ready to run away! And I was dying. So I wondered, have there been

any funny experiences like that for you growing up when you were having sex with women?

R: Yes! One of the qualities of being a stud is a lot of them are touch-me-nots [women who prefer to do all the giving and no receiving during sex]. And because I look like a stud a lot of women just assume that I am, too. So I did have a lot of pillow princesses [women who prefer to do all the receiving and no giving] in my early queer days. I think maybe they found it difficult to [have] those conversations and I also never used to bring it up ... Because then I guess there would be the added pressure of, 'OK, that must mean she wants me to eat her vagina, oh my God!' So I would just avoid those conversations. But, yeah, a lot of people do feel like bisexual girls that are just coming into themselves might be here for an experiment, they might only be here for sex and no romance. So those difficult conversations are there to be had as well.

N: I think with me, I definitely avoided women who hadn't had sex with women [before] because to me it just wasn't inspiring confidence. I want somebody who is down for whatever, you know? I'm not down for the pillow princess stuff. This is equal opportunities here! But I definitely dated a self-proclaimed lesbian who ate my pussy like a cat licking milk! So there's also people who identify as lesbians who don't enjoy an act and that's completely fine, but just tell me, please, before we get into it, before we take our clothes off. Please, please let me know that! But I would say the same, that people assume because you're masculine-presenting that you don't want to be touched. And I think for the most part, we do like to give, we do get satisfaction out of being a giver, but also you want to receive as well. So it's not good to make that assumption.

O: I think the average length of time for heterosexual PIV sex is about seven minutes.[19] But we know that women don't necessarily experience the sexual response cycle the same way that men do, so we don't have to follow that same pattern. What would you say is the longest you've enjoyed intimacy for?

R: Oh, maybe two hours or something? Not now, but then! In my mid-twenties, maybe! Now it would probably be like one hour tops.
N: We've got so much going on in our lives that sometimes the sex has to be like an hour max. But back in the day when we didn't have anything to do the sex would be going on for longer. And the thing about it is that we can re-up. And it's not always about cumming; it's really about pleasuring each other so that the sex can really last for a long time.

O: Do you guys have any other sex tips to share?
R: If you're having sex with a woman, make sure that it is wet, wet, wet, wet, wet! Don't be afraid of lube! Just don't be afraid and communicate as well. Sex is always good when you communicate, even during sex, too. Like, if you're enjoying it, *say* that you enjoy it – it sounds good!

CHAPTER 5

Getting to Know Your Body

I'll be honest with you: this is probably going to be my favourite chapter and that's because I enjoy talking about masturbation. I always have! If I'm not asking my guests when they got laid last on my show, I'm asking how long ago it was since they flicked their bean, wanked, penetrated themselves and with what toy.

Masturbating is very normal and a beautiful feeling that helps shape our sexual journey with ourselves. In my opinion it's a very necessary act that helps cultivate what you enjoy with other people. You can't get an STD or pregnant, and you get to climax! What's not to love?

One of the reasons I'm now so passionate about self-pleasure is that, growing up, I'd heard how masturbation was the worst thing I could do to myself. There are pamphlets, essays and whole sermons dedicated to scaring us into believing that masturbation is a sin and anyone who partakes in the act will burn in hellfire. It was even said it would give you blurry vision ... Sound familiar? It was drilled into me at church that it was a dirty, horrible thing to do. I was completely petrified of something I now know to be a healthy, beautiful thing, but I never understood why it was demonised.

Some Christians will point to the story of Onan in the book of Genesis to explain that masturbation is wrong and a sin. Onan was the second son of Judah and God had just killed his older brother, Er. Onan was tasked with marrying his brother's widow, Tamar, in order to give her a child, and I know that sounds extremely creepy, but this was fairly normal back then.

Onan was not super keen on the idea and so he decided to pull out and ejaculated on the floor. God was angry with this and killed him, too. Was God angry that Onan had disobeyed him by trying not to give Tamar a child or was God angry because he 'spilled his seed on the ground', aka had sex for non-procreation purposes? This story is where the term 'onanism' is derived from, meaning to masturbate or ejaculate outside of a vagina. Either way, throughout this story no masturbation even takes place, and this scripture leaves a lot up to interpretation and misinterpretation.

I feel that the sin is more likely to be when a direct order from God is not followed and not that one chooses to pleasure themselves without harming anyone else. And if we really want to be technical about it, there is no evidence that women masturbating is a sin as we certainly cannot spill our seed anywhere, so we good, sis.

I was 12 or 13 when I first started masturbating – a detail I used to keep to myself when I first started talking about self-pleasure, due to the shame of thinking I was abnormal for experiencing these sexual feelings so young and my hormones being all over the place.

It's only in the last couple of years after talking to other women that I have understood this was actually quite normal. In fact, one Swedish study showed that the average age of masturbating for the first time for girls was 13 years old and 12 years old for boys.[1]

I've also asked this question on Twitter many times and the ages I've heard from women are from around ten years old to their mid to late twenties. We do know that women masturbate slightly less than men, but the 'masturbation gap' is not anywhere near as big as a lot of people think it is. One survey found that 96 per cent of men and 78 per cent of women in the UK masturbate, but when asked what percentage of women they *think* masturbate, participants estimated just 65 per cent.[2]

Even though the cultures and religions that teach that masturbation is wrong tend to teach that it's wrong for *everyone*, we can't deny that, like all aspects of sex, there is more stigma attached to it for women.

I still remember denying ever touching myself at 14 when a friend would ask me during our lunch break in the school courtyard. We'd stare at each other waiting for a sign that the other was lying. The truth was I couldn't wait to race home and play with myself. It's why as soon as I got my first debit card in my mid to late teens I bought my first huge dildo: a veiny, black, 12-inch dildo off this very dodgy and cheap site. I'm sure the material would be illegal to use for toys now. It was fun to use but extremely noisy and constantly needed new batteries. I also got caught with it in bed by my landlady when I went to university.

I was half asleep, having forgotten to put it away the night before, when she knocked on my door. She was visiting to check the heating that I had complained about. I couldn't really make out what she was saying to me because she was whispering and I was still pretty groggy, so I murmured that she could look at the radiator. Then I realised she was pointing at something as she said, ever so faintly, 'You want to put that away?' I wasn't wearing my glasses and I was barely conscious, but through my blurred vision I realised that something was my ginormous dildo, which was occupying the other side of my bed. Once I realised what it was she was referring to, I nearly died with absolute embarrassment. I quickly hid myself and the dildo underneath my duvet in utter humiliation until she left.

Honestly, you couldn't pay me to play with that thing today! While this dildo was an important part of my self-discovery, I understand now that pleasure isn't always defined by the girth and length of a penis (well, depending on who it's attached to).

When I got older and started to feel more secure in my sexulthood (yes, I made that up and I kind of like it) I stopped lying to my friends and admitted to masturbating. I still have photos of when I first showed them my dildo and them being in shock. We laughed, we giggled, and I allowed them to ask me 21 questions about it: *So how often do you use it? Does it hurt? What does it feel like?*

My friends still denied touching themselves, but I think it stemmed from shame and seeing masturbation as something that's wrong and filthy. We hardly had any sex education, so it was no wonder they found it gross, but not me – once I discovered orgasms there was just no going back.

I don't even think I knew where or what my clitoris was when I started to self-pleasure. Because of the porn I took in, I thought a penis-like object was what I needed to help me cum. I made my own self-pleasure penis-centred because I simply knew no better. Of course, once I started exploring myself I soon figured out which areas felt good and which felt *really* good. Over time I learned exactly how best to make myself cum and also what kinds of sensations I enjoyed alongside that.

Once I realised that masturbating wasn't all about penetration, I experimented with other fun toys. I hated some and I loved others, but the ones that excited me were always the ones that focused on my clitoris. These days I always joke that I'm all about the clit. That's definitely where the party's at for me. This isn't to say I'm against penetration play – I'm absolutely not – but discovering a very sensual part of your body you've not been educated on feels like winning a golden ticket, which is why self-discovery is so important when we discuss sexual intimacy.

Without masturbation I'm sure I wouldn't be nearly as clued up on my body and my sexuality as I am. Which is why I talk so openly about it now and am such a passionate advocate for trying it out.

Understanding your body

As young women, we are given such limited information about what our genitals look like and how they work. For those of us brought up in conservative religious families there can be a huge culture of secrecy and stigma around having these conversations. It's vital that we start to dismantle this. I've spoken to a lot of women who aren't even able to locate their clitoris because they're too afraid to look at their vulva due to the guilt and embarrassment they feel. Does that sound healthy?

Even in mainstream education, I don't recall ever seeing a diagram of a vulva. Ever! As I said, when I first started masturbating I didn't know about my clitoris. I mean, I'd literally never been told it existed! And even if I had, I might not have known how I liked it to be touched or stimulated were it not for those formative teenage years spent exploring and playing with myself.

In Chapter 1: My Sex Education I shared a diagram of the vulva and clitoris (see page 15), and while a textbook understanding of anatomy is a good starting point, there's really nothing like getting down there yourself to help you figure out how your body works and what feels good. So go on, grab a mirror and look at your vulva – no, really, really look at her. Talk to her or them and speak words of affirmation. You deserve to celebrate your vulva in a way that empowers you.

Words of affirmation and hype-up phrases for your vulva:

- I am allowed to love you.
- I deserve to experience arousal.
- I love making love to you.
- You are beautifully created.
- My pussy is mine.
- You are deserving of pleasure.
- 'This pussy make movies, wetter than a whale' – 'Pussy Talk' by City Girls
- Look how beautiful you are ANDDD you bring powerful orgasms!

Masturbation helps us to develop agency and autonomy over our own body, allowing us to rediscover our sexuality, especially when we weren't given the education to do so. You have a right to enjoy the clitoris, vagina and any other erogenous zones you were born with, and no one should make you feel ashamed for it.

If you're still surrounded by people for whom the subject of masturbation is taboo then try to find new social groups where you can talk openly about it – either online or in person (visiting a sex shop, for example, can be a good way to have an open conversation with staff about what you're interested in, what kinds of toys do what, etc.).

Getting up close and personal with our own vulvas and realising that they can give us so much pleasure can also help us break down the idea that they need to look a certain way or that there's a 'right' way to enjoy sex. Masturbation is also how we learn what we like. And that, in turn, will help us have better sex with our partners.

There are specific masturbating motions that I personally enjoy in the bedroom when using my toys. What's great is being able to communicate to my sexual partner exactly how to emulate this and also directing them on how to caress other parts of my body, which can add to the sensation. I'm usually direct and tap into my dominant side by saying something like, 'Touch me like this,' or when I'm feeling a bit cheeky I might say, 'I know you can do better than that.'

In my 2020 TEDx Talk, I described how masturbation gives you the chance to learn how to love yourself sexually so that you can, in turn, teach your partners how to show you that same level of love. If you don't take time to really discover what it is that turns you on in the bedroom, by yourself, you cannot really instruct someone else on how to love your body, because you have no clue yourself.

Masturbation allows you to become more confident and develop a sense of authority over your body, because at the end of the day no one understands your pleasure better than you.

Masturbation isn't a consolation prize

I used to work in a sex store, so I saw different people come in and out daily – no pun intended! I remember speaking to a lady who was probably in her twenties and had popped in with her friend. I asked if they needed any help.

'I don't need sex toys, I've got a man,' she told me.

I had the most perplexed look on my face, because this woman thought that a toy was a replacement for her boyfriend. It isn't. But it gave me an insight into how some people saw sex toys. Why was she defensive over a bit of plastic?

I can't tell you the number of times I've heard men say, 'My girl doesn't need that, she's got me' – giving off strong vibes of jealousy and insecurity. I've also heard guys say, 'If she has a toy, she won't want to have sex with me.'

There's this misconception that people who masturbate have no one to enjoy physical intimacy with, but sexual pleasure isn't just about being with another person; it can also be about being at one with yourself – no different to enjoying a movie on your own as well as wanting to enjoy one together with your partner.

Part of the issue, I think, stems from misunderstanding what penises represent in sex. Men have been told all their lives that their dick is all that is needed to make cishet women climax. They ran with this assumption so hard that some still find it unfathomable that we'd need extra assistance, therefore making it about their masculinity. They have run with it so hard that people do not understand the concept of sex that isn't centred around dicks. If we want to experience better sex, better orgasms, better foreplay, then we need to understand what else sex can consist of and change the script we've adopted, because it's clearly not working for many of us.

Masturbation can be a wonderful addition to your life, either as a single person OR if you're in a couple. It's not something you have 'instead' of partnered sex; it's its own separate activity and can be enjoyed alongside the sex you have with other people.

Masturbation is good for you

Today when I see people talk about masturbation it's categorised with wellbeing, alongside exercising, meditating and eating well. They're not wrong either. Masturbation has been shown to have significant health benefits, including my personal favourite, which is better sleep.[3] Oh, how I enjoy a wank just before bed! Orgasm also releases feel-good hormones such as oxytocin, prolactin, dopamine and serotonin,[4] which help reduce stress – one reason why I rush to bring out my favourite suction toy when I'm under a lot of pressure. Other benefits have been said to include reducing period cramps (and other kinds of pain), boosting concentration and lifting mood.

I look for any reason to masturbate whenever I feel like it, because it makes me feel happy after that dopamine kicks in. I feel alive and it also challenges me to look for new ways to enjoy sex with myself. Sometimes I use ethical porn to help when enjoying self-pleasure as the visuals help stimulate me; other times I use audio erotica, but most times I enjoy just closing my eyes and fantasising about some of my most pleasurable sexual experiences or intimate moments that I'd love to tick off my bucket list.

If I'm honest, though, sometimes I get tired of seeing articles listing the '101 health benefits of masturbating'. I feel like it can be overdone to the point where we almost feel like we need to use health benefits to justify masturbation instead of championing it for what it is: a pleasure activity. But I think, again, this is linked to stigma. By focusing on the health benefits, we can avoid accusations of being perverted or abnormal. There's a reason why brands advertise their sex toys and lube as 'wellness' products – because it's more socially acceptable to pay attention to your health and wellbeing than to your sexuality.

I understand all of that, but it shouldn't be something we constantly need to defend. When you or your friend get a new haircut or hairstyle we know it's done because you like it and it makes you feel good! We don't have endless conversations about the health benefits or what a new hairstyle can do for your wellbeing. Instead, we might talk about the latest hairstyle trends. Perhaps we should do that more: talk about the latest masturbation trends!

I mean, I understand why it's done, but we shouldn't be wasting our energy trying to convince people who have absolutely no desire to understand something that is very natural. Enjoy what makes you feel good. The fact that it also comes with a raft of wonderful health benefits is just a bonus if you ask me!

Masturbation should be part of sex education

An important person who comes to mind and was definitely ahead of her time when discussing masturbation is Dr Jocelyn Elders. In 1994, Elders, the first African-American surgeon general, was forced to resign from her role in the United States under President Bill Clinton for encouraging the education of masturbation. Her aim was to help kids understand that self-pleasure was not only natural, but could also help decrease STIs by presenting young people with a viable alternative to partnered sex. She wasn't wrong either!

Elders was dubbed the 'Condom Queen' as she was known for giving out the contraception to public school kids, showing how dedicated she was to teaching children about safe sex.

In 1994, during the United Nations conference on AIDS, Jocelyn Elders was asked her opinion on how she felt on the topic of teaching children about masturbation. She was asked if she believed that self-pleasure could reduce the chances of unsafe sex, to which she responded: 'I think that is something that is a part of human sexuality, and it's a part of something that perhaps should be taught. But we've not even taught our children the very basics. And I feel that we have tried ignorance for a very long time, and it's time we try education.'[5]

Clinton immediately asked her to resign. The audacity, right? And of course we all know how he ... nevermind.

Elders' aim was not to corrupt young minds, but to further educate children on what many of us still aren't taught about sexual education today. As she herself said, ignorance wasn't working (and it still isn't). She wasn't suggesting kids be taught *how* to touch themselves, but merely that they be informed on what self-pleasure is and that it was a safe option. Instead, she was condemned for her very valid opinion.

If we allowed young people to know more about what self-pleasure is, they'd grow up to have a healthier understanding of sex as a whole. Keeping it away from them as a subject just adds to the ignorance and stigmatisation of masturbation.

Elders was vocal about many issues, including female reproductive rights. She did not mince her words. When asked in an interview whether she thought there should be laws against stalking and harassing doctors who provided abortions, she was categorically in favour, adding: 'We really need to get over this love affair with the fetus and start worrying about children.'[6]

She was a real badass, who not only spoke up, but did the work. Thanks to Dr Jocelyn Elders, 7 May is now National Masturbation Day. The idea was started by a sex-positive retail store in San Francisco in 1995 as a direct response to her dismissal and it now extends to the entire month of May. Yes, Masturbation May is an annual international event, which helps create positive conversations about self-pleasure and destigmatise the act of masturbating!

So, are you ready to explore now we've debunked some myths? Well, get your fingers and your toys ready then!

Getting started

Masturbating can be different for everyone or sometimes the same; for example, I'm sure some men wank by using lube, a toy or, of course, their hand. Some men enjoy lying down, others standing, some sitting up. They have their favourite tools to help stimulate their pleasure such as their favourite category in porn and, just like us, fantasies, audio or magazines. But this book is about how we discover *our* orgasms, not theirs, so let's get into how we enjoy masturbating.

Do something that'll turn you on. This might be wearing lingerie for yourself, lighting some vanilla scented candles, playing some music that'll help make you feel sexy, taking a bubble bath, looking at photos of someone you find attractive, watching or reading some erotica, turning the lights down low and watching yourself in the mirror dancing in a sensual and seductive way – whatever it is, do it, because arousal is key. Ooh, and don't forget to lock your door!

This goes without saying but lying on your bed on your back is probably a great way to continue. Make sure your hands are clean. Now, let's say you're watching some great ethical porn that has helped turn you on, you can either continue with it on in the background, or lower the volume as you close your eyes. Remember, be in the moment: take in the scent in the air, the sexual noises in the background, the visuals of the porn you're watching; imagine it being yourself, your breasts, your vulva, your ass. Imagine it's your body being catered to sexually.

Women have several erogenous zones, otherwise known as areas on your body that help turn you on. As well as your clitoris, these may include your neck, ears, breasts, lips and ass. So if you're feeling awkward or nervous about sticking your hand down your knickers, my advice would be to start elsewhere. Touch these different parts of your body using different pressures and strokes – fingertips, whole palm, massage, pinching – just use this time to get used to touching your own body in a sensual way. Not out of necessity, but out of pure pleasure.

When you do finally feel ready to touch your intimate area, start off by using one or two fingers to gently and slowly massage around your vulva. Tease yourself by gliding your fingers up and down your inner labia, pressing lightly on your clitoral hood. Do this repeatedly and when you're ready move your fingers to your clitoris and rub in a motion that feels good to you. The possibilities are almost endless and remember, there are no rules. This is about exploring *you* and your unique body. In their ongoing research of over 20,000 women, sex education platform OMGYES.com have found no less than 36 techniques people used to enhance their pleasure.[7] So if you're not sure where to start, let me give you some ideas and inspiration. You might need to try out a few different techniques to find the one that works for you.

Masturbating techniques:

- Circling – Use your middle finger to gently massage different parts of your clitoris in a small circular motion that feels natural.
- Up and down – Change the motion by gliding up and down on your clitoris with one of two fingers.
- Side to side – Try lightly applying some pressure on your clitoris and use one or two fingers to go from side to side repeatedly.
- Rocking motion with your fingertips – As you use your fingertips to play with your clitoris continuously, use your pelvic muscles to rock back and forth to match the pace.

Focus on your breathing and pay attention to your fantasy as you masturbate. You can also use your toy to rub on a part of your body that feels good. Try applying different forms of pressure while using that other hand to play with your nipple. It might not even be your boobs; it could be your inner thigh.

Try different positions, too, and switch it up. You might want to get on all fours on your bed and place a pillow directly under you. Use one hand to hold on to and hug the pillow as you use the other hand to hold a sex toy such as a wand between your legs from the front, then finally find a vibration setting that feels good and massage your clitoris.

How about sitting on a chair with your legs slightly spread open as you sit in front of a mirror playing with different parts of your body? Start off by using your fingers, then a clitoral vibrator or a suction toy at the lowest setting. Massage your clitoris with the toy; angle it in different ways to help find the spot that makes you even more sexually excited.

Another masturbating position you might really enjoy is kneeling on your bed and resting your back on the wall or headboard. Allow enough space between your thighs so a toy can be centred as you play with yourself. Remember to be patient with your body and to listen to it. If you want to change the setting by going higher or lower, do so and don't forget the lube.

Get to know your orgasm

What I love about my orgasms is that they're never identical. The sensations and emotions you feel from an orgasm after you masturbate today might be totally different from the last three orgasms you've had before. All different but still special and intense in their own way. The beauty is never knowing what sort of orgasm it'll be, but anticipating it will still feel spectacular. I personally enjoy masturbating most right before I sleep at night or just before a quick nap in the middle of the day. Currently one of my favourite ways to play is with a wand, suction toy or a rabbit ears vibrator and by listening to an audio recording of me and my partner having sex. I close my eyes and rely on the sound to help me escape to the moment his body was gently pressed on mine, and when I could feel his breath in my ear and his moans. Don't you just love a moaner, ladies? Whew!

Orgasms do not always need to be the goal of masturbating, but learning what makes you cum when you're on your own should help you explore and understand what your body responds to best. If you know how to please yourself and you have a partner who is patient and willing to learn, then you can teach them. Emphasis on 'patient' and 'learn' here, though! Your body is unique and it doesn't come with a manual so as long as your partner is a keen student, let's try to grant them the same patience.

Research has repeatedly shown that the majority of people with vulvas need clitoral stimulation in order to orgasm.[8] But how else can you orgasm, you ask? Well, I was hoping you might ask. You may also find you can do so through the G-spot, which can be found on the front wall inside the vagina, 2–3 inches up. It's also known as the Gräfenberg spot, an erogenous zone that was brought to the forefront by Dr Beverly Whipple when she realised that inserting your fingers inside the vagina and signalling to 'come here' can unlock another way for women to achieve an orgasm.[9] However, some have argued that your G-spot is also part of your clitoris.

Remember the diagram in Chapter 1 (see page 15)? You see, your clitoris isn't just the little bean that you see with your naked eye; there's a hell of a lot more depth and complexity to it. As I explained earlier, we now know that this incredible organ extends back into the body, where it straddles the vagina. So what we think of as the G-spot might well be the internal underside of the clit.

In some ways I don't know that it really matters as long as it feels good. Anecdotally I know that a lot of people with vaginas report that orgasms from internal stimulation feel different to the ones they get from touching themselves externally. This is why, although I think it's good for us to understand our anatomy, my emphasis is always on getting to know *your own* body. Because what works for me might be different to what works for you, and that's OK.

If you want to have a go at finding and stimulating your G-spot, I recommend starting with your fingers. Place a bit of lube on the finger or fingers you've chosen to use, breathe, relax and dip inside gently. In general, you shouldn't need to insert your finger past the knuckle. Press your fingertip against the upper wall of your vagina and gently move it around to see how it feels. You can change up the pressure or use a rubbing motion to explore how it feels. You might notice an area on the vaginal wall that feels a bit different (some people report that it feels bumpy or more ridged) or you might know from the internal sensation that you've hit the right spot. There are also sex toys designed for your G-spot that can help you locate it and apply the right kind of stimulation. Don't feel annoyed if you can't find it, though. Like I said, G-spot orgasms are not a universal experience and the last thing we want to be doing is making ourselves feel bad for not being able to tick a box.

I've also had women tell me that when they put pressure around 1–2 inches inside their vagina to locate their G-spot, they feel the need to pee. This is most likely because the urethra is directly above the vagina and you're putting pressure on that at the same time. It's nothing to worry about, but it might help you relax if you use the toilet before you start your search. That way you know there's no danger of wetting the bed!

So now we've covered the G-spot, what about the A-spot? This is an area deep inside the vagina, about 2 inches further up from the G-spot, known as the anterior fornix erogenous zone (AFE). A few small studies have suggested that when stimulated for 10–15 minutes, this area increases vaginal lubrication and helps build up erotic sensitivity.[10] (Then again, 10–15 minutes of stimulation on any of my erogenous zones would probably get me wet and horny so I don't know that this sounds particularly amazing!)

Its existence is disputed by other scientists, but anecdotally there are people out there who claim it has unlocked the best orgasms of their lives,[11] so once again, if you feel like exploring, I say go for it! Ultimately, there is no categorical answer on any of this and no right or wrong way to get your nut. Different people will experience pleasure and orgasm through different activities and stimulation to different areas, so it really is a case of *you do you*, sis.

Getting into the zone

Exploring the physical parts of your body is fun, but it can feel a little bit clinical if your head's not in the right place. To experience the full pleasures of masturbation, you really do need to be able to relax and tune into your body.

There are lots of different ways you can do this, from lighting candles and putting music on to taking a bath or shower, doing some light exercise first, or listening to some horny audio stimulation like I do! Another great way to tune into your body is to incorporate some elements of tantra.

Tantra is an Indian philosophy that dates from around the sixth century, with its traditions originating in early Hinduism and Buddhism. Tantric traditions are extremely diverse and a lot of them are not really about sex at all.[12] Still, it's fair to say that most of us in the West associate tantra with sex, so for the sake of understanding that's what I'll be talking about here.

When we talk about tantra in the context of sex, what we're generally talking about is a kind of mindfulness and meditative approach that allows us to get very in line with our partners and help us tap into a deeper connection. It's often done through maintaining eye contact with your sexual partner, being very intentional in the way you connect with each other physically, moving very slowly through touch, massage, and sexual stimulation, and breathwork.

Now, tantric sex can lead you into a toe-curling orgasm, but that isn't its primary aim. It's about truly connecting and enjoying the journey, the exchange of energy and all the feelings that come with exploring each other sexually.

And there's lots of this you can experience solo-dolo, too! Tantric masturbation could take the form of you practising meditation or mindfulness while you touch yourself, incorporating some breathing exercises into your self-stimulation or even playing around with edging, giving yourself pleasure but holding off from an orgasm. Just like mindfulness itself is having a moment right now, so is mindful masturbation – go ahead and google it and see what I mean!

One of the things I love about it is that it requires you to really pay attention to your body (and not just your vulva or penis!), which will help you understand the full extent of what pleasure can look like for you and learn more about how you enjoy being touched, the pace of the intimacy, and the connection you create with your partner and yourself. Whether you use it as a tool to help you relax and be present or just as a way of making love to yourself in a more sensual way, it's a wonderful thing to try.

And as always, don't get frustrated if it doesn't work for you. It's OK if you can't quite get into it or feel like you can't focus. There are so many ways to enjoy exploring your body and this is simply one suggestion.

How wet do you get?

I remember on Twitter when I asked women what their go-to for lubrication during intimacy was, several responded by telling me their favourite type. Their suggestions included water-, oil- and silicone-based lubes from a number of different brands; lubes they vouched for, lubes they recommended for different sexual acts and positions. But others responded by heavily gloating about not needing it. 'The lubrication my body naturally makes,' the smug responses said. I remember one user in particular who just said, 'Good pussy.' Now, don't get me wrong, when someone who has a vulva is stimulated enough, they experience vasocongestion, which is an increase in blood flow to the genitals.[13] This in turn stimulates the Bartholin's glands, two pea-sized areas situated on either side of the vaginal opening, which produce a liquid that helps lubricate the vulva and vagina, helping to make sex feel better.[14]

A lot of us can get wet! For many of us, it happens when we're pretty much horny and turned on. But not always. How wet we get can change depending on our hormone levels, which vary not just monthly, but also over our lifetimes, during and after pregnancy, and as we age. Our level of natural lubrication can also be affected by hormonal contraception and other drugs.[15] And don't even get me started on douching and other vaginal 'hygiene' products, all of which can mess with your natural wetness.[16] And as with everything, we're all different. Some people will be absolutely soaked at the drop of a hat, others will experience something more like a subtle slick of moisture. There's no right or wrong way to get wet, as long as you're enjoying yourself and feel comfortable (and are not in pain!).

So reaching for a lube bottle shouldn't be something to be afraid of or embarrassed about. It was as though the author of the 'good pussy' comment was trying to make other women feel a certain way or get one up on them. The attitude that not 'needing' lube somehow makes you a superior lover is not just bitchy, it's just plain wrong. It's giving ... dare I say it ... 'Pick-me!' vibes. Honestly, I didn't think I'd ever see the day when some women would use pussy secretion to try to make themselves seem more appealing.

In my view, anyone who knows their body well enough to have a favourite lube should really feel empowered by that, not ashamed. Plus, lube isn't just a replacement, it's also an enhancement. Some sexual activities just feel better with lots and lots of lube.

Anyway, since we're on the topic of getting wet, let's take a deep dive into squirting, shall we?

What is squirting?

One of the most memorable moments I've had of squirting was actually a time when I didn't even realise it had happened. I was having sex with an old boyfriend and suddenly the bed was soaking wet and I quickly noticed this huge smile on his face. He was over the moon, grinning from ear to ear like a Cheshire cat. 'You're squirting, I just made you squirt!' he said excitedly. My response? 'Uh ... did I?'

He was convinced I had. 'Yeah, didn't you see it happening?' he asked me. Nope.

But then came the most telling part. Because here we had a man who was overly excited not only about the sex we'd had (which was really great), but his perceived ability to make me squirt. He actually turned around to admire himself in the mirror, flexed his arms and gloated about it for a few minutes. I guess he felt like he was the man and as though his dick was full of tricks! Who was I to take that away from him?

I'm very aware that the reason why he was over the moon that I had squirted is partly due to how it's been glamorised in porn. Millions of videos are dedicated to the subject, which not only make out that any and every woman can experience it, but also that it's down to the prowess of the person who's fucking them, and not (as is more often the case in the experience of many women I know) total fucking pot luck. Still, it's no surprise that many cishet men feel accomplished when it happens. If only they'd put the same energy into trying to help us orgasm, though, eh?

Porn stars, just like any other actor, have tricks to help them look like they're squirting, and to ensure the scene looks authentic. Just as a regular actor may have a specific technique to turn on the waterworks and make them cry when a sad scene calls for it, an adult performer will have tried-and-tested ways to make it rain during sex.

That doesn't mean anyone can do it and it definitely doesn't guarantee that it will look like that if and when you do. Just another example of porn robbing people of their understanding of what real sex actually looks like.

So what actually is squirting? Let me start by saying there's no concrete answer on this one. Scientists still haven't reached a consensus on it, but I'll do my best to fill you in on the information that does exist.

Squirting, or female ejaculation, is an involuntary emission of fluid, which can happen to people with vulvas during sexual activity. It has long been acknowledged that female genitals are capable of ejaculation; in fact, it was even mentioned in the Kama Sutra![17]

But why it happens is a bit hazier. For some it happens at the same time as orgasm, but for others it's a totally separate experience. I have friends who squirt when using clit-sucking toys, and others who need sustained G-spot stimulation to stand a chance.

A lot of people assume squirting is just wee, but I'm afraid to say the jury's still out on that one, too. Studies have found that female ejaculate contains urea (which is in urine) and some have even shown that people's bladders were less full after squirting, leading researchers to conclude that it *must* be wee.[18] But other studies have found that the fluid released during squirting actually only contains very low levels of urea and a lot of other substances that you wouldn't normally find in piss, which suggests it's something else altogether.[19] Helpful, eh?

You might also have heard people mention the Skene's glands when they talk about squirting. These are small glands on the front wall of the vagina, on either side of the urethra, which release an anti-microbial fluid to clean and lubricate the urethra.[20] Some scientists also believe it's the female equivalent of the prostate and there is some evidence to suggest they are also the source of female ejaculate.[21,22]

Just to confuse things even more, some researchers claim that 'female ejaculation' and 'squirting' might actually be different things consisting of different fluids and originating in different parts of the body.[23] If your head is spinning at this point, don't worry, mine too!

The most important thing to know about squirting is that it is normal. But so is not squirting. It's not something everyone can do and it's not something everyone *wants* to do. If you are reading this chapter looking for tips on how to make it happen, don't worry, I'm definitely going to share some. But before I do, please just take a minute to ask yourself, are you really doing it for *you*? Or is it to please and perform for a partner? I'm not saying that exploring something new together isn't valid. It's exciting to find out what your body is capable of and to turn each other on in the process.

But I also know that a lot of guys treat it like an achievement to be ticked off, something they can say *they've* done. They don't actually care about whether it's pleasurable or fun for you, they just want to boast about it to their little friends and feel like a boss. So do take a moment here to check in with yourself and find out whether this is something you actually care about or want to experience, because if the answer is no, that's also totally fine.

But for those of you who are genuinely turned on by the idea, here's what I've learned ...

One of my favourite books on this subject is called *Kunyaza: The Secret to Female Pleasure* by Habeeb Akande. It explores the sexual practice called '*kunyaza*' from Rwanda that supposedly causes women to squirt and have multiple orgasms during sex. The word actually derives from the word '*kunyara*', which means 'to urinate' (uh-oh, this again!), but it can also be translated to mean 'pouring rivers', 'waterfalls' or 'the ocean'.[24]

The ancient sexual technique is also practised in Uganda and Kenya where it is sometimes known as *kachabali.* One of the things I like about Akande's work is that it shows how, in this part of Africa, it's quite common for female pleasure to become the centre of attention, unlike here! Women are actually taught the method by sex educators in order to help teach their husbands, and men are also taught by other men to practise on their wives. According to Akande, it's rare that a woman in Rwanda isn't able to *kunyaza.* What's more, it's thought to show a lack of masculinity if a man is unable to make a woman squirt.

So now I'm guessing you want to know how to do it, right?

It dates back to an old story where the ancient queen asked a royal guard to have sex with her while the king, her husband, was away at war. The guard was so nervous and anxious about what could happen if he got caught that he couldn't bring himself to put his penis directly inside her vagina. Instead of penetrating her, he rubbed and tapped the head of his penis on her clitoris and labia rhythmically. Legend has it that this technique built up such a huge amount of erotic tension for her that she gushed and squirted her pleasure all over the bed.

Nowadays, the method of *kunyaza* focuses on both clitoral, labial *and* vaginal stimulation. It starts with the same kind of rubbing and tapping described in the story (you and your partner can adapt this to find what kind of rhythm and pressure brings you both pleasure), then, once you're *really* aroused and lubricated, you move on to penetration. According to Akande, your partner should thrust in an intense and deep way to maximise the chances of *kunyaza*.

You can also try lying down and gently raising your bottom ever so slightly with a pillow underneath. This will help you move your hips in a way that matches and responds to the movement of your partner's penis on your vulva. Other sex educators have said that squirting is to do with your pelvic floor and doing regular Kegel exercises can help, while others emphasise the importance of a long build-up, either physical like in the *kunyaza* method, or allowing yourself to get slowly turned on by watching or listening to different forms of erotica.

Akande's book is aimed at cisgender, heterosexual couples, but needless to say you could also try all these techniques with a dildo or even your fingers. You can also buy toys specifically designed for G-spot stimulation, which a lot of people say they need in order to squirt. Some people I know swear by glass dildos because it's easier to manipulate the pressure on the G-spot. Then again I also know people who've squirted while using wand vibrators and even clit suckers, so, as always, the key is to enjoy the experiment, rather than get hung up on the 'results'.

I realise I'm starting to repeat myself now, but it is *so* important to remember that our bodies are different so how we squirt or ejaculate might differ, too. These tips may or may not work for you. Again, our bodies respond differently; what's important is your own self-discovery. Practise, play and be patient.

Introduction to sex toys

Sex aids, or what we might think of today as 'toys', have existed as far back as the Ice Age. In 2005, German archaeologists unearthed what is believed to be the world's oldest dildo from a cave in the mountains in the south-west of the country. The 8-inch-long, 1½-inches-wide object is made of siltstone and is thought to be around 28,000 years old. How do they know it's supposed to be a penis? Well, apart from looking extremely phallic, the, ahem, 'tool' is highly polished, which sets it apart from other kind of tools of the era (nobody wants chafing). 'It's clearly recognisable,' confirmed one of the professors who worked on the research project at the time.[25]

But what about more modern inventions? A story you'll hear trotted out time and time again is the one about the Victorian doctors who would help their female patients masturbate to orgasm, supposedly to cure hysteria, apparently in the belief that it was not a sexual act. This is often linked to the invention of the first electro-mechanical vibrator was created by Joseph Granville in 1880.

But exactly how true is this? Now, there's no denying that Granville came up with a contraption that vibrated, but its original purpose was for the relief of pain and muscle tension. And hysteria *was* a real diagnosis given to women during this period.

However, historians are sceptical about whether they were actually being stimulated to orgasm by their doctors as a supposed 'cure'. Firstly because, contrary to what we like to tell ourselves, the Victorians actually *did* understand sex and female pleasure. They knew full well that stimulating the female genitals would lead to orgasm! It seems pretty unlikely, then, that either doctor or patient would obliviously engage in 'pelvic massage' as a form of mental health treatment.[26]

But anyway, Hollywood loved this narrative, because of course! And if you've seen the 2011 film *Hysteria*, you'll know what I mean. So exactly who was this myth created by? Well, I'll tell you. It is attributed to American scholar Rachel Maines, who wrote in her book *The Technology of Orgasm* that 'in the Western medical tradition genital massage to orgasm by a physician or midwife was a standard treatment for hysteria ... When the vibrator emerged as an electromechanical medical instrument at the end of the nineteenth century, it evolved from previous massage technologies in response to demand from physicians for more rapid and efficient physical therapies, particularly for hysteria.'[27]

She has since changed her tune and claimed that she was presenting this idea as merely a hypothesis, but it's no wonder this little piece of medical trivia has been bandied about ever since.

Eventually historians such as Halle Lieberman decided to properly fact-check Maines' work and saw that there was a lot of truth-twisting. In 2018, Lieberman published an in-depth investigation with colleague Eric Schatzberg, which concludes that there is 'no evidence that physicians ever used electromechanical vibrators to induce orgasms in female patients as a medical treatment.'[28] In short, Ms Maines' 'theory' was nonsense.[29]

Let's move forward to 2022, though. Today, there is a wealth of toys on the market, none of which are being prescribed for hysteria! Obviously, when I look back, the idea of using a 12-inch dildo as my first sex toy makes me laugh now. But I just had no clue. As I said, penetration was the only thing I really knew sex to be and so I just assumed that would be how I got pleasure. Luckily, my understanding has evolved since then.

It's interesting because when I think about it, the look and feel of my sex toys has developed along with time. From that very first gigantic dildo, I went from vibrating dildos, to rabbit ears, to wands, and right now I can't get enough of my suction toys.

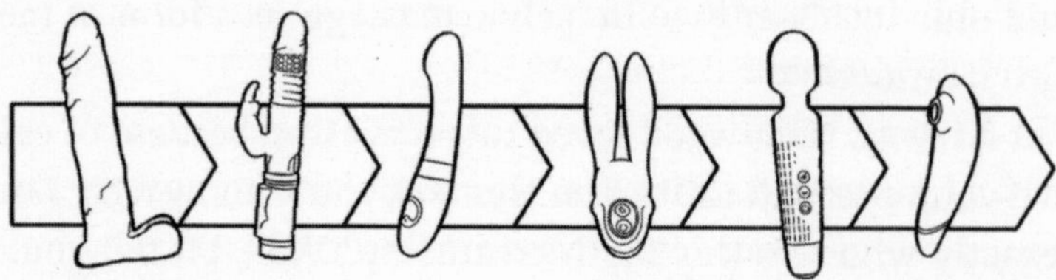

To me, my sex toys tell the story of my understanding and self-discovery about pleasure. I went from looking for AA batteries to put inside this gigantic plastic penis to discreet little suction toys that primarily focus on my clitoris (and have USB points to charge them!).

Nowadays if someone asks me for a recommendation for their first toy, I would probably suggest a small bullet or a sex toy kit, which has numerous toys inside that you can explore with. But, as always, it's very much down to you and your specific needs. So let's talk about some of the main ones ...

Bullet or pebble vibrators

Bullets are usually great for beginners as they're less intimidating than other toys, they come in a variety of shapes and can be found in every adult store. I'd know – I was usually trying to flog them as an add-on when customers purchased other items. They are not to be inserted directly inside your vagina, but used instead around your vulva and to massage your clitoris gently at a pace that feels natural and sensual to you. What's great about vibrators, especially small ones, is that you can pack them in your dick or pussy appointment bag as they're also great to use during foreplay, in the middle of penetration and during mutual masturbation. (If you've never paused physical intimacy for mutual masturbation as a form of edging, well, it's great that you've picked up this book!) Mutual masturbation is extremely hot. Tease your partner from across the room and ask them to watch you play with yourself as they do the same thing. Instruct them that they're not to touch you again till you're ready. Or make them beg!

Think about a bullet as a replacement for your fingers. Find a speed and pulse that feels exciting and natural to how your body responds and use your toy of choice to either stroke, rub or caress around your clitoris continuously. It's important to note again that bullets do not go inside your vagina, just around your clitoris!

Other kinds of vibrators

When you do use a vibrator, big or small, use it in positions that leave direct body space for you or your partner to play on your clitoris. Penetration can be quite intense, so if your partner's body is pressed against yours, you might not be able to get to your vulva – this is exactly why doggy is my favourite position.

Vibrators can also be a tool you use to wake up other areas of your body that bring you pleasure. Gently and slowly run your toy along your inner thigh or in a circular motion around your nipples for a 5–10 minutes before you start playing with your vulva when on your own.

It's fun knowing that vibrators don't just have to be used on you. When having sex with someone else with a vulva you can ask if they'd be up for using it and if they are you can experiment with pulsations and speeds of the toy. Ask what they like and listen to their directions on what they want and what their body responds to best. When giving a blowjob to a person with a penis you can get things hot by asking if you could use a vibrator on their balls when sucking the head and shaft of the penis or when giving a wet hand job with some lube.

Rabbit toys

The original Rampant Rabbit (made famous by that episode of *Sex and the City* where Charlotte gets addicted to it and won't leave the house) came out in the Nineties. Back then these toys tended to be made from pink thermoplastic rubber shaped like the end of a penis, with a kind of arm on the side, which featured a little rabbit-shaped head with 'ears' designed to stimulate the clit. Some of them also had rotating pearls in the shaft for added internal stimulation. You can still get toys like this, but you can also find sleeker versions made of silicone.

The idea is that they offer both G-spot and clit stimulation at the same time, so you'll often find a curved shaft, designed to hit that internal spot, coupled with smooth, pointy 'ears' that offer targeted stimulation either side of your clitoris. Others have dispensed with the ear-shaped design and instead have a small external vibrator, which is curved to hit your clit directly.

Dildos

A dildo is another great toy that is perfect for penetration play, especially as it can hit your G-spot. It can go directly in your vagina, unlike a bullet vibrator, but it doesn't stop there. Dildos can also be used for anal sex or mouth play. So back to when I was talking about mutual masturbation a few paragraphs up, you can use dildos to put on a show so your partner can watch – get creative and do what feels sexy and natural to you. You might want to play with yourself on camera and send a sexy video to your partner so they can see and reminisce about what it looks like when a penis-shaped object is inside of you. No face, no case, though! And always ask for permission first.

Teledildonics

Speaking of letting your partner watch, technological advancements mean that if you're in a long-distance relationship, your lover can watch you play with your clitoris, your vagina or butthole – the choice is yours. And maybe theirs, especially as there are toys that allow them to download an app to have control over the rhythm and the tempo of the vibrations – it's lit, right? I know, I know!

Anal toys

Anal toys, too, can be added to the mix and there is a wide variety. This includes anal beads, butt plugs and dildos! I shouldn't have to tell you again, but lubrication, please! Why not train your anus by playing with toys of different sizes to help prep you for some extra fun? And don't forget to make sure your ass is squeaky clean.

Suction toys

Suction toys are definitely my favourite sexual tool at this moment, as you can probably tell. They basically behave as though someone is giving you head due to the air suction technology, which helps the blood flow rush to the vulva and heightens the sensation. Again, play with different levels and find a pattern that your clitoris responds to positively. You could use this with your partner during a 69 position and possibly ask them to slowly finger you as the toy is caressing your clitoris. You might not fancy the 69 position and could also try it when they're giving you head as you lie down or your back, legs spread enough for them to get in between.

This is when you hover a clitoral suction toy over your clitoris. The magic here is within the wrist and finding a rhythm of motion that works for you. Suction toys include some of the latest sex tech and help achieve back-to-back orgasms.

Kegel balls

Kegel balls are another sex toy I've been asked about before. They're two round balls that are linked together with a string, designed to sit in your vagina. They've been used for many years and help strengthen your pelvic-floor muscles. They're also great to use after childbirth or if you have urinary incontinence. If you don't want to use the balls, you don't have to; you can do your Kegel exercises instead. You know the ones, where you squeeze your pelvic-floor muscles and release non-stop for a few minutes. I bet you just did yours now, didn't you ...? Yeah, I thought so.

Penis toys

Sex toys exist for men, too, and can be really hot, from fleshlights to strokers and penis rings that can help them last longer in the bedroom during penetration.

When purchasing a toy, don't go too crazy and get something overpriced. Explore and see what works well for you and repeat till you feel more familiar with the world of sex toys.

Hygiene

There are several wipes and sprays that I definitely recommend you buy to help keep your toys clean, such as EasyGlide Toy Cleaner or Vush Clean Queen Initimate Accessory Spray. They can be found in pretty much every adult toy store and should be in your drawer next to your vibrators, dildos and wands. These objects come into contact with your genitals and I'm sure you don't want any sort of bacteria build-up, especially as they can create horrid infections. So make sure you clean after every use. Another suggestion is using a condom on the toy when using it with a sexual partner, to help decrease the chances of getting an STI.

Porn, erotica or just your imagination?

All this physical stimulation is fantastic but sexual arousal happens in our heads, too. There's an expression you might have heard, which is that the brain is the biggest erogenous zone. How you might choose to engage your brain during masturbation is, of course, highly individual. Maybe you're very visual and you like to see a few sexy images or videos. Maybe you love the build-up of an erotic story, either read or listened to. Maybe you just want to close your eyes and let your fantasies run wild in your imagination. All of these are great ways to augment your pleasure and level up your masturbation experience. And let's get something clear: whatever you might have been taught or told, there is *no shame* in any of them.

A survey by Ofcom found that half the adult population watched some sort of porn in 2020. The most popular site was Pornhub, which had some 15 million visitors. Of these, 16 per cent were women.[30] If that sounds a bit low, remember, it equates to around two and a half million women. And anyway, this only accounts for *one* website. A study published in the *Archives of Sexual Behaviour* found that around 45 per cent of women reported watching porn with a partner, while 30 per cent said they watched it alone.[31] Either way, the fact remains that women *do* watch porn and they do enjoy it. Meanwhile, audio porn is having a serious moment. In 2019, audio erotica start-ups collectively raised over $8 million in funding,[32] and there are now numerous sites and apps that will pump sexy stories directly but discreetly into your ears.

Many people have made claims that enjoying masturbation or porn can lead to an addiction, and while there is an element of truth in the idea that we can become a bit reliant on certain 'shortcuts' to pleasure (like how a lot of us feel we've developed a reflex for picking up our phones when we want a quick dopamine hit), there isn't actually any scientific evidence to support the concept of 'porn addiction'.[33]

We can develop compulsive habits around anything that gives us a thrill, but I do think when we talk about masturbation and porn it almost feels like an outdated scare tactic to stop us from doing it. As discussed above, we know that a huge proportion of people watch porn, and this can unfortunately mean that they end up on unethical sites that do not respect the rights of those involved, whilst also giving a false narrative of sexual 'pleasure', which is not in line with sexual freedom and empowerment. It is therefore even more important to have these conversations, so that we can educate people about the presence of ethical porn sites and to be more vigilant to any unethical sites that they might come across.

Personally, I love watching porn to help get me in the mood for masturbation. But I know many people have had their hang-ups about it, and do you know what? I get it. The porn industry has not always been kind to women, and of course a lot of it has given us this warped idea of what sex is meant to look like, which shapes the type of sex people are having today. But ethical porn does exist! Now, ethical porn can be described as porn that respects the boundaries of the performers, doesn't include a dodgy contract or work hours, and explores real sex and fantasies such as queer BDSM. This genre is also known as feminist porn and celebrates sexual equality. You can check out Bellesa, CrashPadSeries and PinkLabel.TV.

You can also support a lot of sex workers by subscribing to their content online and paying them directly via ethical sites such as OnlyFans.

Find and watch different categories to help discover what helps get you off. You might want to do this by creating an account; just like any media platform, signing up will help tailor your search and make it suitable to your taste and what you're into. You're likely to be asked questions about what your porn preferences are, allowing the algorithm to work in your favour and not just give page after page of porn you have no interest in, but instead to give recommendations that'll make your clitoris excited.

POV, amateur, scissoring, BDSM, anal, threesomes or orgy are some examples of what you can search for, but what's good to know is that you can also make use of the filters to help whittle down your selection. The filter might include the porn category, the length of the video or even the performer. What I enjoy watching most when selecting a porn category for myself is Black women with other women or men, or both together (depends how freaky I'm feeling) – this is because it allows me to fantasise about the sexual experience when I see someone who might look similar to me.

So, go forth and enjoy yourself! A good relationship with an understanding of your own pleasure is the basis for great sex. You'll be surprised by what you find out about your body after exploring, as we'll see over the course of the rest of the book.

Ladies, shall we have some fun ...?

Scandalous sex stories Twitter thread*

25, London, UK

So I was having a few drinks with my brother and his friends one Sunday afternoon. We all went back to his

---

*Not all the views expressed in the Twitter threads reflect my opinion as the author of this book, but it is important to me to share other perspectives and experiences of peoples' sexual expression and relationships.

friend's house and carried on drinking. Me and one of his friends went outside and this man had me bent over behind his garage. Then his other friend walked down and caught us, then joined in. I had one fucking me from behind and I was giving head to the other and I've honestly never felt so alive. My brother still doesn't know, nothing has been said since!

23, South Africa

Hi Oloni! I have to say it was when I had sex with my ex-situationship (the most mediocre sex I've ever had, and he finished with 'that's enough for you') and I obviously was gobsmacked, so three hours later, a long-time crush of mine and I hooked up and had the messiest, most pleasurable sex of my life. The situationship and I dated, but it was a toxic relationship, and now that I'm out of it, I have to admit that throughout the relationship, every single time I'd have sex with him, I'd always think about that time with my crush.

31, London, UK

Omg so I had been with my boyfriend for like 5 years, we were in love and talked about taking things to the next level, etc. It was all good but I think I got bored and needed a little fun. One day I reached out to an old link who was always a good time, and we started talking, next thing I know he booked a hotel for us. I was hesitant because I'd never cheated before but thought F*uck it, just this once! So we met up at the hotel and, Oloni, OMG we went round after round after round ... it was sensational! So sensational

I had to go back for more and I ended up seeing him on the side for nearly a year! He had a big dick, he was nasty and we did EVERYTHING and tried all the fantasies we'd both been curious about. I even still get flashbacks lol. Anyway I obviously couldn't sustain that and once I had gotten it out of my system ended it and carried on with my bf. I have no intention of ever cheating on him again and hope he'll never know ... We've been happily married for 2 years now with a baby on the way, and can honestly say husband dick > nasty dick alllll the way! x

---

29, UK

Anon: I met the host on Feeld, [a] dating app for kinky people. We met for a coffee yesterday and spoke through everything. I felt very comfortable with him and I think I can trust him.

Him and his mates have done this before. I told him I don't know if I want to be abused or adored, I prefer to be worshipped and he said it's totally up to me. Regardless I'll be sharing my location with my friend and she'll be calling me to check up.

I've not even had a threesome before.

Oloni: Omg and four guys? Are you nervous?

Anon: Yes, maybe even five. I'm more excited than nervous, but I'm living my best hoe life and loving it. I was shown pictures of them, and they saw mine. I'm not one to judge physical appearance so to me it's more exciting to see what they can do for me.

[She came back the next day to tell me about it.]

So I went to [the] hotel and about six guys walked in. That's the moment I shit my pants – not literally. I was laid on the bed, undressed and immediately they all started playing with me ... two dicks in my face, fingers in my pussy, tongue on my pussy and nipple play, I was in literal heaven!

I really connected with one specific guy and might I say he was such a good fuck and those lips, so good looking. I wasn't so keen on a couple [of] guys, I only liked three of them so it was mainly just them fucking me. I came multiple times – I lost count – and I usually don't cum with penetration. I lasted about an hour, which is good for a first timer 😂😂

It was an insane experience, I was the focus of every single one of them.

I walked into the hot guy in the bathroom and he started kissing me, fingering me, then I sucked his cock and left him hanging, he then took my number later and we're going to arrange a one on one. I was on such a high when I left, it was incredible. I definitely won't do it again but I did enjoy it overall and I'm glad I did it.

Btw they all wore condoms, they were all so respectful, they didn't hurt me or even dirty talk; they all cheered me on, haha, it was amazing.

They didn't have bags or anything, they had to put their phones away in the cupboard. Some of them knew each other from previous gangbangs.

33, Ghana

Anon please. My ex and I were texting and randomly decided to do dinner on a Friday night since he was in town for the weekend. Ended up getting tipsy and reminiscing. We checked into a hotel and stayed up all night fucking in front of a mirror. We woke up and he gave me that good morning wood, spooning from the back –

he's huge and the sex was amazing. He came in me, no protection *[please always use protection, ladies!]*. I had a lunch date with my boyfriend so I had to rush home to get ready. We went to lunch and got back around 3pm. The thought of my ex's semen still inside me was turning me on so I mounted my boyfriend and rode him until he came in me. The fact that both semen were mixed up inside me was a turn on for me (and still is). The next day, Sunday evening, I went to see my good friend who I have slept with occasionally. We ended up having sex doggy while he fingered my bootyhole. It was honestly an amazing weekend. Didn't plan to do 3 guys in 3 days. They're all amazing men.

25, Toronto, Canada

I was having sex with my boyfriend and this other guy at the same time, but I have [a] security guard downstairs in my building. I was so scared the security would have snitched on me or made some comment because they always try talking to my guest[s]. I started following them up and down, instead of allowing them to go by themselves.

30, London, UK

Went out on the Monday and got speaking to a guy in the clurrrb. We ended up hooking up and he offered to drop me off home with his cousin in tow. Got to mine and had a 3some (MFM – a family affair but yo I literally had the time of my life). The next morning I noticed a guy had liked a couple of my pics on insta ... me thinking it was the cousin, I DM'd him and told him I'd let him dick me down again ... Cut a long story short, it weren't him, a case of mistaken identity, it was some random next guy. This fool played along until he revealed that he'd never met me before in his life! I was dyinggg. He was cute tho so he came round on the Wednesday and we fucked too. I have a boyfriend ... but just wanted to experience having a 3 before we get married one day.

Lol. (I also sound jobless but this was over the Christmas period so it's calm.)

33, London, UK

This was time ago, but my boyfriend cheated on me so I decided we should go on a break. This was the second time I knew of, so I needed space. A week later a guy who was trying to move to me texted me to chill and hang out ... so we did. I enjoyed the company, like really enjoyed it. I had an idea to call my boyfriend on withheld so he could listen to me get fucked by this other guy. All we could both hear was a 'hello? Who is this??' 'Hellllooo?' then he'd hang up. I'd dial right back so he could hear me moan some more as I was bent over. A couple days later he asked if I mistakenly called him and I just said no.

CHAPTER 6

What Kind of Sex Should We Be Having?

'Donna, sex is how we control men. If they know we like it as much as they do, we'll never get jewellery again.'

Jackie Burkhart, *That '70s Show*

When we think of sex it's usually cishetties in missionary, engaging in PIV sex. A bit of foreplay and then penetration till the man finishes. This is what we've been taught 'proper sex' is, so it's no wonder that's what most of us imagine and indeed do when we're getting down to it. But who is that really serving? More often than not it's the person with the penis who's getting the most out of that scenario. If you're lucky, you might be getting extended foreplay (and I'm going to talk more about this later in the chapter) with lots of focus on your pussy, but I'm going to bet that for a lot of people that part's going to be pretty cursory. Too many guys like to rush through it to get to what they see as 'the main event'. And it doesn't take a genius to tell you that this version of sex is probably a big part of the reason why heterosexual women aren't enjoying sex nearly as much as they should be.

There are other influences on us, too. Think of porn. It's a show designed not to give pleasure to the people *in* the scene but to the viewer! When you're watching porn it's important to remember that the person who's *really* getting off is you. And that's OK, that's literally what it's for! The trouble is, a lot of people don't realise this. They see porn and mistake performance for reality. They think because the people on screen are behaving as though they're in sexual ecstasies (it's called acting, bro!) that will also be the case if they try out those things IRL. Therefore, it's not uncommon for men to replicate what they've seen in porn in reality. Now, I'm not saying porn can't be a good place to pick up tips, but *most of the time* in mainstream porn, it is not the woman's pleasure that's the focus.

So what kind of sex should we be having? The kind that puts our pleasure up front and centre. Because when our pleasure isn't prioritised, we are NOT going to be having our best sex.

Here's an easy question: how many of you have ever faked an orgasm? Yeah, I thought so. It's almost all of us. I know this because any time I ask on Twitter about faking orgasms I get inundated with responses from women.

More recently, I'm starting to have more people come through saying they don't bother anymore. That's a good start. But 'not bothering to fake it' is not the same as actually having an orgasm or getting pleasure. And that's what I want to talk about in this chapter. Because the truth is, women *do* like sex as much as men. So why are we settling for this unsatisfying version of it?

One reason is that for so long we have lied about our orgasms. Sometimes we do this in order to allow the guy to feel like a man. But we also do it because many of us think there could be something wrong with our genitals. We've been taught that 'sex' means PIV so we don't understand why we can't possibly climax from that. We've internalised the idea that we might be broken. Even those of us who know full well how to get pleasure from our clitoris when we're on our own can sometimes fall into the trap of thinking a dick alone should be enough to make us cum.

Don't be ashamed of it. It's not our fault! The fact is, many of us have been lied to about how our bodies and pleasure should work. The so-called 'father of psychoanalysis', Austrian psychiatrist Sigmund Freud, once described clitoral orgasms as 'childish'![1] But wait, it gets worse! He also said that the clitoris was basically the equivalent of the penis (because it develops out of the same organ) and therefore to cum from clitoral stimulation was 'masculine'. The proper, mature, *feminine* way to orgasm, he claimed, was through internal vaginal stimulation. No fucking wonder so many of us think we're broken!

Over the last century, multiple studies have proved Freud wrong. We now know, for example, that over three-quarters of women don't orgasm through penetration alone.[2] In fact, one study, which surveyed people of all sexual identities, found that *only heterosexual men* rated vaginal penetration as resulting in frequent and satisfying orgasms.[3] But the myth that we should be able to cum from having a penis inside us STILL pervades. It still has so much power over us.

That's why I'm so confident in saying that if you're a cisgendered heterosexual woman and you're reading this, you've probably lied about your orgasm before.

I've often asked the question on my podcast *Laid Bare*, 'Are you having sex, or is he using your body to masturbate with?' What I mean by this is: are you acting as a vessel or tool for his pleasure like an inanimate object, or is he allowing you to be present in a mutually fulfilled experience?

When we follow these male-centred 'scripts' on what sex should look like and what it should involve, that is basically what we are doing. We are letting our partners use our bodies to masturbate with. It sounds harsh to phrase it like that, I know, but it will make you quickly re-evaluate all the types of sex you've ever had. I've had sexual partners where I definitely felt as though my pleasure mattered, but I've also had moments when I certainly could tell my gratification wasn't cared about. They might as well have used a blow-up doll.

I'm going to say it again: it's not our fault. As well as the misinformation we've received about what counts as 'proper sex', we've also been supplied with very little information on how female pleasure actually works.

The truth is the female orgasm is both very simple and very complex. The clitoris has a very high concentration of nerve endings,[4] and its sole function is to provide sexual pleasure,[5] so in some ways it's a no-brainer. The vast majority of women orgasm when they masturbate (i.e. when we get to choose how to stimulate ourselves!),[6] so we know it's not *that* mysterious or elusive! But most of us know from experience that getting there with a partner can be a different story. Often it requires a lot more attention and a lot more concentration. And if our partner doesn't understand that and isn't prepared to give us the time and attention we need ... that's when we get the 'orgasm gap'.

If you're not familiar with the orgasm gap, it's a term used to help define the disparity in sexual experiences between men and women. Studies (and there have been several!) show that heterosexual women are much less likely to have an orgasm during partnered sex. One study of 800 university students found that 91 per cent of men but just 39 per cent of women said they 'always or usually' orgasmed during sex.[7] And straight women are not just having fewer orgasms than straight men, they are also having fewer orgasms than lesbians! A separate study found that 86 per cent of lesbian women 'usually or always' cum during sex, compared to just 65 per cent of straight women.[8] So it's not that female pleasure is more elusive ... it's that men aren't putting in the effort to understand and facilitate it.

But wait, that's not entirely fair, is it? I've definitely dated men who were very invested in my pleasure and I'm sure you have, too. Actually, a study of 15,000 university students showed that sex in the context of a relationship (as opposed to a casual encounter) generally leads to more orgasms for women.[9] That isn't to say there wasn't an orgasm gap for those who were in a relationship (there still was by 17 per cent), but the research found that there was an even bigger disparity during hook-ups.

We're going to talk about casual sex in more depth in Chapter 11, but I think this definitely highlights one of the problems with hook-ups for women. It's not that we don't want or enjoy them, but when it comes down to it, relationship sex benefits women more.

Dr Laurie Mintz (who is widely credited with coining the term 'orgasm gap') documented a lot of this research in her book, *Becoming Cliterate*, and concluded that '78 per cent of women's orgasm problems are caused by not enough or not the right kind of clitoral stimulation'.[10]

Does any of this come as a real surprise to you? The way I feel is, we can do research and studies till we're blue in the face about the orgasm gap between cishet men and women, but real, honest conversations with your straight friends are all the proof you need. In short, the patriarchy was established centuries ago by haters who wanted to keep us away from enjoying our best nut, and we have our work cut out today trying to undo that deep-rooted damage.

As we've discussed already, many of us have never been able to speak about pleasure in the way we do today without someone trying to label us a whore. Frank conversations about pleasure and intimacy can be pretty hard to come by in straight culture. In Chapter 4, I shared the conversation I had with *Two Twos* podcasters Ro and Nana (see page 72). During that chat they told me they reckon one of the reasons why lesbian sex is so much more pleasurable is that both partners are really looking to satisfy one another. There's a real honesty and communication about your likes and dislikes, and most important of all, there's no bullshit messages telling you that sex has to be PIV.

By contrast, a lot of heterosexual women aren't allowed to be expressive about what they want in the bedroom and it's due to the sexist double standards around us. I keep coming back to this, but it's true! Some men want a woman who is amazing at giving a blowjob, but they get put off if she's too experienced in knowing how to give one. At the same time, a woman's enjoyment of sex is often seen not as a legitimate sign of her innate sexuality, but as a measure of a man's capacity in bed. When you're operating in an unequal, judgemental environment like this, it's hard to own your pleasure and have the confidence to ask for what you want.

Whether it's in the teachings of our parents, our sex education at school or porn, our pleasure has never been a focal point and with all the shame women have been made to feel around the topic of sex, it's no wonder we don't understand our bodies and pleasure the way we should.

What I love about the work I've done is that I've always encouraged women never to settle in the bedroom or out of it. Never allow yourself to be in a shitty relationship and never stand for shitty and half-hearted sex. Communicate, guide, help and teach your lover how to please you. It's time for us to stop settling for second-best and start getting the MOST pleasure we can out of sex.

Communication

I talked in the previous chapter about how masturbation and self-pleasure is a great way to get to know what you like and understand the type of sex you should be having. And you can bring this knowledge into your communication, too. By centring your pleasure and focusing on finding out where your erogenous zones are, you're able to take what you've learned about your body to help teach your sexual lovers. It's so beautiful and empowering when you can grab someone's hand and say, 'Touching me like this really turns me on,' as you stare deep into their eyes. It sounds sexy as fuck, too. Knowledge over your sexuality is sexy. And let's not forget that communication doesn't always have to be verbal. Using the principle of *show, don't tell* can be a really hot way of letting your partner know what you like. It might feel awkward the first time you touch yourself in front of a partner, but trust me when I tell you he's most likely going to be into it. Why else are there over 80,000 videos labelled 'masturbation' on Pornhub?! (Far more than there are featuring anal sex, by the way, even though we often hear that that's what guys want now.)[11]

But sometimes talking *is* the best way. I think a lot of people consider communication the boring bit you have to do before you can get down to the juicy stuff, but I totally disagree. I actually created the term 'have sex before having sex' after I'd met this guy at a private hotel after-party.

We'd met before but only got well acquainted after wandering off to the hotel bar and having a couple of glasses of wine. He was making me laugh and we seemed to be really clicking, so I gave him permission to do something I don't usually let people I've just met do: talk to me about sex.

Normally, I only have these kinds of conversations with men who are my friends, with sexual partners or with guests on my podcast! But was there a huge attraction between us? Absolutely, and since I'd enjoyed a glass or two, I figured let's talk about sex!

The whole conversation kind of felt like I was recording a podcast ... until it didn't. I think I even remember asking to record parts of it because of how funny I found it. We went from talking about terrible sex we'd both had, to amazing sex we'd experienced with past sexual partners. It slowly turned into less of a podcast episode and more like the beginning of an audio erotica. We spoke all night about what we enjoyed in the bedroom, what he was into and what made my clitoris thump (and, boy, did it thump that evening!). He described the best head he'd received, how he enjoyed it when women used the right amount of saliva, his favourite part of foreplay and his sexual boundaries. I shared my kinks, my love for dirty talk and, in true *Laid Bare* podcast style, I also expressed what I didn't like that some men do in the bedroom! I talked about the double standards of oral sex (which I'll come back to shortly) and the minimal interest a lot of guys show in foreplay. We both laughed as he tried to convince me that he was equally as passionate about good sex as I was.

Now, even if we hadn't had that conversation, I probably still would have fucked him because he was quite handsome. The sexual chemistry between us had already clicked, but the conversation? That was the icing on the cake. The *sex before sex*. It wasn't just a means of communication and a way into understanding each other's wants and desires, it was also a safe place to connect sexually with zero judgement or shame. It gave me an insight into his sexual maturity and fantasies, and gave *me* a chance to let him know in advance what he needed to do to get me off.

Now I'm not saying that you should talk about how you enjoy your nipples being sucked with every person you find attractive, unless you've been given the green light to do so. Instead, I'm encouraging you to get into the habit of having a healthy conversation about sharing what you love and like in the bedroom to help guide the physical later on.

This isn't some golden rule, of course! There's no guarantee that once you get into the bedroom your partner will be able to put their money where their mouth is, but at least you know you are giving yourself the best chance of pleasure. Communication before sex allows your lover to feel more confident and comfortable when being intimate with you. Couples who communicate well generally report better sexual experiences *and* higher levels of desire.[12] And good communication around sex has been shown to be a better indicator of relationship satisfaction than frequency of sex.[13] Yep, how good you are at talking about sex is more important than how often you're doing it! And if nothing else, taking the time to have a conversation can save you from a horrendous dick-centred sexual experience.

It doesn't have to be too serious; you can make it flirty, playful, random – honestly, just try it! You can exercise this with a new casual sex partner or someone you've been in a relationship with for a while. It's never too late to start!

Here are a couple of ways to help start a conversation with a potential or current lover:

- 'Babe, what do you enjoy in the bedroom most?'
- 'I really enjoy when foreplay lasts for a good 25–40 minutes, sometimes longer. What's your favourite part of foreplay?'
- 'I want to experiment more in the bedroom. Are you up for it?'
- 'I want to make a sex playlist. Do you have any suggestions?'
- 'What's a sexual fantasy of yours?'

The type of sex we should all be having is the type where we feel comfortable enough to start conversations about pleasure. The way I feel is that if you can't speak about the sex, you shouldn't really be having it either.

The list above gives conversation starters for chats you have outside the bedroom, but you should also be communicating *during* intimacy as well. What I love about the audio erotica I've been listening to recently is how sexy the communication between the characters is. The way they check in with each other and ask for permission before performing a sexual act is so hot. It really goes to show that consent *is* sexy and it's so refreshing to hear. So if you need a good example of how to do it, I really recommend checking out some audio porn apps.

I've seen some people argue that being asked questions in the bedroom can be a turn-off, and to those people I say, I hope no one else has sex with you! There is so much sexiness in being asked if your sexual partner can go slower or faster. It's not just about how attractive it is in itself, you're also showing that you care how they feel. You should want the person you're sleeping with to be relaxed enough to tell you how they feel in that moment.

Like I said, audio porn demonstrates this so well, but a few other lines to help you check in and communicate during sex include:

- 'Are you OK?'
- 'Tell me what you want.'
- 'Where do you want me to cum?'
- 'Can I go faster?'
- 'How do you want me to suck it/eat it?'
- 'Do you want me to stop?'
- 'How does this feel?'
- 'Do you want to try [activity of your choice]?'

As you can see, it's not rocket science. All these examples are probably phrases you're familiar with. They sound so hot in the moment but are also classic ways of checking in and continuously asking for consent. If in doubt, do not assume. Instead, ask!

Setting boundaries

Sometimes you only figure out where your boundaries are after exploring, but other times you just know what you're not into. It might not be forever, but at that moment it's a limit you've put on how far you're willing to go. Discuss this beforehand so there's no room for confusion and never allow anyone to push it or coerce you into a part of sex that doesn't interest you, satisfy you or make you happy. If you ever do feel like your sexual limits are being pushed, express this immediately. Someone who genuinely cares about your sexual experience will not try to pressure you into doing something that hurts or stresses you.

Remember: *you* are allowed to create your sexual boundaries and they should be informed by *your* interests, *your* needs and *your* desires ... although it's good to know the difference between stuff you're not into and don't want to do and stuff you're not into but don't mind doing because your partner likes it. We'll come back to this in more detail in Chapter 7 where we talk about consent (see page 162), but I have found that what we're up for can change if we know our partner finds it really hot. The key is to give each other the space to decide that for ourselves, not to push or coerce.

I have friends who hate spit play and have absolutely no interest in trying it out, even though I've shared how much I've enjoyed it before. That's their sexual boundary and I respect that. But I've also had sex with a guy who told me beforehand that he thought spit play was gross. Fine. Fair enough. But when we started doing the do, guess what? He asked me for consent to try it out! Yes, spit play – the thing he'd told me he found disgusting! It was kind of hilarious how his mind changed in the moment (of course I gave him permission!), but it does go to show that while we always need to respect each other's boundaries, we should be open to the fact that they can change, and that's OK, too.

Foreplay – the play before the play

In one of the examples I gave above on how to start a sexual conversation I mentioned foreplay. If you ask me, this is an extremely important part of knocking boots. But when I was growing up and watching sex scenes, it was always about ten seconds of kissing, then immediately ripping each other's clothes off to have sex. And what I notice now as an adult is that a lot of people have adopted that fictional version of intimacy, instead of taking time to enjoy being in the moment.

Sex is so much more than just a dick entering and leaving your vagina. Don't get me wrong, I love penetration – a lot of women do. I love being teased as it slides against my walls, but why would I want to miss out on all the other things we could be doing before, during, after and sometimes instead of penetration?

Let's take a look at the word and break it down. The 'fore' part refers to the fact that it comes before something (usually penetrative sex, but it doesn't have to be – more on that in a sec) and the 'play' part ... well, I think we all understand that. Foreplay is fun, it's exciting. It can be a tease, a slow burn, an intense build-up. It's that feeling of butterflies in your stomach and the thump of arousal in your clit.

I honestly can't express enough how important I think foreplay is, but for some reason not everyone is adding it to their sex routine, even though it's proven to increase sexual enjoyment. Remember the orgasm gap study (see page 123)? Well, some of the same research also found that 'women were more likely to orgasm if their last sexual encounter included deep kissing, manual genital stimulation, and/or oral sex in addition to vaginal intercourse'.[14]

Once again, I ask you: is this report really a surprise? Of course not. Think about it like cooking (God knows I don't cook, but I asked my sister and she said this metaphor would work!). Imagine you're about to make yourself dinner. You have all your ingredients: your peppers, onions, seasoning, salmon ... whatever it is you're making. Now, you're not going to serve it raw, are you? No, you're going to go through certain steps and eventually put it on a stove or in the oven to cook. And the best chefs take great care and enjoy the process of cooking, as well as the final result! Are you following what I'm saying? Sex is like cooking. Sure, you can just heat something up in the microwave (i.e. have a quickie!) if you really can't be bothered, but the best experiences are when we've taken our time over the touching, kissing, stroking before we get to a point where we're ready to sit down for the meal.

A quick note! As we discussed at the beginning of the chapter, a lot of people consider 'the meal' to be PIV sex, and it's fine if you do too, but remember, it doesn't have to be. In fact, some sex educators today argue that the word 'foreplay' shouldn't even really exist because it relegates all the things women enjoy most to a mere warm-up act. That's a fair point, but the way I like to think of it is that no matter what kind of sexual interaction I'm having, I still want a bit of warm-up. Contrary to what Donald Trump thinks, no woman wants to have their partner come in and just 'grab 'em by the pussy'; I want to be flirted with, kissed, caressed, long before we get to the part where we're taking our clothes off. We might be talking about 'sex before sex' of the kind I described earlier in this chapter (see page 126), where you and your partner are having a really horny conversation in a bar before going home to lay it on each other! Even sexting could be considered a kind of foreplay. If we look at foreplay as less about preparation for PIV and more about creating a sexy atmosphere, enjoying the build-up, I personally think it's a useful term to have.

So, the next time you have sex, try to enjoy a good 30 minutes of nothing but strictly foreplay. That means no PIV sex or any intense sexual moves that can lead to ejaculation just yet. Trust me, you won't regret it. Start by talking and touching. Ask your partner to kiss the places that help turn you on, whether it's your lips, neck, thighs or even the backs of your knees! Ask each other sexy questions as it's happening and don't forget to check in for consent along the way.

Penetration – more than just P in V

However much we sex educators try to remind people that there's more to sex than putting a dick in a hole, the fact remains that penetration is the bread and butter of a lot of people's sex lives – especially between heterosexual men and women. So let's not gloss over it.

Firstly, it's worth remembering that there are other ways to enjoy penetration that aren't necessarily penis-in-vagina sex. This could include anal play, using fingers or toys, or even switching it up and having you be the penetrator as you peg your partner. Yes, I went there! (Hey, just ask. You never know, they might be up for it.) Whatever kind of penetration you're into, if you're sticking something inside someone's body, you need to make sure they are ready, consenting and comfortable. Don't go ramming your fingers into someone's bumhole with no warning!

Always have lube on deck to gently smother on the outer area of the vagina or massage onto the penis (or fingers, or toy) – right from the shaft to the glans. There are different types of lube you can use, but water-based lube is generally considered the best all-rounder, especially when using a condom. An increasing number of sex educators are warning against using lubes that contain glycerine because some women report that it contributes to yeast infections. There's actually no firm medical evidence for this, but all our bodies are different and what works for one person might not work for another so please make sure you check the ingredients before you purchase and be aware that you may need to try a few different products before you find the ones that work for you.

Other lubrications you can play around with are flavoured lubes, as well as silicone- and oil-based ones (although it's worth mentioning that oil-based lubes do not go well with condoms as they can damage the latex, causing breakages).[15] But in the right situations, all can help enhance your sexual experience. A tip of mine to help warm up the lube in case it is too cold is to place the bottle in a warm bowl of water before using it.

Oh, and try to opt for a reputable brand of purpose-made lube rather than just raiding the chemist shelves for any old thing. Products like baby oil, coconut oil, and Vaseline might feel good but they were not designed to be used internally, are not very friendly to vaginas and can cause yeast or bacterial vaginosis,[16] and we don't want that. If you ever do experience a change or discomfort in your vagina see a health professional as soon as you can.

Sex is not meant to hurt. If penetration hurts, stop. I don't mean you can't ever go out and get your cervix pounded if that's what you're into; I mean that if your partner is trying to put their fingers, dick, sex toy or anything else inside you and you're experiencing an unpleasantly painful feeling, you shouldn't feel like you have to push through it. For example, there is a condition called vaginismus, which is an involuntary contraction of the muscles around the opening of the vagina, and this feeling of being 'too tight' can cause serious pain and discomfort on penetration – not just with a penis or sex toy; it can even be with things as little as a finger. It's very common in women, and although the majority of the time the cause is unknown, it can be attributed to sexual assault, vaginal inflammation and endometriosis.

I've spoken to many of my followers on Twitter about their vaginismus journey and have friends who have also experienced it, and the good news is it can be cured! One friend had vaginismus most of her adult life with no clear cause. She struggled to use even the smallest of tampons, and so after years of suffering in silence she finally went to her GP and was referred to a vaginal physiotherapist. They gave her vaginal dilators and she used them a few times a week, gradually increasing the size once it was tolerable. Eventually she was able to enjoy full penetrative sex, with a lot of lube! Usually, dilators are enough to help, but some private clinicians provide Botox injections to relax the vaginal muscles that go into spasm, although success rates vary in these cases. Vaginismus is so much more common than we think and the more we speak about it and share our stories, the better help we can get. It's important to get seen by a medical professional if you experience pain during sex or have a fear of penetration, because sex is not meant to hurt! And I particularly wanted to mention it here as an example of when it can be important to think outside the box and remember that penetration is not essential to good sex.

For those who do enjoy it, penetration is an amazing feeling. I've made a lot of noise about how penis-centred sex is, but having the right one glide between your vaginal walls is just a beautiful feeling when done correctly (emphasis on the word 'correctly'!).

As usual, I can't dictate what will feel good to *your* body – you will need to play around and see what you enjoy and what brings you the most pleasure – but I can share some of my tips for getting the most out of PIV sex.

Let's start by chucking out the obsession with the size of a penis. The old question has always been: 'Does size matter, or is it the motion in the ocean?'

The average size of an erect penis in the UK is 5–6 inches long, with a circumference of about 4.5 inches.[17] Now, don't get me wrong, I do love the sight of a thick meat, especially if I'm attracted to the person, but I've also had amazing sex with guys who weren't all that well endowed but who really knew how to use what they were given.

All women are different: some of us do enjoy larger dicks and some of us genuinely don't. The far more important thing is that the sex between you works and feels good. I've always felt as though some dicks and vaginas have perfect fits, but that doesn't mean there aren't other ways to also make sparks fly in the bedroom.

You can have a big penis, but if you don't understand the importance of foreplay, lube and teasing, what good is it, really? I'd much rather have sex with an average-sized guy who paid attention to my pleasure and cared about getting me off. Having a big dick is not a golden ticket to great sex, nor is it any sort of guarantee that you'll be able to satisfy your partner. Dicks come in so many different sizes and shapes, circumcised, uncircumcised – as long as it's washed correctly (and I mean correctly, because I know you've read my hygiene threads on Twitter) and being used at a pace that you both enjoy, that's all that matters.

Now we've got that age-old question out the way, we can get to talking about the good stuff!

When it comes to pleasurable penetration, probably the most important part is making sure you're aroused and feeling like you really want it. Lots of foreplay and build-up time will help with this (as well as lube, of course!), but equally it's worth remembering that even when you get to the point where you're ready to switch to penetration, you don't have to just shove it in and start pumping away. You can ask the person with a penis or a strap-on dildo to use the head of the penis to tease the entrance of your vagina, by only going in by a couple of inches and leaving repeatedly, gently, using the head of the penis to slowly rub on other areas of your vulva such as your labia and clitoris. You can also be slow and intentional. When you're at the height of horn for each other and really gagging to feel that dick inside you, it can be amazing to have your partner hold off a little bit more and maybe just continue to tease the edge of your vagina with the tip of the penis.

Of course, there's nothing wrong with a rough fuck if that's what you're into, and sometimes it feels just as good to be flipped over and have your partner unceremoniously fuck your brains out! The key is to make sure it happens at a point when you're *both* ready and want it, and not just when your partner decides it's time.

And don't forget, PIV can be so much more than monotonous thrusting. Some men really do treat it like they're masturbating with a woman instead of their hand and it's just not acceptable. Play around with different speeds and rhythms such as drawing out really, really slowly and then pausing before plunging back in. If you're on top, try alternating between sliding up and down and grinding for different sensations. While doing it doggy style, instead of just letting him hammer away, get him to hold still while you move at your own pace and explore the angles that hit the right spot for you. As a bonus, he gets to enjoy the visual of watching you eagerly push back onto his dick. One of my favourite moves is to do some Kegels as it goes in and out, using your pelvic floor to grip your partner's dick, otherwise known as 'quinting'.

Of course, it doesn't have to be slow and sensual. Some people do absolutely love getting smashed in the cervix during PIV and that's fine, but don't forget you can mix it up, too. Try switching between the wheelbarrow position, with your legs over your partner's shoulders, which allows for a really deep penetration, and a bit of classic missionary where you lower your legs and have them come down onto their forearms to be close to you. Sometimes, when you've been going at it and enjoying some rough sex, suddenly having that level of skin contact again is all the more intense.

One thing I always try to remind people is that sex does not have to follow a set formula. You don't have to go from kissing to foreplay to PIV to orgasm and that's the end. Just because you've moved on to penetration does not mean all other activities are off the table. You can do PIV for a bit, mutual masturbation and then maybe come back to PIV. Or not! You could have penetrative sex for a while and then switch to oral sex if you want to make each other cum.

It's also really important to find ways to incorporate other kinds of stimulation alongside penetration, especially if you're someone who isn't going to cum from that activity. I think it's fair to say a lot of us enjoy PIV even if many of us don't orgasm from it, but there's still no reason why we can't augment the experience. If you're someone who loves nipple play, a great position can be to have your partner sit with their back against the wall or headboard while you ride them. Their head will be at chest height, allowing them to lick and suck on your nipples while you grind. Or maybe you could try out some nipple clamps. They're not as scary as they sound and you can actually get really cute ones that just look like jewellery and can really add a level of intensity to your play, no matter what position you're in.

As everybody knows well by now, I am personally all about the clit, so any position where you can incorporate a toy or use fingers (mine or my partners!) to stimulate my clitoris during PIV sex is definitely going to maximise the experience for me. As always, the key is to speak to your sexual partner and tell them how you'd like to be dicked down.

Positions that are great for penetration and using your toys:

Doggy-style

This is definitely one of my favourite positions because it gives you such easy access to masturbate during penetration. Bend on all fours on a bed as you allow the person with the penis or dildo to penetrate your vagina or anus from behind. You can put a pillow or cushion under your stomach for support and don't forget to arch your back! Grab a wand, vibrator or suction toy to stimulate your clitoris. My suggestion would be a large wand as it's easier to reach your vulva. You can do the doggy-style position lying down flat on your stomach, but the best way to use it with a sex toy is when there is a bit of space for you to play with your vulva. Also ask your sexual partner to grab hold of your waist for support. Use the momentum from your partner thrusting into you to rock back and forth onto their penis.

Missionary

Who doesn't love the classic missionary position? It can be quite tricky to include a sex toy during missionary, because, let's face it, you're up close, leaving little room for a sex toy. However, another sex-toy option is to get the penetrator to wear a cock ring with ears. The ears are able to play and vibrate on your clitoris, helping to increase the sexual stimulation.

Spooning

Both you and your partner lie on your sides, with your back close to their chest. Allow the penetration to take place with a penis or penis-like object and then use a toy of your choice to experiment with. You can gently twist your body to face your partner and enjoy some good ol' smooching during this position, too. Encourage them to play with your nipples and other parts of your body that turn you on.

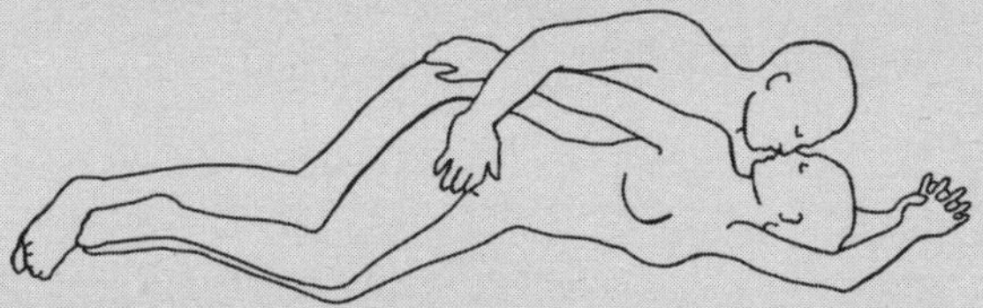

Lap dance

This position is fun and exciting, especially if you do it in front of a mirror! Allow the person with a penis to sit on a chair as you straddle them with your back facing the person. Gently slide the penis into your vagina as you begin to ride, and use a toy of your choice to stimulate your vulva during penetration.

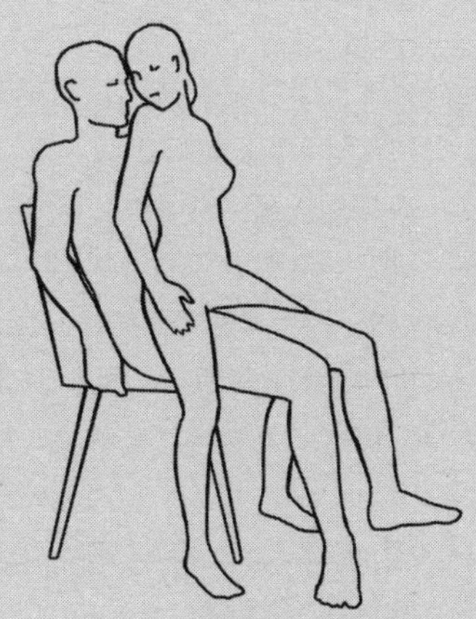

The splitter

This is a missionary hack and a fun one that not only gives you the glorious view of your sexual partner as they penetrate you, but also allows you (or them) to grab a toy to play on your clit bean. Do this by lying down on your back, then, as they're on top, have them put one of their legs over one of your legs (the leg that mirrors theirs), as you allow your other leg to rest on their chest. The splitter is great for deep penetration, so remember to try to do some Kegels to help increase pleasure for you both as the penis slides in and out.

These are some classic introductory sexual positions that are particularly good for learning how to use a toy on your vulva during penetration, to help maximise your chances of achieving the Big O. There are many other toys you can include into your sex routine as mentioned in the chapter before, to add more fun, such as a butt plug! Allow your anus to prepare for its own show by lathering the toy up with lube and siding it into the anus gently. Lube AGAIN, Oloni!? Yes, because unlike the vagina, the anus does not self-lubricate. It's also a sensitive area that we aren't trying to cause any friction or damage to, now, are we?

You can start off by using a finger, but what's amazing about many anal toys is that, other than the different material, shapes and sizes they come in, sometimes the tip of butt plugs or anal beads start off slim and get thicker the further you go in. Now, once you feel comfortable with the butt plug, you can engage in other PIV positions with your partner, giving yourself the chance to experience double penetration.

If you want to turn up the heat, try out a vibrating butt plug that can be controlled by your lover, which is such a fun way to experiment together. How about some mutual masturbation and giving them the control over the type of pleasure you'll feel? Or having your pussy eaten with the toy inside of you? Listen, I won't be shocked if you start to spiritually levitate.

There are so many pretty silicone, bedazzled butt plugs on the market that can be worn just to make you feel sexy in the bedroom, as your partner enjoys the view during doggy-style, or perhaps you might want to try a glass anal bead for a different sensation. Experiment, but note that silicone toys are not to be used with silicone-based lubrication as it can wear down the material of the toy. Instead, try water- or oil-based lube. However, water- and silicone-based lube can be used with glass sex toys.

Remember, the toy can stay in for some time and even be worn outside of the bedroom in preparation for anal sex, but try not to go over two hours just to be on the safe side. It should also go without saying that if you do feel any slight pain, take it out immediately, and if you've been hurt please seek some medical care ASAP.

Other toys you can experiment with are blindfolds, handcuffs, door jams, whips, paddles, ropes and more. I know, I know, I'm going down the BDSM route – we'll talk more about this lifestyle and culture in Chapter 13: Kinks, Fetishes and BDSM (see page 299). But sex toys are not just vibrators and dildos; sex toys are any objects and restraints that help heighten pleasure in the bedroom.

Additional sex acts

Give a hand job:

Giving a hand job is the gateway to giving great head. It can be done during oral sex, or as part of foreplay and in between PIV sex. The best way to give your partner with a penis a really good hand job is by watching them, trying it and asking how it feels. Ask to watch your lover masturbate and see how they position their hands; notice where on the shaft their area of sensitivity is and imitate that with either a bit of saliva or some lubrication.

How to suck dick:

The art of sucking dick includes three things: having fun, absolutely no teeth (unless they say they're into it) and confidence. Always ask the penis-holder how they enjoy their penis being sucked, as people vary. Some people enjoy sloppy head with quite a bit of saliva as it's being sucked on, while some prefer just a bit. Experiment with flavoured lube (such as passion fruit or crème brûlée) as it can help add more pleasure and enthusiasm on your part. Next, you want to gently squeeze the penis with both hands yet rotate them in opposite directions as you slide up and then down the shaft with your hands and suck the head of the penis. Do this repeatedly with and without your hands, but again, ask your partner what else they'd want you to do when sucking their penis. They might want their anus gently fingered repeatedly, or their balls licked and sucked. People have a personal way of enjoying their dick being sucked, so communicate. 'Tell me how you like it.' Giving a blowjob is meant to give you both pleasure in your own ways, so make some eye contact as you play with their dick if you're really trying to snatch their lives sexually. Remember, confidence is key!

Deep throat:

Deep throating a dick is another level of blowjob, but one you should only try out if YOU want to, not because you've been pushed into it or seen it in porn. First think about the sexual position you want to be in when practising deep throat. In most cases, a blowjob is usually given when someone is on their knees or positioned between the receiver's legs when they're lying flat on a bed. These positions are great, but you can also try a position where you're lying on your back, with your head gently off the bed, facing the ceiling, as the person with the penis hovers over you and gently places it in your mouth. No matter what the position is, it's important that you have a safe action, such as blinking repeatedly or waving in order for the other person to stop. Prep to start off with by simply sucking the dick; use lube and take a break until you're ready for the next step. Do not forget that breathing is vital. Do so through your nose and only continue for as long as you want. Start off with a couple of inches of the penis inside your mouth and then give a signal that let's your partner know they can either go deeper or should stop. You can practise with a dildo beforehand to know your limits, but never push the boundary of what your body is comfortable with. Some people have a sensitive gag reflex and others don't. What matters most is your experience, how you feel and if it's exciting. It's also not a sexual act you have to do every time you have sex.

The gag reflex is a very normal contraction of your throat whenever something uncomfortable goes way too far in there. I'm not going to teach you how to stop it as it's there for a reason, such as helping us when choking, and trying to alter it just for the sake of a blowjob, when the orgasm gap needs fixing, is just not part of my ministry.

How to ride:

Riding is a fun penetrative move that can be done in different ways: you can ride like a cow girl, or do it in reverse, otherwise known as the reverse cow girl. You don't need to be 10/10 but if you want to get better you've opened the right page. Even with all the noise I make about getting on top on my podcast, it is a position I enjoy with a vibrator. That's right, incorporate your vibrator on your clitoris when riding or, better yet, ask your sex partner to do so. The magic of riding comes from your hips when you get on top. There's a misconception that you're meant to just bop up and down, and some people might enjoy that. But instead, try rolling your hips in and out. Place your hands on their chest for support to help you get into the motion, but also communicate because people enjoy pleasure in different ways. Ask for support, and for them to hold on to your hips as your booty rocks back and forth. You can even hug when on top and have your partner underneath to penetrate you. You don't have to sit up directly, but instead lean your top half close to the person you're riding and allow your bum to have a rhythmic motion, rolling your hips during each movement as you go up and down. Do this continuously with fast and quick movements or at a slow and medium pace as you squeeze your vaginal walls. The secret is not to put all your weight in your mid-section, but to put it in your arms or legs as you ride the penis. It's all about the power of the hips and how you grind on it. Think about it as giving them a literal naked lap dance that's just nastier and wetter as you stare deep into their eyes. *(Tip: Play some slow, sensual, sexual music that can help inspire your movement.)*

Anal sex:

The anus can be an erogenous zone for many people, especially as it is full of nerve endings. We've got part of the prep figured out with fingers, toys and lubrication, but it's also important to make sure a couple of hours before anal sex takes place that you're extra clean down there to avoid any accidents. You can do this with water or a shower enema set, or just find a healthy cleaning method that works for you personally. Once you're ready, start off by picking a sexual position such as doggy-style and allow the tip of the penis to enter the anus gently. Communicate with your partner throughout the experience as it's important for them to know how you feel. Remember to also relax to help the experience run more smoothly, as a scared bootyhole is an even tighter one, which won't allow room for the dick to go inside. Again, communicate throughout and use some check-in language, so you can tell your partner when to stop, how to continue or when to pause at any time. Once they're inside and you're completely comfortable, ask them to continue penetrating and to add more lube for an even better experience. It's also possible you might want to peg your partner that has a prostate, because when the prostate is stimulated, orgasms can be formed. Ask them if they'd be up for it.

Foot job:

Foot fetishes, otherwise known as podophilia, have been said to be one of the most common fetishes among men, and if your partner has one or just enjoys the act, you might want to try it. Ask if this is something they've tried before or want to try. Make sure your feet are well moisturised, add some lubrication and sit up slightly between their legs as they're sat or lying on a bed. You can also try doing this both sitting on a chair opposite each other. Start off by gently teasing, using your feet to stroke parts of their inner thighs and the lower half of their chest, then work your way back down to their penis. Place the penis between both feet and cup it slightly, but not too tightly, then 'penetrate' by going up and down with your feet repeatedly. It's vital you ask what they prefer and what adjustments they'd like if you try this out.

Tribbing:

This sex act is when a woman grinds her vulva on another woman's body or vulva and it can be done in various positions. For amazing clitoral stimulation try open scissoring – this is when you and your partner open both your legs and grind vulva to vulva to heighten stimulation on your clitoris. There's also doggy tribbing, where you grind and hump on the ass cheeks of your partner, and of course missionary, so you're up and close, allowing room for kissing and more touching.

Nipple play:

Nipple play is such an underrated form of sexual intimacy. It's such a huge erogenous spot for many people. Don't just save this for foreplay; include it during different parts of penetration by licking, softly biting, pinching and squeezing. Ask a check-in question during nipple play to find out what type of pressure they'd like. Studies have also shown that orgasms can form from areas other than the genitals, and research from a 2019 study saw that when the nipples are aroused from stimulation it activates the same parts of the brain where clitoral and vaginal stimulation takes place, called the genital sensory cortex.[18] Some women have also said that they were able to get nipple orgasms during sexual experiences, showing just how important nipple stimulation is to our sex lives. Have some fun with nipple clamps, nipple suckers and maybe some nipple tweezers. Again, don't be bummed out if you're not able to get a nipple orgasm – all our bodies are different, so continue to try out different methods and just enjoy the sensation.[19]

68:

The 68 is a great sexual position to allow your partner to perform oral sex on your vulva. As they're sitting up slightly on the bed, allow your legs to go over their shoulders, knees bent behind them, with your pussy in their face, as your back rests on their legs that are slightly raised. Instruct your partner on how to eat it – talk them through the fun and add some flavoured lubricant.

69:

This is a sexual act for mutual stimulation and pleasure. Allow your partner to lie down as you get on top, but with your body faced the opposite way to perform oral sex and a hand job on their vulva or penis, while they return the favour by either eating your ass or your pussy. There can be a lot going on so don't freak out if you find it a bit tricky!

The Kivin method:
This is an oral sex move for people with vulvas that some have sworn by, yet not enough people know about. Instead of licking the vulva up and down when in between your legs, your sexual partner should position themselves on their side, so they can lick parts of the vulva, especially the clitoris, from left to right as they use their other hand to play with your perineum or finger your vagina. People have testified to this giving them earth-shattering orgasms in under five minutes, but again, do not feel the pressure to orgasm immediately, just think about adding it to your sex routine to see if you experience a new sort of pleasure.

Sex in a digital world

There are so many ways we can heighten how we enjoy sexual moments with our lovers, even when they're not in the same room as us. Sexting, sending nudes or vudes (video nudes), video-call sex and sharing links with each other to a hot porn scene are just some of them.

There are many reasons why couples create private sex video content. This could be simply to admire their performance, for self-pleasure, or to have something to watch if you're away from each other and want to reminisce. On the other hand, if recording intimacy makes you uncomfortable then that's fine – it isn't for everyone.

Personally, I love sending my boyfriend nudes when I'm feeling myself in all my nakedness. I see it as a sex gift that only his eyes are lucky enough to gaze upon. It's also a way to help keep the relationship raunchy and remind my boyfriend of how lucky he is (I'm in my Leo bag right now).

Saying that, it's really important to be careful with who and how you send nude photos of yourself to when sharing a sexual interest. There was a time I used to scream, 'No face, no case!' out of fear that the image could possibly leak online. Sometimes phones are stolen or iClouds hacked, which used to put the fear of God into me. Today, we're lucky that there are vault apps where you can store your images and videos to keep them safe, and you can also hide photos, too. I'm not sure if it's all 100-per-cent foolproof, but it makes me feel more at ease, compared to many years ago when I'd give my phone to a friend to look at a picture and they'd start to swipe! My heart would beat fast, hoping they wouldn't come across endless photos of my boobs. It's also not a bad idea to leave your face out of images and videos that you wish to send, if it makes you more comfortable.

You could try recording audio instead of video clips of you and your lover to play back. Pay attention to the moaning, the dirty words, the creaks of the bed, the breathing, the headboard hitting the wall. Listen to it all. Sometimes the best sexual content is what we allow ourselves to create. You get to analyse the video or audio to express what you enjoyed and how it made you feel. 'I really loved it when we did that position' – or maybe 'That's the last time I ever try that!'

Sending that nude

Just as it can take over 20 selfies to find the one we love for our display and profile photos on social media, sometimes it can be exactly the same with nudes. Experiment with your angles and your nakedness. Find a shot that turns you on! Yes, nudes are fun to send to your sexual partner, but they can also be for yourself and something you look at when you're having one of those 'meh' days.

Use a tripod if you want, and the self-timer to help you get into position. Use your bathroom or bedroom mirror (don't forget to clean that mirror). Play with the filters and find one that really complements you. You don't have to be totally naked either; it could be a shot of you in a sexy bra, a crop top that shows off your underboob, sexy leather lingerie when you're oiled up – it's up to you!

Video nudes could include a slowed-down clip of you doing something seductive, from looking at yourself in the mirror to playing with your favourite part of your body. That might be you squeezing your boobs, turning around to show off your ass in a pretty thong or coming out the shower wet.

If you'd like to see a type of nude from your lover, you can express that by messaging, 'It's your turn now' followed by the eyes emoji.

Ultimately we share our intimate content with people we believe we can trust, but sadly some people break their promises or show their true colours only after you have let your guard down. However, revenge porn in the UK is illegal and has been since 2015 – you can be prosecuted if sexual content of someone is shared online or with other people without their consent. What's more, if someone is also issuing threats they can face prison.[20] Never allow anyone to force or coerce you into sharing intimate images of yourself and if you find that they are, please screenshot the message exchange, block and report them (if done on a social media app) – BUT if this is something you're both consenting to then you do you, boo!

The power of a good tongue

When I was a teenager, so many men I knew either refused to go down on women or flat denied doing it. Some of them continued to deny it till they graduated from university. With hindsight I know that some of them *were* doing it, they were just being secretive about it, but others weren't. I even get straight men on my podcast today talking about how they're saving that sexual act for their wives. (What? Why??) But they still expect oral sex to be part of the package for *them* when sleeping with women whose last names they don't remember.

This double standard shows you exactly how some men feel about our pleasure. Even with the knowledge we have of how we're most likely to cum, they still manage to justify being selfish lovers. Now, I'm not saying all men should go down on women. Some people are simply not into certain sexual acts, and no one should be pushed past their boundaries, but it's important to understand what the refusal is rooted in. If the reason for not eating pussy is rooted in misogyny, if the guy claims to find vaginas disgusting or believes your pleasure is less important, then really, is that someone you should be sleeping with? If it's rooted in toxic masculinity and a fear of being seen as submissive for wanting to please a woman, I ask you again: girl, do you really want to be fucking this guy?

Women, let me tell you, there are plenty of men who enjoy eating pussy. Please go and find them immediately or at least the ones who are willing to learn and want to get better. We shouldn't be sharing our sexual energy with people who are saving the most basic act of pleasure for a woman they haven't yet met and want to marry. Some men are French kissing buttholes to help the woman they're sleeping with reach the height of her pleasure and yet some of us are still sharing our vaginas with men who are doing the bare minimum. It must stop immediately.

There's no 'correct' way to go down on someone, so if you're having sex with a person who needs some guidance when eating you out, just say what feels good to you (if you've spent plenty of time masturbating, you'll have a few ideas!). Maybe you like a really light touch, or the gentlest of flicks of the tongue. Or maybe you want your partner to get right in there till their face is covered in juice. Maybe you want a nice long build-up of kisses around your stomach before they move all the way down to your inner thigh. Think about what kind of sensation you like on your clit – sucking, flicking, gentle lapping, or long, full licks? Do you want them to add pressure with their lips or keep things light and delicate?

If your clit is very sensitive, you might not want it to be stimulated directly. In that case, try getting your partner to use their lips and tongue just above the hood – to provide pressure to the internal parts of the clit, without touching the glans itself. Or some people like to be licked on the part of the vulva just below the clitoris so the sensation comes from underneath rather than right on top. For clits that need more direct action, you can also take control by spreading your pussy lips with your fingers and allowing them to go to town. Or ask your partner to use a small vibrator at a mid tempo on and around the clitoris to help heighten the sensation.

Ask them to talk nasty to you when they're down there, too, if you're into it, to tell you how good you taste or how much they love it. I love to ask nasty questions when their face is buried in my vulva and have them try to answer me without breaking their rhythm!

Having your partner put their fingers inside you at the same time can also feel amazing. One thing I've enjoyed is stroking the side of my partner's face with two of my fingers, gently sliding them back and forth on his beard at the exact pace I wanted him to finger me, at the same time as he was eating my cooch – and it felt so beautiful.

And it goes without saying, we should be putting this much thought into reciprocating, too! If you want to know how a person with a penis enjoys oral sex, you must be vocal and ask. If they're not circumcised, always pull the foreskin back so you can really stimulate the head (that's the most sensitive part). If they are circumcised, make sure you focus on the head area and use both your hands with a bit of saliva, or flavoured lube (lube is your best friend when playing with a dick that's been cut!). Ultimately, as always, you have to ask because ... yep, you guessed it, everyone is different.

Most importantly, don't make the mistake of thinking that oral sex is only reserved for foreplay. It isn't! You can incorporate it at any time and even go back and forth with other sexual acts, including penetration. It can be a great way of edging each other, helping you delay having an orgasm, and drawing out a longer sexual experience. Mix it up by asking to sit on their face in the middle of intercourse. Or lie flat on your stomach with a pillow underneath you and say you'd like your vulva played with from the back. How many times have you had sex with a guy and been asked to suck his dick randomly during different points? Set those very same standards for your vulva, ladies! Your pussy requires attention, too.

Speaking of eating it from the back, remember that tongues can feel good on and around the anus, too. If you're into ass eating (also known as rimming), it's vital that you make sure your bootyhole is clean, not only for your partner's sake, but also so that you can relax and enjoy it without worrying. And if you're planning to reciprocate, make sure your partner is following the same protocol. You don't necessarily have to douche (although it may make you feel more comfortable if you're planning to stick fingers, tongue, toys or dicks up there), but washing with a very mild soap and warm water should be the bare-minimum requirement.

The big oh, ohhh, OHHHHH!

Orgasms are one of the most intense and euphoric feelings we can experience. In fact, the French have a term for it called *la petite mort*, which translates as 'the little death', meaning a 'brief loss or weakening of consciousness'. Today it's used to mean 'the sensation of post-orgasm as likened to death', which in a way makes sense as an orgasm can make you feel as though you have been reborn! They are the peak of the sexual response cycle, the point when all that delicious sexual tension is finally released. Your heart rate will speed up,[21] your muscles will contract and you may find yourself breathing shallower and faster, too. People with a penis will likely experience ejaculation and almost all of us will have some sort of involuntary reaction, whether it's making incoherent noises, screwing up our face, curling our toes, grabbing the sheets or just screaming, 'Fuuuuuuuuuuuuuuuck!' Your brain will also release the happy hormones dopamine and oxytocin,[22] the latter of which is linked to increased social bonding (which is why you sometimes feel extra loved-up after you cum).

How you orgasm and what helps get you there will be pretty individual to you. Over the years I've seen lots of people claim there are different kinds of orgasm and give tips on how to achieve them, but when it comes to scientific research, the jury's out on whether there actually are distinct 'types' of orgasm or whether we just experience them at different intensities and alongside different sensations. Personally, I don't think it really matters. What matters is that you feel empowered to explore your body and figure out what feels good to you. There are people out there who jizz just from doing crunches in the gym, but that doesn't mean we all have to aim for that (and thank God, because I, for one, am happy to keep my workout and my sex life separate). If you're someone who cums just from nipple play or from anal sex or from cervical stimulation, great! Keep doing your thing. But if you've never experienced orgasms from these activities, there's really no need to worry or to feel like you have to figure out how (unless you want to, of course – experimenting can be hot in itself, even if it doesn't result in an orgasm).

Sometimes, the feeling that we need to be ticking off a bucket list of orgasms can actually make it harder for us to experience even one. Focusing too hard on the orgasm itself can sometimes do everything *but* bring you to an orgasm. So instead of trying to rush yourself to the finish line, enjoy being in the moment of arousal.

And never put pressure on yourself to orgasm if it's just not happening, as stressing yourself out about it is almost guaranteed to make the possibility disappear! And remember that sometimes it takes patience and a lot of practice. And that's no bad thing. When we stay in the moment we can enjoy the practice just as much as the 'final performance'.

One tip to help stop your brain worrying, and increase your chances of orgasm, is to allow your imagination to take over. Yep, I'm talking about using fantasies during sex. Think that sounds weird? It's not! Lots of women do it, so let's normalise it. In fact, a 2014 study found that women who'd had erotic thoughts during sex had a higher chance of climaxing.[23] When sexual wellness platform OMGYES.com partnered up with Indiana University and world-famous sex research hub the Kinsey Institute, to look into how women achieve orgasm, they found that a huge percentage use something called 'framing' – which often takes the form of fantasising.[24]

Should an orgasm be the barometer of enjoyable sex? In one of the orgasm-gap studies I mentioned earlier, researchers wrote that, 'Our decision to treat orgasm as a central measure of the quality of young women's sexual experiences may be controversial. Some might see this decision as flowing from male-centred and medicalized views of sex and argue that women are not particularly concerned about orgasm'[25] – and while I understand this disclaimer, why can't we treat an orgasm as a central measure? Imagine if cis men were having sex and never got to nut. Would that sex even count in their eyes?

That's not to say that you can't enjoy sex without climaxing, because you can, you really can; it's just about being honest about your desires and not feeling as though you should have to settle sexually. No one should. We should all be enjoying intimacy and leaving the bedroom satisfied, knowing we had sex with someone who understands our pleasure and cares enough to help us reach the highest form of it.

Aftercare

Sex is a very intimate act, and the best kind is where we take the time to check in and look after each other *afterwards*, too. Don't rush into looking for your underwear that's been scattered around the room and don't just turn over, pull up the bedsheets and try to snooze. Have some manners! I remember a guy I had sex with who would take forever to get me a wipe when he went to the bathroom. Perhaps I was a little impatient, but I never understood why he didn't just have those wipes on standby, by his bed, so his partners could do a timely clean-up. Nobody wants a line of dried-up crusting cum decorating their inner thigh!

That's just one example of my personal preferences, but aftercare can look like many different things, so again, make sure you ask your sexual partner what they enjoy doing when the height of intimacy is over so you can both meet each other's needs. Aftercare could consist of cuddling, spooning, some pillow talk about the experience and what you enjoyed, having a shower together, ordering food, getting a glass of water for each other (because, let's be honest, sex can be a workout), getting a clean, wet towel, laughing together or just lying there staring into each other's eyes. My boyfriend and I are quite playful, so when we finish having sex we mostly cuddle for a couple of minutes and start to engage in a bit of light banter when we get in the shower together. This can extend out to texting as well. I personally love to spend a few days after a good hook-up messaging each other about our horny flashbacks, telling each other what we found hottest and generally prolonging the enjoyment of the sex.

Aftercare is a way to show appreciation when the sex is over, so continue to be thoughtful to one another. Compliment your partner and continue to make an effort to be considerate and show you care about their needs. Blurting out, 'Don't you need to get the last tube?' is not ideal here, but you could use the opportunity to ask if they'd like you to get them a cab or if they want to hang out for a bit longer. If you don't want them to stay the night (and I totally understand that we all need our space sometimes), just explain this honestly rather than passive-aggressively kicking them out.

The afterglow is also an opportunity to check in and make sure everyone feels good about what went down. This is something we can learn from the BDSM community, where aftercare is a step they take very seriously to ensure individuals are feeling comfortable with the experiences they've had and feel safe to 'come down' from the hormonal high that results from intense kink scenes. Even if consent has been given before and during, checking in afterwards is still vital. If you've tried a new sexual act for the very first time, use that moment to ask them how they felt about it and if they'd be open to doing it again. When you show an interest of care it can leave the person feeling good, because it shows you truly care about their experience.

In my opinion, however, aftercare shouldn't only be reserved for people who enjoy blindfolds and whips. I'd argue that we can experience a hormonal come-down from intense vanilla sex, too. In fact, a 2015 study found that many women have experienced postcoital dysphoria (PCD), also known as 'post-sex blues', at some point or other in their lives. Participants reported experiencing anxiety, tearfulness, a sense of melancholy or depression after sex.[26] When we spend time together after sex we show that we care about our partner's wellbeing and that we respect them as a person.

And let's be honest, mistakes can also happen during sex, like not using a condom properly (or at all), so just as you will have talked about sexual health before sex, use the time afterwards to discuss any follow-up measure you might need, such as the morning-after pill.

Finally, ladies, some believe that peeing after sex can help flush out any bacteria in your urethra and helps to avoid getting an infection, so you may wish to do this just in case.

What kind of sex should we *not* be having?

The only type of sex we shouldn't be having is the kind that doesn't meet your needs or centre your pleasure. We should only be sharing our sexual experiences with those who are passionate about pleasing us. There is no perfect way to have sex – we're all different and need to be cared for differently – but a good sexual partner will listen to your wants and do their best to act on that. We're going to talk more about consent in the next chapter, but for now let me just say that if you ever feel like you're being pressured or coerced into having sex then it's important you know that that isn't a person who cares about you or your boundaries.

We also shouldn't be sleeping with people because we believe it'll keep the relationship together. It's unlikely to work and ultimately you're selling yourself short out of fear, and that doesn't sound healthy. If you find yourself repeating your wants and needs in the bedroom over and over again, then it's time to stop wondering why you're not being heard and simply stop having sex with them. If nothing else, remember this: you are worthy of amazing sex that has you having random flashbacks in the middle of university lectures or important work meetings.

Ladies, shall we have some fun ...?

Amazing sex upgrade Twitter thread*

34, Nairobi, Kenya

Hi Oloni, so here is my story. I was born into a culture that does not allow women to enjoy sex and [believes] that one should have sex in marriage only. Got married and, girl, the sexual experience I got was the worst that could ever exist in this world. Glad I am no longer married. Fast forward, 3 months ago, I met this man of a totally different culture and giiiiirl! I experienced the BEST sex ever. He literally took over my entire pussy. Owned it. Ate it! He'll alternate between tongue and dick. Took me fully and I think I came from the moment he put his huge dick inside me, taking breaks in between ... Taps were opened! That was the day I believed I could get multiple orgasms. We had sex multiple times that day and I'll cum every time. Oooh and the best part is, we are keeping it a secret coz I look forward to being devoured again.

24, London, UK

Oloniiiiiii. It's been a month and I still get flashbacks even at work! I thought my vagina was broken before because I

---

*Not all the views expressed in the Twitter threads reflect my opinion as the author of this book, but it is important to me to share other perspectives and experiences of peoples' sexual expression and relationships.

hated penetration but noooooo, she's alive and I love penetration now! The other bodies were just shit!!! He worshipped my whole body, kissed every single part slowly, took his time, fingered me while licking me out and rubbing on my bum hole! Sis, he dicked me down until I beg[ged] him to stop by tightening my pussy so he buss! I usually can go 5+ rounds in one night but boiii 3 or 4 is enough. I can't wait for him to destroy me – I mean dick me down again.

33, Canada

My ex-boyfriend of 5 years did not eat pussy and delivered boring-ass sex. And apparently, his ex-gf had an issue with that as well.

Fast forward [to] today – my man enjoys pleasuring me and eating me out. Missed out for 5 friggin years!! I learned from the hubby that the pleasure is also from pleasing your partner. He is also the only person to make me orgasm [–] the first time I did that with him, I would apologize bc I didn't know my body can twitch like it was an exorcism [–] it was embarrassing to me coz I thought it wasn't normal.

He also mastered how to give multiple Os too because he read sex books. He makes me orgasm from eating me out and eating my kitty. And 2 babies later we still got it!

23, UK

Ahhh, sis, it was simple but this was like guy no.6. Broke up with my ex multiple guys ago but then one sweet Iranian guy I hooked up with [–] he was the first guy I've ever been with that asked me throughout if I was okay, checked in on me, making sure I was enjoying [it.] [H]e was big on consent and made sure I came, was patient with me, which most guys prior weren't, not even my ex of 3 yrs. After him I made sure to be vocal with what I want, especially making sure they're giving long enough head, and my sex life has been A1 since! Finally made it out the hood with dry sex.

26, Texas, USA

I recently started having sex with a new partner and when I tell you I felt seeeeennnn like never before. I have a lot of body insecurities so idk if he could tell but it's the way he intentionally touched, admired and kissed every part of my body that really got me. He took time to know my needs, did not assume what I wanted and made sure I came a thousand times. Then [he] fed me later and we had a good night's sleep. I know this is the bare minimum but it was the first time someone actually saw me and prioritized me in bed. These older men are the real deal!!!! No longer dating anyone under the age of 40.

30, Philadelphia, USA

My sex life has had THE BEST upgrade. My new partner is attentive and always willing to try new things and is invested in my kinks. I'm always one to push the envelope and he tries every single thing I want. Finally found a man that lets me lick his ass and maybe use a toy or two. Also got him to be down with a MMF 3sum – best experience everrrrrr. Aftercare is [a] top priority for us. We lay together and discuss what we liked, want to try again, and just genuinely check in to make sure we both got what we wanted.

24, London, UK

Hello Oloni. So this was when I was with an ex. The actual seggs was fine, no problem. But this man could not do foreplay well at aaaallllllll. Just be moving his fingers around in there any how, and it was like my clitoris didn't exist, would not go near it. I tried to softly make suggestions, but his ego wasn't really tryna hear it. I used to fake an orgasm so we could skip that part and move on to the main event. Didn't know how much I suffered/ missed out on until I met someone that did foreplay on poooiiinntt every time. Changed the whole experience.

32, London, UK

Hi Oloni, I was dating this guy last summer and our sex was incredible. We were so sexually compatible and our bodies were always in sync, he knew how to please me and paid attention to my body well. He used his mouth on my pussy, fucked me great in doggy and missionary as he stared deep into my eyes ... the sun would glisten on our skin from our morning sex sessions. A lot of guys I've been with have been selfish lovers or wanted me to do all the work, but this guy, he was a sex present from the greats whose dick deserved to be shared with other women. He always filled me up with pleasure and cum ... we could fuck all day ... I think actually used to. He really had me dickmatised. Damn, I think I might call him.

CHAPTER 7

Consent

⚠ **Content Warning: Sexual violence.**

What is consent, and why does it matter to understand it?

Consent is absolutely essential. In case you think I'm joking, let me start out by saying again very, very clearly: consent is mandatory. Sex without consent is not 'sex', it's rape, it's sexual assault, it's a violation and it's not OK.

But once we get that into our heads, I believe there's also room for consent to be more than just A Thing You Have to Have ... it can also be a thing you genuinely want, a thing you *enjoy*, a thing that is actually part of the turn-on. Yeah, that's right, consent can be hot!

You've probably heard the phrase 'consent is sexy', right? In fact, you might even have heard it from me. I say it a lot! I do believe there's nothing hotter than knowing that both you and the person you're having sex with *really wants it.* And the best sexual partners are the ones who listen to what each other like and are genuinely interested in each other's pleasure.

But how do we actually do it? How do we make sure the sex we're having is truly consensual? Because it's all very well to say that sex *should* be consensual, but lots of us don't even have a proper understanding of what consent looks like.

It blows my mind how often I get women DMing me dilemmas or stories in which they describe sexual scenarios that aren't consensual. They'll say things like, 'I was so still and then he did this,' or they describe a scenario where they went along with something because the guy begged them to, or they tell me they were not of age when it happened, and I'm thinking, 'Woah, wait, back up, do you realise what you just said?' I obviously never post or share those stories, because I believe I have a duty of care, but it really makes me realise how badly we need to talk about consent. Because too often I'm seeing that the people IN the scenarios don't even realise that what's happening to them is a form of sexual assault.

Of course, it's not just down to us to identify it and call it out. We also need other people to understand and care about consent. And sadly many don't.

Legally, in the UK, consent is understood to be present 'if [the person] agrees by choice, and has the freedom and capacity to make that choice'.[1] The second part of this definition has to be considered carefully in sexual assault cases and it is arguably the hardest thing to figure out. Even if the person said yes to something, we need to be sure they fully understood what they were saying yes to *and* didn't feel pressured into saying yes.

I've spoken to women who were unsure whether some of what they had experienced was sexual assault, and the first thing I asked them was whether they fully knew what they were saying yes to. A story I hear a lot is of a woman who is having sex with a guy when she suddenly realises (either during or afterwards) that the condom has been removed – a mortifying experience that puts her body and health at risk. But is this assault, she wonders? She consented to the sex, after all. But she didn't know he was going to remove the condom and that's the crucial part. She couldn't consent to something she didn't know was going to happen, something that was done secretly. The consent she gave was conditional on using a condom and by removing it her partner has broken the conditions of that consent, so yes, this *is* assault. In fact, this scenario is called 'stealthing'; it's recognised as a form of rape in the UK and you can be prosecuted for it.

When I'm not causing havoc on Twitter with my threads, sometimes I visit secondary schools to teach children about consent. I don't go into too much detail like I do in this book, but instead teach them the basics of what consent looks like. I have a PowerPoint and it includes this very popular video about tea and consent. It uses tea as a metaphor for sex and breaks down how you should recognise when not to give someone a cup of tea. You can find it on YouTube and I encourage you to share it with the young people around you.[2]

This wasn't a talk we had when I was younger, when we all really needed it.

Do you remember growing up with boys or girls who couldn't keep their hands to themselves in school? I do. I remember when boys would play with my school skirt and my bra strap and just didn't understand that 'no' meant 'no'. I also can't pretend I didn't see boys trying to escape from a bunch of girls who were trying to hug them during lunch, when they just wanted to play with their boys on the basketball court. Touching people who hadn't given us permission was a big part of being a teenager and I wish I'd known then how wrong this was. I knew it was annoying and made us uncomfortable – and sometimes we would complain to the teachers – but neither we nor our teachers understood that it broke the rules of consent, so most of the time we didn't make a fuss and the teachers just ignored our complaints. Instead, their dismissal contributed to our collective belief that being touched without permission wasn't 'that big a deal'.

Consent doesn't begin in nightclubs, when someone walks past and tries to feel your bum or dance with you without your permission; it should be taught from childhood. How many of you can remember being told you had to give an aunt or uncle a kiss or felt under pressure to accept hugs and physical affection from other family members or friends that you didn't really want? Most of us learned from a very young age that it was OK for adults to violate our personal boundaries, so no wonder we sometimes struggle to recognise it as a problem now. I'm not being overdramatic – when we let kids know that they don't need to hug an aunt or uncle, it instantly allows them to understand and create boundaries. And once they're aware of their boundaries, they can call it out immediately if someone oversteps them.

When we understand from a young age what agency over our body looks and feels like, we can carry that into our adult lives to help protect us and reduce non-consensual encounters.

To me, it's really clear that the women in my DMs are feeling pressured and coerced into doing things they don't really want to do. But they don't even realise that's what's happening. And it's possible their partners don't either, because a lot of the time men don't realise that women are just saying yes and going along with it because they're afraid that their partner will get angry. Sometimes that's about avoiding an argument or a rejection. And let's be honest here, in the worst-case scenarios women have been killed by their partners for resisting or saying no to them and it's really hard to just let go of that knowledge. Even if we feel relatively safe in our relationships, that power dynamic between men and women is never totally erased.

I also often hear women talking about being tired or not up for sex but feeling like they have to because their partner is expecting it, because they feel like it's their duty. But it's not! I honestly can't say that enough times. It is *not* your duty. You don't have to do anything. A relationship or marriage is not a contract to have sex whenever one of you feels like it. It does not equal automatic consent. You can still be sexually violated by your long-term partner or spouse.

I talk about consent a lot because I don't want to live in a world where women are sending me messages unaware that what they're describing is sexual assault. But I also feel strongly that we need to be able to open the conversation up and acknowledge that navigating consent is sometimes tricky, that it can feel complicated and that we don't all experience it in the same way.

Mixed messages about consent

If you were a girl growing up in the early 2000s then I'm gonna bet you heard the phrase 'no means no'. It was coined by the Canadian Federation of Students in the early Nineties as part of a campaign against sexual violence.[3] The message is clear: if someone says no to sex, that 'no' must be respected.

If you were lucky, you might have also been told that 'yes means yes'. This is called affirmative consent. The idea of it developed because women felt that the argument that 'she didn't say no' should not be enough to get a guy off the hook. Instead of waiting for a 'no', people should get a clear and enthusiastic yes, they argued.

On the face of it, this sounds like a good thing, right? Focusing on saying 'no' turns sex into an exercise in gatekeeping where women (and it *is* mostly women – 84 per cent of sexual offences in the UK are against women[4]) have to be constantly on their guard. Affirmative consent acknowledges that we're there to have fun. It's a more sex-positive approach to consent.

But for all that consent is supposed to be this clear-cut thing, we get a lot of mixed messages about it. I see a lot of content on the subject of consent and, frankly, some of it can be confusing. Some people will tell you that you can't consent when you're drunk (I've even said it myself!), but in the real world many of us have had drunk or tipsy sex with our partners, who were also just as intoxicated as us, haven't we?

My honest opinion on this is that it's all to do with intent in a situation. Now, intent doesn't absolve anyone, but it plays a part. If someone is purposely trying to get you intoxicated because they believe it will help sway you or push you towards a decision they want, then they need to be arrested. This person understands what alcohol can do to your body and is taking advantage.

If you meet someone at a club and they insist on taking you back to theirs because they can see you're inebriated, and instead of allowing you to get some rest they push your sexual boundaries, they need to be arrested also, because that is rape.

Another message we sometimes get is that consent has to mean we go into every intimate encounter 100 per cent sure of what we do and don't want to do. But what about when we don't feel sure, or we haven't tried it so we don't honestly know yet if we might be into it?

My feelings are that if you feel neutral or curious about something, it's OK to say yes to it even if it's something you're not typically into. Perhaps you want to try it out. People try out new sexual activities all the time and decide if it's for them or not. Or maybe it's something they'd rather just do from time to time, not all the time. All of which is maybe why the 'yes = yes' thing doesn't work so well, because sometimes you can be like, 'OK, sure, why not?' and that's all right. However, just because someone gives consent once, that doesn't mean it's a yes all the time, which is why communication before, during and after sex is so important.

Is there ever a grey area when it comes to consent?

To the extent that we get taught about consent, we're usually told that it's a black-and-white issue: we either said yes or we said no and there's no grey area. But I think most of us know from real-life experience that it doesn't always work out that way. First of all, the answer isn't always a definite yes or no. I've definitely had partners suggest things where it's felt like more of a maybe, like anal sex, or where I didn't think I was up for it but then later, when we were in the moment, I thought, 'Fuck it, let's give it a go.'

And on the other side, I've had situations where I've slept with someone, had a good time and then found out some information about them afterwards that made me feel differently.

When I was in my late twenties I met a guy at a brunch party who told me he was 26. I didn't question it, because I knew some of his friends and they were all my age. We really clicked, and after a couple of glasses of prosecco we went back to his place and had sex. After talking more, it finally hit me that something was off. He just didn't seem 26. But I think it was the following conversation we had that allowed me to put two and two together:

I asked him over the phone, 'Have you ever lied about your age before?'

He hesitated. '... Y-y-yeah ...'

I replied, 'Did you lie to me about your age that day we met?'

He admitted that he had, and that was how I found out he was in fact 24.

If I'd known he was 24 I don't think I would have slept with him and I'm sure he knew that, too. Or maybe I would have. It still gave him no right to try to influence my decision based on a lie. So does that mean the sex we had was non-consensual? Honestly, I'm not sure. Some people would say it definitely was. The 'terms' on which I'd agreed to have sex had been violated and his intent was probably to deceive me and increase his chances of intimacy.

But it didn't seem so clear-cut to me. I definitely felt weird about it, but I think it was more about the deception than the sex itself. After all, I'd feel angry and uncomfortable if I found out a friend lied to me, too.

While I might not view it as sexual assault, lying to someone to get them into bed *is* unethical. And that's really what we're talking about when we talk about the 'grey area' – the huge range of shitty or not-OK things people do or say.

Another good example is the storyline in Michaela Coel's drama series *I May Destroy You*, in which Arabella's best friend Terry, played by Weruche Opia, has a threesome with two random guys she meets in a bar. As far as we can tell, Terry is totally up for this threesome – it's definitely consensual. But then there's a moment after the hook-up is over when she looks out of the window of her apartment and sees the two men chatting and congratulating each other as they leave, and she realises they actually knew each other all along and potentially conspired to sleep with her together. At the point when she took those two guys home with her, Terry felt like she was consenting, but it turns out she didn't know the full story. Yes, she consented to the sex, and she consented to it happening with both these guys at once. And they had a good time. But that moment when she realises she's been manipulated muddies the waters. It turns it into a grey area. To me, it comes down to intent again. The fact that they deliberately deceived her in order to orchestrate a specific sexual scenario makes this an example of sexual assault and I think we can tell from Terry's face in that scene that it feels like a violation to her as well. But it's also clear that she's confused and not sure how to react, how big a deal to make of it.

On the other hand, the realisation that someone has pushed your sexual boundaries might not come to you instantly sometimes. It could set in afterwards – years later in some cases. Maybe it's because we try to push it to the back of our mind or because we believe it might not be all that serious. Some women do not want to be seen as victims so try to shut it out. This might be due to shame or it might be because many of us have a very narrow view of what rape looks like: a dark alley and a stranger. But sexual assault doesn't only look one way. In fact, according to figures from the Office for National Statistics (ONS), only 15 per cent of sexual assaults are committed by a stranger. It's far more common for sexual violence to be perpetrated by someone the survivor knows, whether a partner or ex-partner (44 per cent), or someone else they know (37 per cent), such as a family member, friend or someone they're dating.[5]

Realising years later that a sexual encounter was not consensual can lead to a lot of different feelings and I don't think it's helpful to police what those feelings should be. Some people might decide they want to seek redress, or they might want to speak out and talk about the impact of it. Others might very understandably feel like they'd rather just get on with their lives. Either way, please, never blame yourself if you experience any form of sexual assault. It isn't your fault, and I've included some places you can go for help in my Resources section at the end (see page 311).

I've also spoken to women who have admitted to sleeping with men even after their sexual boundaries have been pushed, without understanding why. Some of our sexual experiences can be so heavily complex in how we deal with the situation afterwards, but again, it isn't your fault.

There is no 'correct' way to react to sexual assault and in some scenarios different people may interpret the same events differently. An example I've been asked about a few times is when a guy finishes by ejaculating somewhere on his partner's body (and in the scenarios I hear about it's usually her face). It was not agreed in advance that he could ejaculate there, but he helps himself and does it anyway. Some women do not feel violated by that, merely annoyed or surprised, but the ones that do aren't wrong to. It's a completely different sexual act to what you consented to (plus it can actually be dangerous – if you've ever had cum in your eye, you'll know!) and as such you should always ask first.

Another example is when people have agreed to have sex without a condom, on the condition that he will withdraw right before he reaches climax. But instead of pulling out, he cums inside her. Now, accidents do happen and in those situations immediate aftercare needs to take place. This includes apologising, discussing how to help with the situation and what precautions you'd both like to take. It might be, after that, that the person feels OK about it. However, if it is done purposely or the 'accident' is clearly a pretence, this too is a sexual violation.

I think what we find hard to acknowledge is that in these situations it comes down to you, what you understand the situation to have been, what the dynamic was and how you feel about it. I want us all to understand consent fully so that we can recognise when boundaries have been crossed and never second-guess ourselves. My aim is to provide information, to lay out some of the different viewpoints and scenarios, and to hopefully help you understand your own relationship with boundaries and consent.

It's OK to change your mind

One really important thing to understand about consent is that it can be retracted at any time. Let's say you told your partner you were up for trying deep throat. Maybe you watched some porn and found it hot, and you want to give it a go. But when you start you quickly realise your gag reflex isn't up to the job! Yeah, your partner might be disappointed and that's understandable – he was probably looking forward to having his dick swallowed – but how he behaves in that moment will be very telling. Of course, we all know that carrying on anyway, forcing you to do the thing you've said you don't want to do, is abuse. But it's also a violation of your consent if he tries to get you to continue on the basis that you 'promised'. When it comes to consent there's no such thing as a promise. People can and do change their minds, and pressuring or coercing you based on what you might have said 'earlier' or 'yesterday' or 'last time' is not OK. For what it's worth, in my view, a guy who wheedles or sulks to make you feel guilty is just as bad.

Until 2019 the US state of North Carolina actually had a horrid legal loophole around rape, which meant it was impossible to revoke consent once sex had started. For four decades, the state law was that if a person agreed to have sex but changed their mind, and were forced into continuing, it wasn't seen as rape.[6] Disgusting, right? It has finally been changed, but I can't imagine how many people must have been harmed and affected by this. And that is just one example. Beliefs like this are still common in our cultures and religions, and it's plain mad. Sex is supposed to be FUN, it's not supposed to be a battle of wills, for God's sake. So to the people who maintain that this shit is OK, I ask you: *Why on earth would you want to sleep with someone who no longer wishes to proceed?*

You can say yes to something 99 times and it's *still* OK to say no on the hundredth time. For sex to be truly consensual, you need to be approaching each new encounter totally open to what each person might or might not be up for. That's not to say you can't discuss your fantasies and agree to things you want to do beforehand; you definitely can and you should because that can be really hot, as long as you understand that none of it is set in stone. Just because you spent the entire Uber ride whispering into his ear what you were going to do to him when you got home, that does not mean you've committed to doing that stuff.

But let's not forget that changing your mind can go the other way as well. Remember the guy I told you about in the last chapter, who told me he thought spit play was disgusting ... right up until he was asking me to spit in his mouth? (See page 130.) The fact is, people can and do change their minds about what they're up for and sometimes things we thought we'd never do can seem really hot in the right circumstances with the right person.

When we accept that not being sure, wanting to wait and see, sitting on the fence and changing our minds are just as much a part of healthy consent as enthusiastic yeses and unequivocal nos, we open up the door to safe experimentation. This is something that kinky people and BDSM communities understand well, and I'll talk more about it in Chapter 13: Kinks, Fetishes and BDSM (see page 299), but I think we can all learn something from it, even if we're vanilla.

A lot of consent education assumes that we all know exactly what we like and don't like and that we are confident about our boundaries. And my aim with this book is very much to help you figure that out. I want all of you to be going into your next intimate interaction feeling really good about yourself and knowing how you want to experience and enjoy pleasure. But I also know that it doesn't always work like that. Sometimes we don't really know what we want or don't want until it's right in front of us. Sometimes we don't know if we like something till we try it. If consensual sex relied on us being 100 per cent certain about everything we do, we'd never step it up.

And I can't tell you how many times I've had guests come onto my podcast and make faces of disgust when myself or my co-hosts have shared what we're into, but who have later messaged me to say they finally tried it and really liked it!

It's OK to feel disappointed

Let's say you've got up the confidence to let your partner know you're into something. Maybe they seemed like they might be up for trying it, but when the moment comes they decide they don't want to after all. Is it OK to be bummed out? Yes! Of course it is. It's OK to feel disappointed if someone changes their mind about something you were excited for.

I have a friend, a cis woman, who had always fantasised about having a threesome with two guys. But I'm not just talking about a spit roast. I mean, yes, she wanted that double dick, but she also wanted to see them together. She broached it with her boyfriend and he was up for it, with a few boundaries (touching/oral was OK but he didn't want to have penetrative sex with another guy), so they went on a few dating apps together to look for someone to join them. Soon enough they met a gorgeous guy who said he was bicurious and looking for a couple to experiment with. Jackpot! The three of them went out for drinks to check whether there was chemistry and there definitely was. My friend was buzzing – this was really going to happen! Her fantasy was about to come true. But back at the flat something shifted. Just as they were all getting naked, the guy they'd met suddenly announced he wasn't up for it after all.

Obviously my friend was gutted but what could she do? She and her boyfriend told him it was fine. They all got dressed again and they offered him a drink (though by that point I think the poor guy was feeling so awkward that he just legged it to the Tube). They felt frustrated but, crucially, they didn't let on. They even texted the guy afterwards to check he was OK and that he'd got home all right. I'm pretty sure they probably also bitched to each other about the frustrating experience, but that's OK. Healthy consent doesn't mean you always have to be OK with other people's decisions, but you do have to respect them. You can feel disappointed, you can even feel hard done by – that's normal. It becomes a problem when people start using their disappointment to cajole, emotionally blackmail and even bully their partners into things they don't feel comfortable with.

I've had women telling me how they have to plead with their boyfriends to give them head and I know the struggle can be real when it comes to getting your pussy eaten, but I also have to be honest and say that if he *really* doesn't want to do it, you need to respect that. I'm all for asking for what you want in bed, but if you're at a point where you're literally pleading with someone to do something, you have to ask yourself whether it's truly consensual. Look, I get it. He might not have the best reasons for refusing – it might be rooted in misogyny – but it's still not OK to pressure him.

Sorry to state the obvious but if you really can't find a compromise, the best course of action in a situation like this is probably to break up. Of course you don't have to stay in a sexually incompatible relationship. But no one should feel under pressure to do things they don't want to do either.

How to shift our understanding of consent

One thing I'd love to see people doing more of is stop looking at consent as this boring thing you have to tick off before you get down and dirty. When I say 'consent is sexy' I really mean that consent and all the communication we have around consent can be sexy. You already know that I love me some dirty talk and you can easily build your consent communication into that. I think people imagine it as if they've got to ask, 'Please may I have my dick sucked, ma'am?' but you don't at all (well, unless you want to!). Instead, you can make it filthy and phrase it like you're sharing a fantasy:

- Can I feel your mouth on my dick/pussy?
- I've always wanted to try out this position, are you up for it?
- Can I taste your pussy?
- Can I go in deeper?
- Do you want me to stop?
- Do you want me to go harder?
- I want you to finish on my breasts.
- Touch me like this [you could also demonstrate here].

On the flip side, it's important to know that revoking consent doesn't have to be heavy either. Remember, you don't owe anyone an explanation if you don't want to give one, but if you do know why you've changed your mind and you want to share it, that can help. Some of the ways you can revoke consent include:

- Stop (or any other safe word given).
- I don't want to do this anymore, can we do X instead?
- I'm actually not in the mood for this.
- I've changed my mind – I thought I was up for this but I'm not.
- This isn't working for me, can we stop?
- I'm a bit uncomfortable, shall we do something else?
- I'm not feeling this, let's switch it up.
- Actually, this doesn't feel so good, let's not.
- Can we take a break?

If you're in the middle of intimacy and just need an easy check-in to make sure what you're doing is OK for both of you, you really can just say, 'Is this OK?' or 'Can I?' or 'How does that feel?' or 'You want more?' (And trust me, there's nothing boring or perfunctory about hearing someone panting 'Yessssss' in response!) You can even just use one- and two-word questions like 'Harder?' 'More pressure' 'Deeper?' It doesn't have to be complicated as long as you're properly paying attention to their responses and are prepared to stop, back off or slow down if they indicate that.

And that's really where the biggest shift needs to occur, I think. Because there are times in sex when words only go so far. Really good consensual sex happens when we're paying attention to our partner, both to what they're saying and how they're reacting, non-verbally. At the start of the chapter I told you about the women in my DMs describing encounters where they just lay there silently while their partner did stuff to them. Sorry, but did those women's partners really think that was a good sign? Why were they OK with having an unresponsive sexual partner? Sex is supposed to be a thing we do together, for mutual pleasure. Guys, if your sexual partner is just lying there not doing anything and not saying anything, THAT DOES NOT SUGGEST SHE'S HAVING A GOOD TIME. She might not be saying no, she might not be pushing you away, but trust me when I say that this is not the intimacy she wants to be having. My suspicion is that a lot of guys know this deep down but they put it out of their minds in the moment so they can get theirs. But thinking about it now, guys, can you honestly say you're OK with that? Do you actually want to be having sex with someone who isn't really consenting? Who isn't really enjoying herself? Who's just going along with it so as not to piss you off?

Consent is not just about a yes or a no. It's not just about knowing what you want and don't want. It's also about caring – caring what kind of experience your partner has and treating them as an equal in the interaction, rather than someone you're trying to get something from.

CHAPTER 8

Letting Go of Sexual Hang-ups

'Ninety per cent of life is confidence. And the thing about confidence is no one knows if it's real or not.'

Maddy Perez, *Euphoria*

One theme that comes up time and time again when I'm sent dilemmas is hang-ups – hang-ups about our bodies, the way our genitals look, the way our bodies work and whether we're 'normal'. It honestly breaks my heart that so many amazing women think there's something wrong with their body or are stressing out over whether it's up to the standard (they believe) their partner expects from them. I say it all the time on the podcast: anyone who gets to be naked with you is *lucky* to be there.

But I understand what it's like to feel insecure, to feel uncomfortable about a certain feature or a part of your body, and I know that the little thought at the back of your mind can really distract you from enjoying pleasure. This is why I think it's important to talk about and work on letting go of our sexual hang-ups.

Common sexual hang-ups include worrying about how we look (particularly the appearance of our genitals), as well as the faces we pull and the noises we make during sex. People can also feel shame around what we need to help us cum (I hear from a lot of women who worry that they can only orgasm using a specific technique or a certain vibrator and think that they 'should' be able to orgasm another way) or how long it takes us to cum.

The glamorisation of porn when I was growing up made me feel as though if I wasn't shaped a particular way I wasn't allowed to be confident about my body. I think a lot of us felt like that. Getting undressed with someone else can feel daunting if you're not confident about your body, even if you've been together for years. I guess that's why when I lost my virginity and my friend asked me, incredulous, whether we'd kept the lights on (we had), it was because the thought of getting naked can be scary, and I get it!

It's why I always encourage women to find lingerie that makes them feel confident and sexy in the bedroom. You know how I told you I used to work in a sex store? Well, I've also worked in a lingerie outlet. What can I say? I had many retail jobs in my early twenties and slowly they all started to gravitate towards the things I love most now – sex, confidence and pleasure. Anyway, I'll never forget when I did this bra fitting for a new mum who'd just had her first baby. She explained that she hadn't felt like herself for some time, but we chatted and I showed her some of our styles and once we found a bra that hugged her boobs and made her feel like the snack she is, she burst into tears of happiness. Sometimes all it takes is the right lingerie to help make you feel good again.

We have to work to let go of these ideas about ourselves or else they can become self-fulfilling prophecies. If you have it in your head that your pussy doesn't taste nice then you're going to really struggle to enjoy receiving oral sex, which in turn will make you less likely to ask for it and less likely that your partner will offer it, which might end up feeling like a confirmation of your fears (for what it's worth, this is not true – trust me when I say your pussy tastes exactly how it's supposed to, but I'll come back to that later).

I know it's not going to happen overnight. As I described in the opening chapters, there are a heck of a lot of forces at play that lead to us taking on unrealistic expectations, as well as shame and stigma around sex and relationships, and our appearance.

Most of us have grown up with a very clear idea of what society considers beautiful, what sort of body counts as sexy and appealing, and while I think Instagram can be a powerful force for good when it comes to seeing different bodies, I think we can agree that having a feed showing us women who have had BBLs and lipo doesn't do much for our self-image. (There's nothing wrong with getting any sort of surgery that makes you happy, by the way; I just think it's important to bear in mind that it IS surgery. This is not what most people's bodies naturally look like.)

Just 15–20 years ago having big lips and a big bum was looked down on to the point where I remember looking in the mirror as a kid and feeling certain that I wanted them reduced when I got older. The beauty standards that were celebrated around me in the early Noughties were all skinny, white, thin-lipped women with bony fake-tanned hip bones sticking out over their super-low-waisted jeans.

Finally, a glimmer of hope on the horizon came in the form of Jennifer Lopez. But even as we danced to 'Love Don't Cost a Thing' it did not escape my notice that she was being praised for the body that many – not all, but many – Black women have. Funny how it took a woman who looks like JLo to make it mainstream. My point is how it was overlooked on Black women and praised on her. Fast-forward to today and as we know women are going under the knife to get those bigger bums and injecting fillers to get fuller lips.

It can take a while to let go of the ideas we learn growing up and the things we believe about ourselves. Even when we have plenty of evidence to show us they're wrong.

I remember in sixth form a friend was convinced we both needed to lose weight so we'd have a better chance of getting a boyfriend. Looking back, I realise how stupid it was and how misguided we were, but back then pop culture was full of bitchy Perez Hilton blog pages on the Lindsay Lohans, Victoria Beckhams, Paris Hiltons and Nicole Richies. The infamous size-zero era! I remember her getting us diet pills and doing some other awful things just so we could lose weight – a very harmful thought process we thankfully grew out of.

Similarly, a friend of mine who grew up in the Nineties when fashion was all about Kate Moss and the 'heroin chic' look (aka skinny white girls with greasy hair in tiny slip dresses and plaid shirts) spent years hating her bum. It was too big, she thought. She was convinced she would never get a boyfriend because no boy could possibly be attracted to such a huge ass. Imagine if she'd known back then that in a decade or two people would be getting implants and fillers in their backsides to make them look rounder. Needless to say, as she grew up, she dated and hooked up with guys and guess what? Not only were they not put off by her size, it was actually part of what attracted them to her. The thing she'd spent years thinking was a flaw was actually a legitimate plus! But our hang-ups aren't always rational and even when we're presented with 'proof' of this, it can still be really hard to shake them off.

Usually, our hang-ups stem from an external influence. It might be fashion or beauty trends we see around us, or implicit messages from our culture about how we should aspire to look. It might be things family members have said to us over the years that have made us feel self-conscious – especially if you're Nigerian, because you know those aunties don't know how to mind their own business and like reminding very healthy-looking people that they've apparently put on weight! Or it might be things we've overheard at school, or seen people say online. I will never forget the time I heard a boy at university refer to a girl's vulva as looking like 'a badly packed kebab'. Now, I don't know if he was actually talking about someone he'd slept with, or whether he was just repeating shit he'd heard to make his friends laugh, but my goodness that comment stayed with me. As a sex educator I know that all vulvas are unique (something I'll come back to a little later in the chapter) and that labias especially come in all shapes and sizes. I was able to give this guy the side-eye he deserved and move on with my life, but it's not always so easy. The trouble happens when we let those things get under our skin and become a problem for us.

I'll see people on Instagram talking about how they've always hated their stretch marks or criticising their soft bellies, and half the time I'm thinking, 'Girl, what are you talking about? That is natural and normal!' To me that doesn't seem like a big deal at all, which just goes to show that when it comes to hang-ups about our bodies, yes, society plays a part, but often it's us who are our own worst enemies. We can be so hard on ourselves and really obsess over things no one else would even notice. And no matter what your personal insecurities are, I can guarantee there is someone out there who would be only too delighted to have the opportunity to get intimate with you and see those stretch marks or that beautiful belly close up.

We're fed a lot of messages about what a 'sexy' body is. And guess what? Almost none of us actually tick those boxes. Which means that whether we're young, old, fat, thin, cis, trans, able-bodied or disabled, we've pretty much all felt insecure and down on ourselves at some point in our lives.

In reality, none of these things actually affect whether we have good or bad sex – all human bodies are capable of pleasure – but our hang-ups can have a big impact on how we experience sex. Which is why I'm so passionate about helping people, especially women, let go of them.

Your vulva is totally fine, sis

One dilemma (although I really don't think we should even call it a dilemma) that makes me rage every time is when I have a woman writing in worrying that there's something wrong with her vulva. Maybe she doesn't like how it looks, maybe she's worried about how it tastes or smells, or maybe she's concerned that it doesn't function the way she thinks her partner expects it to.

The reason this particular hang-up bothers me so much is that it is not only total bullshit, but it's the kind of bullshit that people are able to make loads of money from. Every day in magazines, on social media and other platforms, you can see irresponsible companies offering questionable products and cosmetic treatments that will supposedly help people but really are just preying on their insecurities.

In 2017 an international survey of plastic surgeons found that labiaplasty (an operation to reduce the length of the labia) was the fastest-growing type of cosmetic surgery.[1] Elsewhere, companies advertise labia fillers as well as plasma injections and 'radiofrequency therapy' to supposedly 'strengthen and tighten' the vaginal muscles. These treatments can cost from £900 for a single session (and most say they require repeat sessions and top-ups). Just the other day my friend sent me a screenshot of a 'three-step skincare routine' for her vulva that she was being advertised on Instagram. It cost £69.

Don't fool yourself. This corner of the sexual wellness industry is making top dollar off your insecurities. But one analysis published in the *British Medical Journal*, which examined the information communicated in adverts for such treatments, concluded that 'the quality and quantity of clinical information is poor, with erroneous information in some instances'.[2] Yes, you read that correctly. *Erroneous information.*

These companies have no real interest in helping you with your sexual hang-ups. If anything, they want to keep subtly reinforcing them so you'll continue to spend your hard-earned money on their snake oil.

Listen, I won't pretend I've never had a 'vajacial' before. You caught me! I have! I did it out of curiosity and because it seemed exciting. And it was, I won't lie. It was also very relaxing, just like getting a facial. I wanted my mons pubis catered to, especially as a Black woman who naturally deals with hyperpigmentation. Now, vajacials have been said to help treat ingrown hairs, remove dead skin cells, help with hyperpigmentation, smooth bumps around bikini lines and more, so I admit I wanted to give it a try. But let me be clear, this wasn't done for anyone else but me. And it certainly isn't something I do just before I sleep with my boyfriend. It was a one-off curiosity thing that I enjoyed at the time. Who knows? I might do it again, I might not.

However, I'm not naive, and as I said, there is a lot of money that's made from creating beauty problems from our insecurities. But as long as you go in with your eyes open and you understand that it's just for fun, curiosity or relaxation and not because you believe there's something wrong with your body, then sometimes it's OK. Just like anything else in life, if it makes you feel good, and isn't stopping you from feeling confident, I don't see the problem.

But there are other things I feel more conflicted about. For example, cishet women face a lot of pressure to have a freshly waxed vulva, to the point where we fork out hundreds of pounds for lasers and waxes. Why? Because someone somewhere decided that women should be hairless down there. Doesn't the idea actually creep you out a bit? Because if you really think about it, only one type of body is hair free: one that hasn't yet hit puberty.

The social pressure to have your vulva look a certain way can blind us to the reality of what we're putting ourselves through. I remember one young lady sent me a message to read on my podcast in which she explained that she kept getting a rash on her mons pubis when she shaved and what should she do about it? Obviously, we all told her to stop shaving! Seriously, when did we get to a place where vanity and living up to perceived expectations was more important than health? I can't imagine a straight guy freaking out, thinking he's got to remove the hair on his body even if that meant getting a reaction every time he did so, can you? But again, it's not our fault. When magazines and TV screens are full of hairless women, we do our best to emulate those women so we don't seem abnormal. And for what it's worth, if you're reading this and getting a rash or a reaction from something you're doing to your body in the name of beauty, please see a doctor ASAP! And please stop doing whatever it is you're doing. No man is worth putting up with an unhappy vulva.

I'll go into more detail about how to look after your pussy in Chapter 12 when we talk about sexual health (see page 275), so for now just let me say that you do not need to put yourself through any kind of cleaning or freshening regimen beyond what you'd normally do in the shower or bath. Please trust me when I say your coochie can take care of herself.

Popular penis preoccupations

Let's not pretend that men don't also experience hang-ups about their bodies. While it's fair to say that this book is mostly aimed at women and describes the sexual experiences of people with vulvas, it would be unfair to ignore the issues that men and penis-owners can face.

A lot of women describe to me their awkwardness when it comes to speaking up for themselves in the bedroom. But, on the flip side, men can struggle with the idea that they're supposed to always take the lead. I think we're so used to seeing men being constantly ready – wherever, whenever – to have sex that we forget they're human, too! Do not be fooled. Men are sexual beings, they're not sexual robots. Now, some of this might be partly down to porn (I mean, have you ever seen a soft dick in porn?), but it's also society that has confused and convinced us that the mere existence of testosterone is enough to turn someone into a raging sex machine. And the worst part is, a lot of men believe this, too!

Masculinity is very much linked to being confident and knowledgeable in bed, and for a lot of guys this can lead to some very real performance anxiety. This can show up in a number of different forms, including psychological and physical manifestations. One obvious example, which is hardly spoken about (except maybe as a punchline to a joke), is erectile dysfunction (ED). This is when a person finds it hard to get or maintain an erection.

Conversations around this tend to be very quiet, with the men themselves trying to sweep it under the rug, saying it's a one-off, or finding other excuses. And the women I hear from who sleep with people with ED often feel embarrassed about it, too, either for themselves (many think it's a reflection on them) or on behalf of their partner.

In fact, it's a very common problem. Around one in five men (that's over 4.3 million people) in the UK experience erectile problems,[3] so it really shouldn't be such a big source of shame. Plus, it's very treatable! You've heard of Viagra, right? These days you don't even need a prescription – you can buy it directly from the pharmacy.

I do understand why people feel so insecure about it, but whether it's affecting you or your partner, it's so important to communicate instead of avoiding the topic, particularly as some experiences of ED are connected to stress and anxiety. Avoiding the subject or refusing to engage with it could actually end up contributing to the problem.[4] If you're someone who has experienced erectile problems, sharing your experience could potentially help lift the weight off your shoulders. And if you think it might be connected to larger mental health issues, that conversation might also help you take the right step towards speaking to a health professional.

Another common problem for penises is premature ejaculation. Back when I was working in a sex store, a common request was from men asking for a toy or supplement that could help them last longer in bed. Now, again, some of this might be down to the pressure society has put on men to 'perform' in bed (interestingly, one survey of 4,000 American and Australian men and women found that 81 per cent of women care more about the quality of sex than how long it lasts,[5] but still the pressure of being able to 'last longer' is very powerful). Often, though, it was because they were experiencing premature ejaculation.

Premature ejaculation is when a person with a penis ejaculates too quickly. Now, people are likely to have different definitions of what 'too quickly' means. When surveyed, almost one in five men in the UK said they'd had repeat experiences where they 'reached orgasm more quickly than they would have liked'.[6] But the medical definition of premature ejaculation is regularly climaxing in under a minute of being inside your partner.

If this happens as a one-off it might well be down to nerves. I have a friend whose new boyfriend came in seconds the first few times they had sex, but to his credit he owned it. 'I'm sorry, it's always a bit like this with someone new, but once we get to know each other better, it'll stop happening,' he said. Naturally, she was a bit worried. Was he just feeding her a line? But a few months down the line, sure enough the problem has vanished and they're having a great, satisfying sex life. Which just goes to show how powerful it can be when you engage openly and honestly with your partner instead of trying to pretend there's nothing wrong.

Other times, though, there might be something more going on. If someone has always experienced premature ejaculation, it could be down to a psychological issue, such as having had a traumatic sexual experience. If it's something that's started happening recently, it could be psychological or it could be down to something physical, so it's important to get it checked out. Ladies, do not let him feed you stories about how exceptional your vagina feels when it grips his dick to explain away the issue. He might need medical attention and that's perfectly OK, because guess what? It's common, and those with penises should be allowed to have honest conversations about it.

Back to my sex-shop story, though. In those cases, my go-to was always a cock ring, the theory being that the pressure of the cock ring around the base of the penis helps restrict the blood flow and helps the person last longer. These days you can also get special toys that help penis-owners 'edge' themselves. By providing stimulation but then stopping before the point of orgasm, they gradually help people build up to being able to last longer and longer.

You could also try edging at home – either alone or you could turn it into a sex game together. Masturbating an hour or two before you have sex could also be helpful, and again, if you need more help, for goodness' sake lose the bravado and just speak to a professional! Having better sex means doing what you can to avoid what might be holding you back.

All bodies are sexy bodies

Having a body that doesn't fit society's 'ideal' does not mean your sexuality is less complex or important than other people's, or that you don't deserve to explore and enjoy pleasure.

But some bodies are put through procedures deliberately designed to limit their experience of pleasure. This can include female genital mutilation (FGM). The NHS defines FGM as 'a procedure where the female genitals are deliberately cut, injured or changed, but there's no medical reason for it to be done',[7] and according to the World Health Organization (WHO), it affects around 200 million girls and women alive today. Despite being categorically defined by the WHO as a breach of human rights, FGM practices occur in over 30 countries worldwide, most commonly in Africa, the Middle East and Asia, and it is usually done between infancy and the age of 15.[8]

There are different forms of FGM, but all are harmful and they have absolutely no health benefits whatsoever. Defenders of the practice will say it's cultural, it's just a tradition, but given the deeply harmful side effects, which can include bleeding, urinary issues, infection and even death, either at the time of the procedure or later on when the woman has sex or gives birth, I can't accept that as an answer. It's clear that it's done to police the sexuality and bodily autonomy of women.

But while it's an abhorrent abuse of power, it needn't be a source of shame for the victims. There is actually an increasing number of people speaking out about their FGM experiences and raising awareness of the fact that it doesn't have to exclude them from sexual pleasure.

Twenty-six-year-old Ryaihanny Sahrom, a bisexual woman from Singapore, was just four years old when she experienced FGM. As a child she was taught by religious leaders that it was a way of preserving her cultural identity, as well as an important means of lowering the female libido so that she didn't 'become promiscuous'.

Outside her community (and particularly in white Western circles), her experience was framed as standard Islamic oppression of women, 'even though Islam and the Qur'an specifically have never mentioned anything about this'.

Over the years she's been told by countless people, including medical professionals, that sexual pleasure and orgasms will likely be out of her reach. 'Throughout my life, I've received way too many comments on how it is almost impossible to orgasm and that I shouldn't even try,' she says. '[They told me] it'll be incredibly tough for me to have a sexual life. All these comments feed directly into a kind of generational and cultural trauma that as FGM survivors we're still navigating.'

In fact, this has not proved to be the case and over time Ryaihanny has discovered that she can experience orgasms, although perhaps not in the same way as other people with vulvas (although, when you think about it, don't we all cum in different ways?). It's fair to say that Ryaihanny's journey towards a good sex life has been one of ongoing discovery. 'There were feelings of missing out and a personal desire to learn to love sex for myself. This manifested itself in different ways – wanting to be more present during sex, achieving orgasm and [to] experience what I felt like I had been missing out [on]. I was fortunate to have a partner who supported me in my own sexual self-discovery and afforded me the space to learn for myself and not focus on pleasing others.'

Now, this book is all about orgasms and pleasure, so I just had to ask how she would describe her orgasms. 'Akin to ... feeling flushed, yet [a] closeness to myself, and mind-blowing,' she says. Self-stimulation, for Ryaihanny, feels 'very fluid, [it] differs from time to time depending on my state of mind, feelings and emotions. It's always about having fun for me to experience different sensations instead of simply the majorly erogenous zones like my clit.'

FGM is practised both legally and illegally in various parts of the world. Sudan, where some 87 per cent of women have undergone some type of genital mutilation, only criminalised the procedure in 2020.[9] Even in Singapore, which Ryaihanny notes is often seen as very cosmopolitan, there's no legal ruling against FGM.

'There's still a desire of patriarchal society to control women's bodies even at infancy – it's a sign that one's body is not theirs, but the society's,' she says.

I asked her if it's always something she brings up with potential sexual partners. She says it depends. When she's comfortable and secure and feels a connection with someone then yes, she will tell her potential sexual partners about it. 'I'm pretty open, forthcoming and honest about it,' she says. 'But I don't feel like it is a necessary thing to disclose or share, unless I feel safe about sharing.'

For Ryaihanny, this kind of honesty and refusal to feel ashamed or disqualified from sexual pleasure has been a key part of how she's figured out what good sex looks like for her. 'Sometimes, the road to re-establishing our personhood and autonomy and reacquainting ourselves with our bodies, especially when they have been violated, can seem like moving almost impossible mountains,' she admits. 'Honouring our growth and experience, while processing trauma at our own pace, are ways we could work towards acquiring a positive relationship to our bodies – regardless of how that looks ... for people. We're lovable, fuckable, and we can still reach the full capacity of sexual pleasure.'

I'm sure I don't need to tell you how much I love this last line! I fully believe that all bodies are potentially sexy bodies, and we need to work towards dismantling the idea that pleasure is only for people who fit society's mould.

Joy Addo has been registered as 'seriously sight impaired' since she was ten years old and regularly writes about living, dating and having sex with a disability, as well as what it's like to be a blind single parent. She is also the host of *Joy's World*, a podcast which, in her words, offers 'a unique insight into the life of a fat, Black, blind, SEXY, single mother of one'.

She uses a long white cane to get around ('Actually mine is pink and purple because I'm a pimp,' she laughs) and posts some seriously smoking lingerie selfies on Instagram. Joy's a really good example of someone who is not going to let society's idea of 'the perfect body' stand in the way of her owning her sexuality. But as a teenager, she says, the idea that sex education applied to her too just didn't really register.

'When I was growing up, when I was a teenager, I was so [much more] concerned and focused on the fact that I was losing my sight than sex ... It wasn't even really a question,' she tells me. 'I didn't even feel like it was something I could talk about. It just was so far out there. It was never relevant to me as a teenager. It took me a long time to even feel like it was something that I could do, or wanted to do.'

This was also down to a lack of representation. Disabled people have long been left out of conversations about sexuality and I can count on one hand the number of disabled characters I've seen in romantic roles on TV and in films. Joy says the work she does now is to ensure that gap in representation is being filled, to prevent more young people feeling that the concept of a sex life doesn't apply to them and wrongly believing their body can never be viewed as desirable. 'I am plus size, and then I have a disability. I never really saw that. I didn't see people that looked like me, or had the same condition as me, speaking about their sex lives. I want young people to be able to see somebody that is speaking about these things, and actually understand that they can have a good and healthy sex life. It's not off limits to them,' she says.

Visibility matters, not just to disabled people themselves; it's also needed to educate able-bodied people who might have a negative stereotype in their head of what it means to be disabled. Too often, Joy says, people with disabilities are regarded as kind of asexual, as though having a body that works differently removes your need or desire for sexual pleasure and fulfilment. Obviously this is not true, but it's amazing how many people still think it.

'I've definitely faced those kinds of assumptions,' agrees Joy. 'People just assume. So as soon as they see that I have a visual impairment they just feel pity. They don't see me as a sexual being at all. And so it doesn't cross their mind to think, "Oh, I wonder if she's single," or "Oh, I wonder if she's into this or into that." They find it hard to see beyond your disability. And that's why, again, I feel like it's very important that we speak about these things, because people need to understand that disabled people are definitely having sex, too.'

Hearing and seeing people in different kinds of bodies talk about dating and sex is how we start to break down our prejudices and assumptions. In general, Joy has found that dating online is easier because you can share pictures and it's a bit easier to spark a conversation, but she says it is extremely rare for her to be approached in person. Because of the lingering stigma around disability, she also acknowledges that there are extra challenges when it comes to figuring out a person's motives.

'I think some people worry about it being a fetish. I haven't really experienced that, but I definitely feel like there are some barriers there,' she says. I agree. I've talked a bit already about the fetishisation of Black bodies in other chapters (and I'll discuss it again in the chapter on kink), and I understand the concern. Nobody wants to be the object of someone's fetish, whether it's for being plus size, for being Black or for having a disability. I mean, sure, there might be some people who don't mind – I obviously can't speak for everyone on the planet – but to me, I think it's always important to know where the root of a desire is coming from. As always, you can only really do this by talking, and Joy is keen to stress that disabled people absolutely like to be chatted up and flirted with as well!

'It's absolutely OK to approach someone with a disability. If you find someone attractive, and you want to get to know them, regardless of their disability, it's absolutely fine,' she says. 'Just try to get to know them and understand that they are not their disability alone. There is more to people than disability and I think that's really important. I think that's where it all begins, because we're not going to get to the bedroom if you can't even see that I'm a whole human.'

It's no real surprise, then, that Joy's sexual experiences are very relatable. Like a lot of straight and bisexual women she started out having a lot of crappy sex with men who didn't care much about her pleasure. 'I've gotten to a stage where I am very much having sex for my pleasure as well as theirs, whereas before I was literally having sex, probably, just to please them,' she admits. 'My orgasm did not matter at all. And it was all about them getting their nut and that was it.

'There's been times I've had a guy and he was really big and now, looking back at it, I probably should have just stopped or asked him to use lube. But I didn't say anything, because I was just like, "Well, it's not about me, it's about them."' She scoffs at herself as she recalls this.

'Now I've got to a point where if I'm having sex with someone, and it doesn't feel good, I'm going to tell them to either stop, or we're going to do something else. It is very important that it has to feel good for both of us. But you have to be confident enough to say that. And when I was younger, I wasn't. I wasn't confident enough to say to these men, "Oh, can you stop?" or "Could you move?" "Could you do something else?" "Could you change position?" "It doesn't feel that great for me."'

As for most of us, it has also taken her time to get to know her body and what brings her pleasure. She laughs as she recalls mistaking her first orgasm with a partner for an urge to wee. 'It took me a very long time to even realise what an orgasm was because a lot of the time I'd be having sex and I just kept being like, "Oh my God, I need to go wee. Like, I need to stop, I need to stop,"' she says. 'And there was one guy, he was just like, "Wee on me." He wasn't bothered! He was like, "It's fine," so I just released. And then I was like, 'Ohhh! Like, OK, OK, this is ... this is it! This is what this is!"'

These days she says she's no longer a people-pleaser in bed and she puts the same amount of importance on her own pleasure as on her partner's. But she admits she still experiences her best orgasms on her own (her favourite toy is her magic-wand vibrator, which just goes to show that she's a girl after my own heart!). Again, I feel like a lot of women can relate to that – after all, you're the person who knows your body best! If that's the way you get your best nut, go for it! As long as you're not doing it out of a mistaken belief that no one would ever want to give you pleasure or that your body is somehow unfit to receive intimacy. As Joy said earlier, sexual pleasure is not off limits to anyone, regardless of what they look like or how their body works.

As with all stigma, one of the best ways to get rid of negative assumptions about disability (or any kind of body that doesn't meet society's standards of beauty or sex appeal) is to shine a light on it, talk about it and bring it out into the open so people can see that it's bullshit. Images help, too, which is why Joy is so adamant about using her social media platform.

'That's why I do what I do and that's why I'll post pictures in lingerie on my Instagram,' she says. 'It's not for no reason. It's because I am very aware that people don't see me as a sexual being. So I'm gonna force them to!'

I hope this chapter can help, too, and I hope that you will go and follow people like Joy on Instagram and listen to her podcast so that you can start to challenge the stigmas *you* might have internalised, both about other people and about yourself. Because, as Joy acknowledges, it can be so easy to fall into the trap of believing that you don't deserve to explore and enjoy your sexuality if you don't fit society's mould of the 'ideal' body.

'I was insecure. I felt like I just had to accept whatever it was that a man wanted to give me. So [if] they didn't want to give me a relationship, but they wanted to have sex with me, I was like, "All right, I'll put up with that then,"' Joy admits. 'I also remember there was a time where I used to think that because I was disabled I can't be bisexual. I can't be a lesbian. I just felt like it would be too much. But now I'm like, "No, I can do what I want, I can do *who* I want, and it's OK to want to explore your sexuality and you deserve that as well."

'I've put up with a lot of shit because I was just insecure. I'm bigger. I was blind. I was like, "Who's gonna want me?" That's what I thought. Whereas now I'm just in a very different mindset.'

I think in some ways we all experience this feeling from time to time (especially when we were younger). Even if we don't have a disability, most of us have probably had a moment of thinking, 'Maybe I'm not good enough,' or 'No one will want me.' But you know what? There are billions of people in this world today. It's not even about finding 'the one', because actually there are *plenty* of people out there who would love to get with us. None of us has to settle for crumbs.

But, as I always say, sexuality is a journey. That's been my vibe for quite some time now. And I think your relationship with your body is a journey as well. It's really important not to beat yourself up if you can't feel 100 per cent positive about your body *right now.* Instead, maybe just focus on letting go of some of the shittier feelings around it. Don't make it your goal to love your body unconditionally because, let's be honest, that's not very realistic, but treat it with love. Honestly, even Lori Harvey probably has days when she feels a bit *meh.*

The key to letting go of sexual hang-ups is to do it bit by bit. Don't expect an overnight change, but *do* start to pay attention when you can feel those insecurities rising up in you. Maybe next time, instead of letting the negativity take over your thoughts, just say to yourself, 'Oh, that's my hang-up. I know it's not real, but it pops up to bother me sometimes.' Acknowledging what you're feeling but *also* reminding yourself that it is only a thought, not a reality, is a good way to start diffusing the insecurity.

Or maybe just make your aim to stop trash-talking your body. At some point this week, look in the mirror and find one thing you DO like instead of focusing on the things you don't. It's these little steps away from our hang-ups that make the real difference.

Oloni's top tips for body confidence in bed

- Spend more time naked. Research in the *Journal of Happiness Studies* concluded that going without clothes, either in public or private, can improve body image and self-esteem.[10] And a study published in the *Journal of Sex Research* found that naked social interaction actually improves appreciation for your own body.[11] If you don't feel quite ready for naked speed-dating, you could simply spend a bit more time naked at home. Try sleeping naked, for example. Or after you've had a shower and moisturised, take an extra ten minutes to wander around your room before getting dressed. If you're someone who always grabs her underwear as soon as sex is over, try waiting a bit longer and having some pillow talk in the nude. It all helps.
- Follow some body-inspiring accounts on social media. Interacting with people who have different body types, whether it's people with disabilities or differently sized bodies, and seeing pictures of everything from underarm hair and bikini-line stubble, stretch marks, cellulite and mastectomy scars, can be a really powerful way to start chiselling away at the idea of the 'perfect' body. Unfollow

or mute the pages of people who don't make you feel good about yourself. Who is going to beat you?

- Treat yourself to some sexy new lingerie and have fun! Play music and take photos of yourself as you try on different ones. Create your own personal haul and pick any favourites you might possibly want to reveal to a lover.
- Try some sexual mindfulness. If you're stressing about how long it takes you to cum, that is definitely going to stand in the way of you having an orgasm. There are apps that offer coaching and guided masturbation to help you let go of negative thoughts that distract you from intimacy and will help you be more present in your body during sex.
- Refer back to Chapter 5: Getting to Know Your Body and read those affirmations to speak to your vulva over and over again (see page 87).

CHAPTER 9

Relationships and Heartbreak

I've been blogging about relationships since I was 18 and sometimes I look back and laugh at how my opinions have drastically changed. I used to think monogamy was the only answer to dating, and can you blame me? That's all I knew, from religion and culture to what I saw in the media. I grew up watching teenage girls who were obsessed with boys on Nickelodeon, and don't even get me started on Disney.

We see so many cishetereo monogamous relationships on our screens that are meant to last forever. It's also drummed into us that cheating is wrong, and although I agree that it's not OK to deceive and hurt each other, the fact remains that a lot of us continue to do it. Or else we stay in situations and partnerships that make us miserable, simply because we don't believe we can find anything better, or because we're scared of being alone, or we've somehow convinced ourselves that unhappiness is 'normal'. So are we all just terrible, greedy, ungrateful, indecisive people? Or is the problem that we're following a 'script' that we've been shown – either by our culture or religion or Hollywood (in some ways as bad as each other!) – while not being given the chance to decide for ourselves what actually works?

Start by raising your expectations

As well as wanting the pleasure gap to be discussed in schools, I also feel strongly about teaching kids what healthy relationships should look like: how to identify healthy connections and intimacy, what red flags to look for when dating, when to know it's time to walk away and not stay in a relationship that isn't working just because you've 'put in the time'. I think if I'd been given this perspective, I would have benefited from it a lot, and I know many others would have, too. It would have saved a lot of heartache, trauma, abuse and gaslighting.

Looking back, a lot of the things that felt good at the time I now recognise were merely the bare minimum. But sometimes it felt as though that was good enough, or as good as it was going to get. As a Nigerian woman who was brought up in London (and I know many other African women can relate), I was expected to have the skills to be someone else's wife. Someone else's childbearer. Someone else's cleaner. Someone else's chef. Someone else's **everything** (with not enough space to have it reciprocated).

It's no wonder I have many dilemmas sent from ladies who are determined to hold on to a relationship that doesn't serve them, because a lot of us have bought into the idea that we can't do or get any better.

When I was 22, I wrote a blog that is still one of my faves today, entitled 'The Girlfriend Fluffer'. It was about single women who found themselves in situationships with guys who weren't interested in commitment, only to realise that they'd actually been preparing the guy to be with his actual girlfriend. I related to this and found that so did many other young ladies, because we all had similar upbringings and a similar understanding of what love was meant to look like and represent. We bought into the idea that men were the prize and that our worth was only truly met in marriage. It didn't matter how many degrees you had, what businesses you had set up, how amazing your character was. Where is your ring? Where is the piece of jewellery that is a testament to your desirability? Because of these beliefs we often ended up sticking around, trying to make the relationship something it wasn't ready to be (and trying to make *ourselves* into someone *we* probably weren't ready to be) instead of either allowing ourselves to enjoy it for the casual thing it was or else move along.

I love encouraging women to want more in the bedroom, but I love encouraging them to want even more in their relationships. Be ridiculous with your expectations, ladies, because someone's son has been taught to be ridiculous with his. Set your standards high and let the people you date know the expectation they have to meet. With any luck, the ones who can't won't even bother to waste your time. Don't just take my word for it. Psychologist Donald H. Baucom has spent decades studying marriage and relationships and in his research he found that people with high expectations tend to report higher relationship satisfaction.[1]

As I grew older, I learned a lot about relationships through my friends, but, to be honest, many of us didn't know what the fuck we were doing. The things we felt were OK in our early or mid-twenties are certainly not things we'd accept today. That's not to say there weren't any success stories, there were (*-ish*), but like a lot of people I learned slowly and sometimes painfully through experience. A lot of my relationship dramas helped me figure out what I was actually looking for, where my boundaries lay and – crucially – when it was time to walk away.

Whether it's the expectation that 'true' love effortlessly lasts forever or that monogamy is easy and natural, whether it's the pressure to fit someone else's mould in order to find happiness or the belief that 'all you need is love' to make a relationship work, the messages we get taught about relationships can end up standing in the way of us finding something that really works for us. And without any education on the subject, it can take a really long time to realise that.

In order to find the right relationship for us, we need to let go of these ideas about how relationships 'should' work and start paying attention to what *actually* works for us and our partners.

I do understand that it can be difficult. Whether you feel like you've been a serial dater for a decade, or you've just had a string of bad luck with partners, it can seem like you're never going to find a good one. It's easy to blame ourselves in these situations or repeat to ourselves the internalised messages we've received from others, which tell us we'll never 'find a nice husband' if we continue to do whatever society/family/friends say we shouldn't do. I don't agree with this. There are millions of people in the world that will get you, you just have to find them. But I know that feels hard sometimes, too. In my opinion, it comes down to one of three things:

1. Dating in 2022 is hard and many of us struggle to identify healthy intimacy.
2. Long-term relationships take work.
3. We're either looking for the wrong things, or the relationship we're in just isn't right for *us.*

I'm going to come back to all three of these things in more detail shortly, but first I want to make something really clear: no relationship is worth being miserable for. Regardless of what you've been taught or the pressure you feel to be partnered up, if a relationship isn't making you happy, then you need to leave.

No relationship is better than a bad relationship

Relationships aren't always easy, but my goodness they are not meant to be extremely hard. If you constantly find that you and your partner are miscommunicating with each other, if it feels like they never really get you, if you just can't seem to find your common ground, isn't it better to accept that you're not compatible, instead of trying over and over again to make it work?

The problem is, many of us feel a huge pressure to be coupled up. Either that or we've conformed to an idea of what we believe a relationship should look like and so we resign ourselves to it, even when it's not making us happy. Or – worse! – we've actually taken on the idea that suffering is part of the package.

Understand that as I type this I'm also indirecting my past self! But this struggle has become so heavily normalised that sometimes we're unable to identify it even when we're in it.

I was in an unsuitable relationship from my early to mid-twenties. We had our ups and downs, but the majority of those downs wouldn't have existed had I just left. I think the reason I stayed was the belief that maybe this was as good as it was going to get, because the streets are truly scary. I loved him, but I discovered that love isn't enough, especially if it has you questioning your sanity and second-guessing yourself. If I'm extremely honest, it didn't hit me that I needed to get out of that relationship until the day I accidentally fell pregnant. I discuss this in Chapter 12: Sexual Health (see page 285). In that moment, I watched my life flash before my eyes and said to myself this could not be my destiny. Admittedly, I didn't leave immediately because I was healing from two different scenarios – a life that nearly became and a love I was scared of losing – but I'm so glad I did eventually leave.

I'm tired of watching brilliant women battle to try to turn 'OK-ish' relationships into the Real Thing because they've been taught that so much of their value lies in their ability to 'keep a man'. In truth, I almost kind of admire the way many cishet men create boundaries for themselves in relationships or even casual flings. If they aren't fully into you, they will not hesitate to keep you at arm's length – just close enough so you stick around, but not so close that they feel any sort of duty towards you. I want to say that we need to adopt the men's attitude, but I don't actually think we want to copy these toxic behaviours; and I also understand the privilege that they've been given to move on to the next one, or two (or even two at the same damn time!) without any social repercussions. We're too ashamed of being on our own, reluctant to increase the number of men we've slept with or scared we can't do better.

I'm going to talk more about letting go and ending relationships towards the end of this chapter, but I do think people are often afraid that ending a relationship looks like a personal failure. It's not. It's just part of your journey to figuring out what works for you. And even though it can come with pain and sometimes embarrassment, I do believe the experience is important. I have definitely been in some bad situations with partners, and I'm not going to sit here and tell you I'm so glad I had those experiences, but I will say that they helped me get to a point where I feel confident about what I want and strong in my expectations.

Dating culture

While I'm all about moving on if a relationship isn't working, I do sometimes wonder whether hook-up culture has made us blasé about what it takes to find, develop and sustain a connection. Dating apps have given us access to such a huge pool of people, which is amazing, but at the same time it can seem almost like the wealth of choice has made us bored of each other. It's like it's taken away the excitement somehow. Or perhaps it's made us feel like it's not worth the effort. There's always another person to swipe, another potential match, another date, so we don't try to find ways in which we can work it out with each other and instead fall into a pattern of just moving on.

According to YouGov data from 2019, 21 per cent of couples between the ages of 25 and 35 met online.[2] And some experts reckon that number will rise to 50 per cent over the next decade.[3] But I can't tell you the number of times I've had my friends tell me about their horrible dating-app experiences. They swipe and swipe,

swipe some more and continue to swipe again, till they find someone who piques their interest, and even when they do the conversation doesn't really go far. It becomes a list of idle chats; a couple of exchanged words with no real intentions behind them. We forget that there are real people behind these profile photos, so we hardly care about how they feel.

This isn't just my perception. It's a real psychological phenomenon. Numerous studies have shown that having *more* choice actually makes people feel less satisfied with what they pick.[4] Like when you go to a restaurant and the menu is three pages long. You might choose a cheeseburger but you have a little doubt in your head. Maybe you should have ordered the pasta instead ... You look around to see what other people are eating, trying to keep your food envy at bay. By contrast, a café with just three or four options makes it much easier to make a decision you feel confident about.

This attitude can lead to us treating each other really disrespectfully. Today, there are so many different bad behaviours witnessed on dating apps, and in dating culture more generally, that we've literally had to invent new words for them. 'Breadcrumbing' is when someone leads you on by sending messages here and there but without properly engaging or truly pursuing you. 'Benching' is a sports analogy, meaning you're sitting on the sidelines but not actually getting to play right now. In dating it means the person wants to keep you around as an option, not the *first* option, but one they'll pick up if they ever get bored (or if their first choice is unavailable). You might talk via text and DM, but that's as far as the effort will go. And of course, everyone's old favourite, and something I know we've all experienced: 'ghosting' – aka when someone just seems to fall off the face of the earth after showing a romantic interest.

I won't pretend I've never been guilty of these behaviours, because I have. But I've also been on the receiving end of them, and it sucks. We have to stop treating each other as if we're just numbers. Whether we're dating to find love or just to get laid, we need to start acknowledging each other as real people, including ourselves! It's as though we're in a silent competition with each other to see who can care the least.

Dating is meant to be fun! You should be spending that time getting to know new people, trying new experiences and using those experiences to discover yourself and find what it is you're looking for in a person.

I'll share a secret with you: when it comes to dating, like most things in my life I've always been a true believer of manifesting and doing the work in order to get the results I want. During the pandemic I opened up my Notes app and created a list of everything I desired in a partner. I'd dated for a while, so I knew exactly what I wasn't looking for.

I realised there were three levels of what I wanted in a serious love interest. The first, most basic level was attraction, of course. The second was more down to personality, career, attributes that I'd admire and need in a partner, such as being supportive, intelligent, wise, charismatic, funny and loyal. Level three was sexual and emotional compatibility and the ability to tend to my personal love languages. I also created a level four, which said 'maybe add what you're willing to compromise on and what you definitely won't' – I never did get round to filling in that part!

It became a thing between me and my girls that we all had a list and would sometimes sit around and drink wine and even tell the other what type of person would work well with them romantically. We'd do the same with our dating-app profiles. We'd take the other's phone to look at the photos and answers on the profile to make sure we were putting our best foot forward and to also make sure we weren't embarrassing ourselves. Just girls looking out for each other. We'd then start laughing about some of our dating experiences because, let's be real, some of these matches did make for some funny-ass stories, even if we weren't going to pursue them ever again!

Two years later and I'm actually so happy I made that list with the stages I mentioned. It genuinely helped direct me into the happy relationship I'm in today. It allowed me to explore and to realise why things had never worked out with anyone else. I visualised what I wanted and what I felt complemented me, and eventually it found its way to me.

Sometimes when we're dating we don't even know what we're looking for in a romantic interest, we just go along for the ride. Now, that's not necessarily a bad thing. Again, dating is meant to be full of adventure, romance and hilarious stories you can't wait to tell your friends. It's just important to acknowledge that not every person you hit it off with is going to be someone you jump the broom with, or someone you should introduce to your parents, or have a baby with. And if that's the case it's OK to just enjoy being in that moment and to learn from it till it's time to move on and discover something different.

It's also OK to talk to and date multiple people! If you're in a space where you're trying to meet someone new, you should be spending part of your free time doing just that – going out to bars, spending time in new places, going to different events to help increase your chances, because, let's face it, if you do the same thing over and over, you won't see new results.

Identifying healthy intimacy

As I've mentioned before, it's important to recognise that some relationships aren't meant to turn into committed partnerships. It's OK to have a casual, short-term thing (and I'll talk more about this later in Chapter 11: Casual Sex) as long as you're both having fun, being honest and treating each other with respect. But it's not OK to stick around with someone who isn't treating you well.

However, the pressure to be seen to be 'in a relationship' means women often ignore the red flags. It's not always our fault. As I've described many times, we aren't taught how to identify healthy intimacy, and many of us are also raised to believe that the 'job' of making a relationship work is entirely on us. But it's not. If our partner is not willing to meet us in the middle and to find ways to communicate, and instead just dismisses our needs or concerns, then honestly? You need to get out of there. I'm not saying they have to unquestioningly do whatever you tell them, but if they are ignoring you or making you feel crazy for having doubts, that is *not* an example of healthy intimacy.

When I was with my ex, I once decided to be open and honest about my insecurities over a friend of his who was a woman. I didn't want him to end his friendship with this lady ... nah, fuck it, I did – I didn't like the girl! I didn't tell him that, obviously, because I knew it was unreasonable. However, I admitted to him that I believed that if he ever cheated on me, it would be with her. Their closeness bothered me and the way she seemed to depend on him for emotional support made me uncomfortable. It also didn't escape my notice that when we got together, it took him forever to tell her he had a girlfriend. (Sometimes I laugh and scream about what I let these n*****s get away with back then!) Anyway, in a moment of vulnerability, I shared my feelings because I wanted to be real with him. Little did I know this would turn into a knife to be used later to stab me in the back.

You see, one time after they hung out, she posted a picture on Instagram of her wearing his jacket. My spirit didn't take to it, so I asked him if he could tell her to remove the post. You could argue that I was an overbearing girlfriend, and I wouldn't say you were wrong, but something about it didn't feel right to me. To what I *thought* was his credit, he agreed and asked her politely to remove the post. She refused. So I decided to call her and ask her myself. In the course of our conversation she repeated back to me what I had told my ex in confidence, word for word, bar for bar.

Ladies, let me tell you this: the moment a guy has you talking to another woman about him, leave. Please. What was meant to be a secret shared between a couple became a trump card for another girl to use. Why would she remove the post now? She was clearly assured of his loyalty. He had given her enough ammunition to completely disregard how it made me feel. He had made her comfortable enough to disrespect our relationship.

It probably seems childish that I was so upset about a picture and a jacket, but I *was* young. And truth be told, I was *not* secure in that relationship, so it only took the most minor thing to tip me over and act up. I don't think I was completely wrong to feel uncomfortable with their friendship either. And in the end my discomfort proved to be well founded because here was this guy going around using my name to tickle the ears and do pillow talk with other women! I pride myself on loyalty and would never, ever make another person feel the way he made me feel. Imagine if I hadn't spoken to her. I'd never have known he'd been talking to her about us; I'd always have just had this unsettled feeling about it.

I will say, my ex cut her off after the incident (or so he says sha), but it added to our eventual break-up. It was very hard for me to trust him, and do you blame me? How can you keep a relationship thriving and your boat floating if the person you're with keeps trying to put holes inside of it when you're not looking?

But as I said, I have learned from these experiences. And I think that's the reason I've been able to help so many women with their relationship dilemmas. Most times, when I read or hear about a scenario, I find I can relate and so I'm able to spot those nasty red flags immediately. Even if I haven't been through it directly, I've been answering dilemmas for several years and I've seen the same type appear over and over and over again. It usually looks something like this:

> 'Dearest Oloni ...'
> [OK, not dearest, but I like how it sounds, OK? So go with it!]
> 'Dearest Oloni, my boyfriend of three years keeps speaking to his ex-girlfriend. It makes me uncomfortable and I've told him. He says I'm being insecure. I trust him, but I don't trust her. Help!'

This sort of dilemma really annoys me if I'm honest, for two reasons: 1) She has done the communicating and her feelings have been ignored. 2) She insists it's the ex-girlfriend she fears, not her boyfriend who is entertaining this disrespectful madness. In this situation it's clear to me the boyfriend knows his girlfriend is not going anywhere so is doing as much bullshit as he's being allowed. Sometimes, you have to peep shit for what it is and exit a relationship.

It's important we understand what it feels like and means to be in a relationship with someone who has the same values as you do, or else my inbox will continue to be flooded with unbalanced relationship scenarios.

All commitments take work, but they also need to be realistic. You cannot date a serial cheater and believe that he will change and then, when he doesn't, continue to disturb your friends on what you should do about the relationship.

The dilemma above is just an example. I'm not saying being friends with an ex is always a problem. If you're in a secure relationship with healthy communication, you might not care if your partner talks to their ex. There might be context, they could have dated them ten years ago and stayed friends. You might understand that this friend was there before you and can tell that they're not trying to threaten your relationship. I don't think being territorial about our lovers is inevitable and I think it can sometimes become quite toxic in itself (something I'll come back to a bit later in this chapter – see page 216 – when we discuss monogamy more broadly). But when the foundation of our connection with someone feels shaky or we don't feel like our feelings are being respected, it's only natural that situations like this would prick at our defensive instincts. Healthy intimacy doesn't mean ignoring those feelings for the sake of keeping the peace, it means being able to talk about it with them honestly and feeling confident that your partner will engage in good faith.

There are probably people who will read that and think it sounds boring. What can I say? Some of you are addicted to the drama. Maybe a relationship doesn't feel exciting unless there's some chaos involved or a dilemma bothering you, and in some ways I get you. I probably used to think the same way. It's certainly the sort of thing we thrive on in TV and films – it's what pushes the plot along – and it always makes for the juiciest stories we hear from our friends. Constant drama, however, does not equal a healthy relationship. Whether you're right at the beginning or several years in, love is not supposed to be a struggle. But it does take work. The question is, how do we get the balance right?

Sustaining healthy relationships

A lot people know what it's like to fall in love, for sparks to fly and what the butterflies feel like, but most people don't know what the work and emotional labour that comes with being in a healthy relationship looks like. And how would we? We don't get taught that. I know I keep saying this but that's because we need to be reminded!

It ought to go without saying that relationships need to include *like* as well as love. There are people out there in relationships with someone they're just used to and possibly, deep down, even hate. They may not have always hated them, but it's understandable that, with commitment, resentment and an unhealthy amount of confrontation can build up and turn love to hate without the person even noticing it.

Sometimes things just fizzle out. The reality of everyday life takes over and the spark that was there at the start dies out. This is one reason why people might start to wander elsewhere. But that shouldn't be an excuse. Because if you are serious about the relationship, you can work on maintaining it. As humans, we are all drawn to the possibility of the new and exciting. Novelty is a big motivator. We enjoy the experience of freshness, newness, the unpredictable. But instead of trying to explore that with someone else (duh, lol), why not do the work and find a way to bring that back to your relationship? Have a conversation with your partner and say, 'Babe, we need to find a way to put a spark in our relationship again.'

In a 2019 study, psychologists found that couples who do what they called 'self-expanding activities' together report higher relationship satisfaction *and* higher levels of desire for one another (which can be a big part of relationship satisfaction, too).[5] What counts as a self-expanding activity really just depends on you and what you're interested in, but basically it means anything where you experience something new or learn something. So it could just be taking trips together on the weekend, learning a language together, going to salsa or boxing or a cookery class together, or deciding to get into cooking at home, or figuring out how to do some DIY. Really, it could be anything. What these activities do is they bring back some of the exciting feelings of novelty and discovery that you most likely had at the start of your relationship, which can help inject new energy into things.

Meditate or pray together if you're religious or spiritual. You might want to use this moment to just be still and find a way to share an energy that can bring you both closer. No matter what it is, just experiencing a moment of stillness might help awaken your relationship.

You can also broaden your horizons by exploring new sexual activities (and I'll come back to the importance of sexual compatibility and how to foster it in the next chapter – see page 233). Even if you think you've done every sexually exciting thing there is to be done, there's always more. And don't forget to make space for erotic moments, even if you're both busy with the day-to-day grind (in fact, as life gets busier and full of other responsibilities it becomes even more important to prioritise time together where you actually get to connect romantically, instead of just lying on the sofa half asleep).

Plan a date night/double date that is new to both of you and a moment you haven't shared together. After all, isn't that what romance is meant to be? Sharing new moments that add to your love story. Create them together! You might also want to go on a baecation or somewhere out of town where you can experience a different place other than your back garden. When you're able to temporarily put yourself in a new location it can feel romantic and fun, allowing you to make the most of being able to reconnect with each other.

Flirt, touch and be playful just like you did in the beginning of the relationship. These things are not just reserved for a new love interest; they should be a natural part of your relationship. This is what some sex and relationships experts call 'sexual currency'. If you have sexual currency in your relationship it means you find ways to relate to each other that carry sexual undertones, or which hint at your sexual relationship, even when you're just going about your day-to-day life.[6] For example, do you just move around each other in a platonic way or do you find ways to exchange little looks and acts of affection or make flirty jokes and innuendos? Do you still kiss each other goodbye when you leave for work or do you just yell 'See ya!' from the bathroom? Sexual currency can be anything from a little bum slap as you walk past each other, to complimenting each other's appearance – it's about continuing to acknowledge the sexual side of your relationship even when you're not actually having sex. And therapists say that people who do this find it easier to maintain their connection long-term.

Remember, life's not always about being serious with your lover. Sometimes it means play-fighting, other times it's being intimate by gently rubbing the lower back of your partner or enjoying a cuddle, or flirting like they're your teenage crush and just being silly. We don't completely realise it, but there are moments when we become complacent and take our partner's presence for granted, forgetting how to keep that side of the relationship – the innocent, easy side – open.

I also really recommend learning each other's love languages. If you haven't heard of 'love languages', it's a term coined by American author and pastor Gary Chapman to describe the different ways people give and recognise love. Chapman set out five main ones: words of affirmation, quality time, gift-giving, acts of service and physical touch.[7] You can usually tell from just thinking about it what your primary love language is, but there are also several quizzes you can take online to help you figure it out.

Understanding your lover's love language can allow you both to connect in a way that speaks to your needs. Once you realise what your partner's primary languages are, you can actively try to cater to them more. Doing so shows them that you're trying to communicate in a way that really resonates with them. And it helps you appreciate what they do for you as well. I'm an acts-of-service girl myself. Don't get me wrong, I do also appreciate quality time, but when my boyfriend randomly gets me something I mentioned in passing or solves a task I need help with, it really makes me feel cared for and understood. And that's very powerful.

I am also a big fan of vocalising your appreciation for each other, long after the initial 'wow' factor has worn off. After all, who doesn't want to feel good and hear compliments from the person they love? They reassure you, make you glow, and exchanging compliments reminds you of how attractive you find one another so you never find yourself having to fish for appreciation or second-guess your partner.

You should have noticed the theme of communication throughout this book by now. In my opinion, *all* healthy connections require good communication, whether that's for a single night or the rest of your life. But when it comes to sustaining a relationship in the long-term, understanding how to communicate with your partner is obviously something that holds a lot of importance. But many of us have no real idea what 'good communication' looks like.

In my former relationships, I used to wonder if I asked for too much. I tried every form of communication, from being an empath to being assertive, to writing it down, to expressing my feelings in person. Nothing changed. In fact, sometimes I felt as though communicating made it worse. I started to believe that talking about the things that upset me was just handing my partner ammunition. Remember the guy who used my vulnerable moment to score points with his female friend? Situations like that made me feel like I was just opening myself to someone who didn't care and giving them more tips and tricks on how to play me. Consequently, a relationship that should have been full of love and joy became about me constantly figuring out how to ask for what I needed without upsetting the other person, and without feeling like I'd made myself too vulnerable or shared all my cards. That's not healthy!

And asking for communication can be just as hard. If your partner hasn't worked on themselves and they don't understand their own needs and feelings, they are going to struggle to communicate back. Communication has to go both ways so if this isn't something your lover is prepared to work on, then maintaining that relationship is going to be really hard. And yeah, I'm afraid to say that if you're fucking with someone who just doesn't care about your needs then no amount of communication on *your* side is going to solve that. You see, you can communicate about something a hundred times, but it does no good if the person you're communicating with doesn't understand how to receive it, or doesn't want to engage with it. The number of times I hear, 'Oloni, I explained how I feel and now he has told me I'm nagging him!' Are you his mother?! Sis, leave!

Communication shouldn't feel like a code you have to crack. It should be about two people being able to show up and say what they feel and need without it being taken as an accusation, without it setting off the other person's defences, and it should never be something that's used against the other person, to undermine or ridicule them. Indeed, the relationship I'm in now showed me why all my other relationships didn't quite click before. There are no mind games. It's just two people who respect the hell out of one another's boundaries and aren't using what they're insecure about to drive the other mad.

I will say, though, that knowing how to speak to each other is vital. You cannot meet someone with aggression and expect them to receive that neutrally or be forthcoming in their response. You cannot be passive-aggressive and after numerous, increasingly frustrated occasions when you ask your partner, 'What's wrong?' expect to have a good conversation. If you don't want your request to be taken as an accusation, you need to find a way to word it so that it doesn't turn into one. Therapists talk about using 'I sentences' instead of 'you sentences' in situations like this. By focusing on your feelings and beliefs rather than what you believe the other person has done wrong, you're less likely to make them defensive and more likely to have them empathise and understand what it is you need.

Instead of saying, 'Why don't you ever invite me when you're going out with your mates?' try saying, 'I'd love to come along sometime when you go out with your mates. It would feel really good to be included.'

Being transparent and learning how to talk to your partner with respect creates a habit for maintaining a relationship that is blissful. It makes it easier for you both to speak your minds without overthinking. When you establish a pattern of openness and honesty, you find you get to know each other better; you can anticipate how something might make the other person feel, and it stops you having to strategise or second-guess. You may even find that there are situations that don't require words for your partner to understand how you feel because they know you well enough to formulate what would and wouldn't ruffle your feathers.

You also have to be able to trust each other, to be honest and to be open about what you both want and need. Now, trust isn't a fixed thing ... you can develop it, earn it, break it and rebuild it. Only you can know where your boundaries lie, what you need from people in order to trust them and how flexible you are prepared to be as time goes on and you understand each other better.

I've always believed that trust is not something you just hand out to people freely, especially with regards to something as precious as your heart. However, if you're dating someone exclusively, over time you start to get a better understanding of what they are and aren't capable of. You learn what you can rely on them for and how dependable they are, and that builds trust. And hopefully they feel the same way about you. When your level of trust in one another is built around who you are as individuals and not some idealised notion of what a relationship 'should' be, you'll find you're able to do a much better job of maintaining it. It also allows you to be transparent with each other about your expectations and limitations in a way you know you will not be judged or shamed for (I hope, at least). No human is perfect and sometimes trust can be broken, and if that trust has been tested and the result is one that affects you, you're not wrong for wanting to pump your brakes and put up a bit of a wall until said person earns back your trust. They have to genuinely want to earn it, too; words hold very little meaning if they're not matched with action and consistent change. A week of improvement before returning back to their old tricks will not cut it.

Finally, the healthiest relationships are ones where each person recognises the other as an individual. I know that feeling of it being just the two of you, in your own little universe, can be intoxicating, especially at the start of a relationship, but that kind of insularity can turn into co-dependence over the long-term. Trust me when I say that expecting one person to meet all of our needs is a direct route to dissatisfaction over time. Having strong relationships with friends, family members, colleagues (even exes if it's appropriate) are actually a big part of how you sustain a healthy connection with your romantic partner. It's important to respect and make time for each other's different interests, even when you don't understand or relate to them. Maintaining a sense of self is actually key to long-term satisfaction in a relationship.[8] Rather than seeing his monthly 'boys' night' as an annoyance or barrier, see it as a potential benefit!

Time apart as well as time together is also good for your sex life. A lot of us are led to believe that closeness is the key to sexual intimacy, and that is definitely important, but we need distance, too. Sex and relationship therapist Esther Perel noticed that when she asked the couples she worked with to describe the moments when they found themselves most attracted to one another, it was always times when they were able to take a step back and observe their partner as a separate being. So it might be while overhearing them talk confidently on the phone to a work colleague; it might be while watching them play a sport or play the guitar, or do something else they're passionate about; it might be watching them interact with their friends and make people laugh; it might be seeing them play with their nephews and nieces, or it might just be that moment when you see them walk into the bar to meet you but they haven't clocked you yet and so they're still in their own separate world, taking off their headphones, greeting the doorman and looking round to find where you are. Independence, as well as intimacy, is essential for sustaining long-term interest and desire.[9]

Maintaining any sort of romantic relationship past the honeymoon stage isn't always the easiest. Life happens, we're tempted, we question, we love, we doubt. No relationship is full of butterflies and laughter 24/7, and that's OK. I think what's important above all is being true to how you honestly enjoy relationships, identifying the work you're prepared to do in order to maintain the relationship and exploring other options that fit with what you truly desire.

And in some cases, you might realise that what you truly desire isn't monogamy at all ...

Monogamy is not the only option

I know this subject is highly controversial. I know that because every time I bring it up, whether it's on Twitter or on my podcast, I get flooded with messages from people stressing out because they think I'm telling them they have to be OK with their partners sleeping with other people. I'm not saying that. At least, I'm not *dictating* that. But I am saying it's maybe worth thinking about.

There's a joke that sometimes gets levelled at people in monogamous relationships, which goes a little like this: 'You're in an open relationship, you just don't know it.' The implication here is that, actually, people in supposedly monogamous relationships cheat all the time and there's no real way of knowing for sure whether your partner is being faithful.

I'm sorry to say the stats bear this out. When surveyed, almost a quarter of men and just under a fifth of women admitted to cheating during their current relationship.[10] Now, I'm not saying that if you're someone who is constantly unfaithful, you should just opt for being in an open relationship, but I think we need to be honest with ourselves about the fact that clearly a lot of us find monogamy hard.

Of course, plenty of people would say that we should overcome these instincts. But history has shown us over and over again that we're quite shit at it. Think about it: even when adultery is illegal, when the penalties are imprisonment, flogging and death, as they are in many countries around the world, people still cheat.

Some people do achieve monogamy and if that feels realistic and doable for them and it makes them happy then fine. I also know that some people aspire to sexual exclusivity, even though they know it could turn out to be an insurmountable challenge. Again, if they are happy that's fine. I'm not saying monogamy can't work or that we should all give up on it, but given how hard many people find it, I think it's worth considering the alternatives.

And this is not to say that open relationships can't also be deceitful. Ethical non-monogamous relationships require honesty, and it is definitely possible to cheat in a non-monogamous relationship if you cross someone's boundaries or break the rules you've set for yourselves. Betrayal of trust is never OK. It doesn't matter what sort of commitment you're in; an open relationship can't fix your lack of integrity. So I am definitely not going to sit here and tell you that non-monogamy is the answer to everything, but in general I feel like if you start out on the basis that you can be open and honest about your attractions to other people, it seems logical that there are going to be fewer ways in which you can end up hurting each other.

I personally don't think we were all meant be monogamous. I mean, how can we be? If we all have different needs when it comes to our lifestyle, how can monogamy be a one-size-fits-all? I used to think I could be with one person for the rest of my life, but honestly, if my partner today wanted us to open things up in any sort of way I don't think I'd be totally against it. We'd need to have several conversations and I might chicken out of the idea at the last minute, but I wouldn't be mad if he did want to explore it several years down the line and vice versa. Spending your forever with someone is a very hard ask, especially if you know deep down you desire a different dynamic in your relationship.

How can we ALL possibly want to experience one type of love and one type of sex? It just sounds unreasonable and forced.

So much of monogamy propaganda (yeah, I know it's a strong word, but it sometimes feels that way) is rooted in the idea that our partner is our property. Once they have committed to us, whether verbally or through their actions or even legally through marriage, we are taught that they are *ours*. We forget that we do not own anyone, but instead are meant to experience the love, laughter or sex they share. And it's perfectly OK to experience that with other people, too.

Sometimes I actually think it's kind of selfish to ask one person to be everything and more to you in a relationship. We're human, not super-mono-heroes. When I was much younger I believed that you were meant to be with one person for the rest of your life, but as I got older and more experienced when navigating the dating world, I began to understand why people set their own rules or had non-traditional relationship set-ups. Plus, as I discussed in Chapter 2: Society, Stigma and Slut-shaming, there are actually many cultures around the world and throughout history where monogamy is NOT the norm (see page 36). People openly and consensually take other partners and it isn't seen as being destructive. Their societies don't fall apart! In other words: it *is* possible to do things another way, if that's what works for us.

So what if I told you that hundreds of thousands of people who have created the rules of their non-monogamous relationship are just as satisfied within their relationship as those in happy monogamous relationships? Let's talk about some of the ways that might work ...

You've probably heard of terms like 'open relationship', 'polyamory' and 'swinging'. You might not really understand them, though, and have probably used them in the wrong context (I'm sure I have!). That's hardly surprising in a society that places monogamy on such a high pedestal and doesn't encourage us to talk openly about anything else. So let me break down a few of these terms for you ...

Ethical non-monogamy or consensual non-monogamy

When we talk about 'ethical' or 'consensual' non-monogamy, it's basically an umbrella term. It broadly refers to any kind of relationship that doesn't have sexual or emotional monogamy as a core value. But it's important to understand that this can mean vastly different things to different people. The part that really matters is that it's 'ethical' or 'consensual'. Whatever the dynamic, it has been agreed and negotiated and openly discussed by everyone involved.

Open relationship

When people talk about having an 'open relationship' they are usually describing a set-up where sex with other people outside the primary relationship is involved. The emotional side and the commitment (falling in love, cohabiting, building a life together) is usually reserved for the 'main' partner, but sex with other people is seen as OK. So, for example, you might live with your partner, but if one of you is out of town for work, it's OK to have a hook-up. In my experience this is the set-up that sparks the most curiosity from people. In fact, why not have a little fun right now?

Ladies, if you're in a cheeky mood (and you know your partner can handle it!), text the person you're dating this: 'Hey, babe, can we both try being in an open relationship? I think it'd be so exciting.'

Then screenshot their response to me in a tweet using #TheBigO. Let's all laugh. (Please do also follow up to let them know it's a joke and that you're reading *The Big O* ... unless you're not actually joking, of course!)

Swinging

Swinging usually refers to you and your partner having sex with other people, often together but sometimes separately or with one of you watching the other. It could also include having threesomes or foursomes or any kind of orgy or group sex. This can be done at sex parties or organised privately among yourselves with other couples or singles. There is usually no romantic involvement and is purely for fun and sexual gratification.

Swinging isn't a new concept, although the word itself has kind of gone out of fashion and I think a lot of people would find it a bit cringe to call themselves 'swingers', but actually having a threesome is one of the most common sexual fantasies. Around 95 per cent of men and 87 per cent of women have fantasised about sex with multiple partners,[11] and around one in five of us has actually done it.[12] When we look at it like that, swinging is probably one of the more common and socially acceptable forms of ethical non-monogamy.

Polyamory

Polyamory is where someone has numerous romantic and/or sexual partners. Where this differs from an open relationship is that the people involved are OK with the idea of forming emotional intimacy with more than one person.

So you could possibly have a primary partner who you live with and share most aspects of your life with and a secondary one who you enjoy date nights, sex or travelling with. Or you might have two partners and you're invested in them both equally. There are people who live alone and have multiple relationships with different people, which are all of equal importance to them (they just don't involve the commitment of cohabiting). There are also people who live in 'triads' with two partners at once. Polyamory could also include a group of three or four (or more!) people where everyone is dating each other consensually. Not everyone's version of polyamory may be completely identical. You can create the rules and define the terms and conditions.

You make the rules!

Being in a polyamorous relationship also doesn't necessarily mean you're currently *in* multiple commitments; it can simply just describe your relationship style and the fact that you're open to forming those connections. It's not always just about fucking either. Lots of polyamorous people also include their platonic friendships as key relationships because they acknowledge the importance of these connections in their lives and don't see why a relationship should be considered more important just because it includes sex and romance. There's this idea that consensual non-monogamy *always* includes sexual intimacy with other people, but that isn't always the case. It's more to do with making the right romantic and lifestyle choices that benefit and suit your needs.

And those can change, too. Remember, *you* create your own set of rules and your boundaries. Just because you try ethical non-monogamy, it doesn't mean you have to spend the entire relationship that way. Most consensually non-monogamous people I know have regular conversations about what's working and what's not, and their relationship structures shift over time.

I'm constantly encouraging individuals to find a relationship that works for them, but when I talk to people I often find that it's the men who want to dabble but vehemently don't want their partners to. And even though I roll my eyes at that, I have to check my own prejudices and acknowledge that there *are* women out there who are OK with this kind of arrangement. Just this week I read an account from a woman who said she liked how it took the pressure off her to be *everything* to her partner. She didn't feel like she had to consistently fulfil all his romantic and sexual needs because she knew he had other people he could go to.[13]

Ultimately, when you delve into the world of non-monogamy you are going to find some people who do things in a way that doesn't sit right with you. I get that – I feel the same way sometimes – but we have to remember that if both those people have truly consented to that situation then it's not our place to judge them. That being said, I also won't pretend that problematic behaviour never happens. Some people manipulate their way into unequal relationship dynamics because they want to control their partner but still get their own way. They'll set out their 'terms' and then it's up to the other person to be OK with that. *Ethical* arrangements involve being open to negotiation and compromise, so if something is presented as a 'like it or lump it' situation, that's unethical if you ask me. You are using the threat of abandonment to take away someone's agency, which in my opinion is awful.

And just as people create their own definitions of what might count as being unfaithful in a monogamous relationship, those in ethical non-monogamy set-ups might have their own version of what each term means to them. I think what's vital is understanding that multiple types of relationships can coexist and it shouldn't be something we're all hush-hush about.

I'm not going to pretend I'm the expert on ethical non-monogamy. I've never tried it (yet!) and I know from friends and other sex educators that it's not something you should just dive into without thinking really hard about what you want and how you'd like it to work. But the older I get and the more experiences I have with sex and relationships, the more I feel that monogamy isn't for everyone. And the more, in fact, I feel that lifelong monogamy may not be right for us all, and that's OK!

If you are genuinely interested in exploring some of the ideas and relationship structures I've shared here then I recommend you check out the *Multiamory* podcast as well as the *Monogamish* podcast, which are great places to start if you want to find out more about how to open up your relationship in an honest, shame-free and *ethical* way.

So now you know the options are almost endless, how do you go about choosing the right sort of relationship for you?

Figuring out what you want

We're taught to feel bad for wanting to experience our sexuality in a way that's outside our society's norms, when plenty of cultures navigate dating in different ways. And that can make it hard to figure out what we actually want or what really piques our interest.

In truth, I think the best way to figure out what you want is simply to try different things and see how we feel about them. I think we sometimes feel like 'not knowing what you want' is a bad thing, but we all look and yearn for different things when it comes to sex and romance so it's OK to dabble, and you're not wrong for wanting that MFM, MMF or FFM. As long as you are going into things consensually, you are communicating well with your partners and you feel emotionally prepared to deal with any new feelings that may arise, I think it's fine to explore. After all, why should sexuality only be discovered or experienced in one way? Why shouldn't you get to experiment and decide whether or not you like it?

Oh, and in case you're wondering ...

MFM = male, female, male threesome with no contact between the two men.

MMF = male, male, female threesome where everyone touches each other.

FFM = female, female, male threesome with sexual play among everyone.

In Chapter 4: Sexual Identity I mentioned some of the tests and quizzes you can do to see where you fall on the Kinsey Scale, learn about your sexual accelerators and brakes, and discover what kind of kinks you might be interested in (see pages 63, 64 and 67). Well, guess what? There's also one you can do to learn more about the sort of relationship that best suits you.

The relationship structure quiz

Certified sexologist Shannon Boodram created a relationship structure quiz that I really recommend you try with your friends, as well as with your romantic and sexual interests. It can help you better understand what kind of dynamic works for you and open you up to a better understanding of what it is you desire. You can find the quiz online and it will tell you which of the following nine relationship structures are most likely to suit you.

I love these categories and definitions so much that I asked Shannon if I could share them with you.[14]

Casual dating

Here's someone who enjoys the art of dating and isn't afraid of jumping from one person to another if it makes them happy. Usually never there for the long-term.

Serial non-committed dating

A type of romantic or sexual relationship that is fun, and not exclusive, and also has some form of an emotional connection. Each person can be dating each other alone or have other people in their life they're also getting to know.

Traditional monogamy

Traditional monogamy is where both people in the relationship have no desire to be with anyone else sexually or romantically and continue with the intention that they will be together forever.

Modern monogamy

This is the type of monogamy that is probably the most popular and one we're most likely to be familiar with. A commitment that is just between two people, until someone decides they'd like to move on.

Monogamish

As a whole the relationship is monogamous, but there's room for sexual gratification that doesn't come straight from your partner. This might look like watching porn or going to a strip club and getting a lap dance but still remaining faithful physically and emotionally.

Free relationship

This type of commitment can be all about monogamy and sometimes the relationship might be open sexually. You create the boundaries and decide when the rules change. It also includes open relationships, polyamory and swinging.

Ultimately, whether we're monogamous or not, I think one of the keys to relationship happiness is understanding that we don't own our partner. They are not ours to claim. We *choose* who to share our lives with, who to have experiences with and who to share sexual intimacy with, and it's important to remember that this never stops being a choice, whether we've been together six weeks or sixty years. Being in a relationship with someone does not mean you get to say how or with whom they choose to experience other parts of their life.

Sadly, though, this does sometimes mean that our relationships will come to an end.

Heartbreak and letting go

One of the reasons I think people hold on to their partners so tightly and feel tempted to try to control their behaviour is fear of the relationship ending. That's really normal. Fear of abandonment is one of our primal instincts and a lot of us still struggle with it in adulthood. But it's not just the idea of being dumped that pricks our insecurities. Many people are equally afraid of walking away from relationships.

Sometimes I worry that it's because as a society we see a relationship ending and classify it as a failed relationship. But the journey and the experience are also important, not just whether it lasts 'forever'. You can have a successful relationship that ends. It doesn't mean it wasn't a success. Our lives and circumstances change. We grow and learn. What worked for us at 25 might not be suitable at 35 or 45 and so on.

As with many things in life, sometimes it's just time to move on. If you switched careers you wouldn't see that as a failure. Same with a friendship that has run its course with no malice involved. Sometimes we're just here to experience people temporarily and those experiences can be just as valuable as the ones that last a long time.

I stated earlier that no relationship is better than a bad relationship, and I stand by that. But it's also important to know that even good relationships can reach a natural finishing point and that doesn't mean that it turned out badly. There's an odd culture in monogamy that makes us feel as though we have to be almost ashamed to admit it if we want to move on with our life separately. But trying to hang on for dear life to something that no longer serves us can eventually become toxic or lead to co-dependency. It's vital that we know when to let go.

Deep down I think we all know when it's time to move on from anything that no longer makes us happy. We know this with friendships and work, so why don't some of us trust ourselves enough to know when a romantic relationship isn't quite working? Sometimes we believe it might change, but if you constantly find yourself thinking, 'This will get better,' and it doesn't, you're just running away from the truth out of fear – and, worse, you're wasting your time.

When I meet with relationship dilemmas from people who want my advice on a situation that clearly isn't great, I sometimes wonder if they're waiting for a magic spell that can help transform it. They'll tell me about someone who isn't affectionate, can't communicate, doesn't take them out on dates or, even worse, keeps them a total secret from friends and family. They'll ask what I think they should do as though I can help them change someone's entire attitude and personality, when really the only advice I can give is: dump him.

You deserve to be with someone who is as passionate about you as you are about them. Someone whose face glows when they see you, who makes you feel like you're part of a team, a confidante, a source of amazing energy. Trust me, this person exists. But I know that when people are desperate for a relationship they will entertain anyone regardless of whether that person is meant for them or not. Be patient with your heart. Do not return to someone who has hurt you after doing the work to move on. A man who only wants you when you decide to be with someone else, after giving them enough chances to act well, does not truly want you. They just hate to lose.

Part of self-love means treating yourself to such a high standard that you refuse to allow any sort of mediocre love near you. It's loving yourself enough to understand that the love you have for yourself will always override a situation that doesn't make you feel good or blissful.

So with that in mind, below are some signs of when it's time to say, 'Boy, bye!'

1. You have become repetitive in your wants and they're never being met or even acknowledged.
2. The relationship effort isn't equal. You're putting 100 per cent in and they're barely putting in 40 per cent.
3. You've been cheated on. Once someone can betray your trust and loyalty, you really need to send them packing. No ifs, no buts!
4. You know you do not see a future with this person, and they don't make you happy.
5. They constantly make you second-guess yourself and your feelings.
6. They post their whole lives on social media yet refuse to show you off on special occasions (or, worse, they intentionally try to hide you, especially if they are not hypervisible on social media).

7. They're controlling and abusive, and continuously disregard your opinions.
8. They lower your self-esteem and do not make you feel good about yourself.
9. Words they've shared are hardly ever followed through with actions.
10. You have mentally checked out and don't care much for the relationship any longer.

How to heal from heartbreak

Healing from heartbreak isn't always the easiest, because it's a form of grief. But it's a part of life that many of us will experience. When you've been in a romantic relationship and have been so used to being with a person who you suddenly have to be without, it can be difficult to get your head around.

First, understand that the hurt is normal, so allow yourself to process the pain in a healthy way. This might include crying and talking about how you feel, but also maybe writing down what you've learned about that relationship and yourself. Do this in your phone notes or diary or send a future letter to yourself to read back in three, six or twelve months. There are plenty of free online websites that can do this for you, such as futureme.org.

Listen to break-up music that you can relate to but also includes feel-good tracks. But mainly, do whatever you feel can ease your pain. When I was going through past break-ups and heartbreak I'd spend some time on my own and other moments with my closest friends, who'd keep me company, remind me how great I was and just be there to help comfort me. My sister Temi is my greatest soldier as she would shower me with words of love and wisdom, and remind me that this feeling wouldn't last forever. She shared encouraging words of affirmations that I started to repeat to myself daily; we listened to and sang the lyrics to Billie Eilish's 'Ocean

Eyes' and Sade's 'The Moon and the Sky' to the point where it felt cathartic, and with time it helped me reach the healing stage.

Here's a list of affirmations that I've created, which might help you:

- 'This too shall pass.'
- 'I will be fine.'
- 'I deserve to be happy.'
- 'I'm a bad bitch and this pain is only temporary.'
- 'I am deserving of the type of love that will make me laugh at this current pain one day.'
- 'I deserve more.'

One of my favourite Yoruba proverbs is '*Ile oba t'o jo, ewa lo bu si*', which translates as 'A king's palace burning down will allow the creation of a newer and more beautiful palace to be built.' This also means that every cloud has a silver lining and that just because something bad might be happening, you have to believe and trust that something good will follow.

Now, if you have close mutuals with the person you've broken up with, you're allowed to make it clear to them that you'd prefer it if your ex wasn't a topic of conversation or ask that they don't invite you to the same places for a while. That's not you being petty, it's just a sensible way to create the space you need to process your feelings. Set your boundaries and continue to protect your heart.

Like grief, there are different stages to heartbreak, but in order to heal you have to really want it. Although I mentioned I'd generally spend some time on my own to get my emotions out privately, do not completely isolate yourself from your loved ones. Keep yourself busy with new hobbies. In fact, why not use this moment to do something you've never quite had the chance to do before? Be kind to yourself and your body. Eat well – and I don't mean diet, I mean food that makes you feel good as well as nourishes you – and if, like me, you constantly put off going to the gym, use this chance to be serious about it and go. I'm not necessarily talking about getting a revenge body, I'm talking about the very real benefits exercise has on our mental wellbeing. Exercising is not only something to focus on in its own right, it is also proven to help relieve stress,[15] and it provides a physical outlet for anger and other negative emotions you might be holding on to.

You could also try talking to a professional who might be able to help you further, depending on the type of break-up and depth of heartbreak you are experiencing. A therapist or counsellor will be able to help you dissect your feelings about the relationship, but also help you walk in the right direction to becoming a better version of yourself.

Most importantly, know that an ending is not a failure. As I said at the start, we need to let go of the idea that there's only one 'right' way for a relationship to look. And we need to throw out the idea that we should be satisfied with the bare minimum, or that it's unrealistic to want more. I'll say it again: be ridiculous with your expectations, ladies. Set your standards high. And look for a relationship *you* want, not just one you can scrape together.

Conclusion: What does the future of dating look like?

I think we can say with some certainty that ethically non-monogamous relationships are becoming more common and less stigmatised. The UK's biggest survey of sexual attitudes and lifestyles, which takes place every ten years, is even planning to include a new question on 'acceptability of agreeing to have sex outside the relationship' in its next round of research to reflect this.[16]

I know, I know, this might seem beyond the norm, especially if monogamy is all most of us have known, but it's about time we all started being honest about what we really want from a relationship instead of just swallowing what we've been fed. Maybe then we'll be better at monogamy and dating, too.

We all enjoy being loved and desired, but it's vital that we're upfront not only with other people but with ourselves as to what that really looks like. If we continue with bad habits, we'll only be left with bad results, but if we make a habit of communicating and staying true to what we want in our romantic life, we'll attract others who are just the same and allow us to be just that.

I think we'll be very surprised by what might become the future of dating. There was a time when online dating wasn't something people liked to admit they partook in, yet now every other week someone on social media is sharing their love story of how they met their life partner online, or telling their followers that they've deleted the app for the 456,757th time after someone with soup on their shirt in their profile photo tried to match with them.

Being a single woman past the age of 30 will not be something to be ashamed of because we understand that a woman does not need a man in order to have a fulfilling life, nor does a relationship define her. Women are winning in so many ways and they should not be feeling an unhealthy pressure to be in any sort of romantic relationship. Single women are happy women, too.

I hope we'll also stop seeing women who want to perform for men to show they're worthy of being with them. Just be yourself and understand that is *enough.*

CHAPTER 10

Sexual Compatibility

I've been quite fortunate to *mostly* have partners I've gelled well with sexually. We've had similar libidos, similar kinks and shared the same excitement for my favourite sexual positions. The very best encounters were the ones where my partner was dedicated to making sure I was beyond satisfied and receiving pleasure, and I felt the same towards them.

Saying that, I've also had sex with people who weren't open to my sexual interests, who didn't care for my sexual role plays in the bedroom or whether I came or not. I've also had partners whose masculinity was too fragile to allow them to moan or to engage in sex fully and confidently. This is who you should avoid. Anyone who doesn't care about making sure you reach your climax shouldn't be given another opportunity. Selfishness is something I've railed against throughout this book. Right now, I want to talk about compatibility and in my eyes compatibility goes a bit deeper than that.

There's a guy I used to call 'school boy' on my podcast, because even though he was a fully grown man he would have sex as though it was his first time. We were both at university and I was extremely attracted to him. I just *had* to fuck him, and I know he wanted to do the same. But when he came over and we got into it he just lay there like a bad bitch and let me do all the work. 'Foreplay' with this guy only went as far as kissing, and then he just lay there as I straddled him. He also did this weird thing with his hands where instead of holding on to my hips and guiding me (or touching my body in any way!), he put his thumbs to his forefingers together in that chin mudra move they do in yoga. Like, bro, is this a meditation session or are we getting it on? I didn't get it then and I still don't get it now. Maybe there are women out there who would totally be into that, but to me it was very clear that we just weren't compatible, and not just because he was shit at giving me pleasure (although he was), but also because we clearly had very different approaches to sex and he wasn't interested in finding out what mine were.

Really great sex happens when we feel physically *and* intellectually excited by and connected to the person we're sleeping with. Now, when I say intellectually, I don't mean they have to be a total nerd (although if geeks are what turn you on then absolutely you do you). It also doesn't mean that we have to be in love with them or that we have to know each other inside out. We don't even need to have loads in common, but on some level we need to feel like we *get* each other. We need to feel like we're on the same wavelength, sexually.

So how do we achieve this Holy Grail? Well, truthfully, we can't always. Some of it comes down to sexual chemistry, and that is not something you can manufacture. It's visceral and often surprising – you know those times when you hook up with someone new and the sex *just works*? Even though you didn't necessarily do anything different. Somehow, you just seem to get each other. It goes the other way as well. Sometimes we meet someone and no matter how much we fancy them, no matter how perfect they seem, the chemistry just isn't quite there. You're going through the motions, busting out your best moves, but somehow the atmosphere between you feels a little ... flat.

Now, there might be good reasons for this. For example, it's hard to have good chemistry if one of you is holding back out of a lack of confidence, or hang-ups about your body, or not really knowing what you want, or feeling ashamed or worried that they're going to judge you or reject you if you fail to look or behave a certain way. Many of these things can be worked on and released. That's why so much of this book is dedicated to helping you understand those things and build the confidence to go into every intimate encounter as your truest sexual self. But in the moment, they can be a real barrier.

However, sometimes a lack of chemistry can't really be explained. The spark just isn't there. Sometimes you might get that feeling right away on the first date, other times it might be a relationship that started out well but seems to have lost its edge somehow. This can be really disheartening, but it doesn't have to mean the relationship is doomed. Like I said, sexual chemistry isn't really something you can talk yourself into, but you can do a few things to try to facilitate it, to try to create that spark. One really good way to try to get that sexual chemistry between you going is to focus on finding your sexual compatibility.

Things that can stand in the way of finding your compatibility

As I mentioned, there are various things that can prevent you and your partner being able to connect intimately. Feeling insecure, embarrassed or just not confident enough to speak up for what you're interested in can definitely stop you experiencing true compatibility. If you're having to guess at what your partner wants, or they're having to guess at what you want, and neither of you is communicating well or giving much feedback, that can make for awkward, clumsy encounters.

I've tried to include my tips for better communication all the way through this book and I'll share more at the end of this chapter. I know it's hard, especially if you've spent your whole life being told that talking about sex is nasty or being into certain things makes you a slut. But there's a reason we sex educators bang on about communication all the time: it's really important.

I saw an Instagram post a while back from sex educators Afrosexology. It said, 'Closed mouths don't get head,' and I am here to tell you that is the truth (obviously feel free to switch out 'get head' for whatever it is you want but can't bring yourself to ask for). We can be quick to blame our partners for not magically knowing how to give us pleasure, but sexual compatibility does not include being able to read each other's minds. It's easy to put a disappointing sexual experience down to our partner's lack of technique or interest in our pleasure, and let's be honest, that is sometimes the case. But if we haven't even said what we want or talked about what makes us cum then we have to take at least a little bit of the blame.

That being said, selfish people do exist and, ladies, I'm sure we've all had experiences where giving oral sex to a guy felt like the norm, but he came up with a very stupid, stupid reason as to why he didn't want to reciprocate. Don't shoot me, but remember 'school boy'? Well, guess who decided to be a dummy and sleep with him again? Yes, it was I. Again, he was really fine and I think I was more obsessed with trying to give him another shot and not increasing my body count. This time it was clear he expected head and was assertive in how he asked for it. I'm not even talking role-play type of assertive – it was very much presented as a deal-breaker, like the sex wasn't complete if I didn't suck his dick. My lack of voice meant I was too afraid to ask him to do the same, because I knew what the answer would be: a strong no. All in all, he wasn't someone I should have been sleeping with and I'm so glad my attitude towards sex and men has changed drastically since then. I've grown up, and these days I'm not afraid to speak up about what I want in the bedroom.

(As an aside, I hear from cishet men all the time on my podcast that oral sex is something they'll only do once they're married or with a long-term partner. I'm sorry, but what?? Imagine how silly we'd sound if we told *them* we were saving head for our husbands!

So this is just my regular reminder to you to not put up with lines like that even for a moment. Someone who is withholding pleasure from you or creating a hierarchy whereby certain kinds of activities are off limits to you because of your relationship status, that is not a person you're going to find sexual compatibility with.)

So, yeah, it can be tricky. Maybe there's been a time when you had sex and you wanted to continue foreplay just a bit longer, but he was more concerned with just sticking his dick inside. I can relate, I've been there, I get it, sis! But if you don't find your voice sexually you won't know for certain if you work well between the sheets. Someone you can't speak to during sex isn't someone you should be getting naked with.

I understand that naturally some people can be shy, so set yourself a challenge when next having sex with your lover. If you want to ask for head, don't do so immediately. Try saying, 'I enjoy it when you kiss my neck, do it again.' This can help give you the confidence to then say, 'I want to feel your thumb rub on my clit.' Start with things you know they're going to do anyway, create your own variations and work up to asking for more and more. Soon enough you will be able to say, 'I want to feel your mouth on my pussy.'

The fact that talking about our desires can be difficult partly comes from the idea that sex is something we give and take from one another. I've talked about this already in the chapter on virginity (see page 43). For a lot of us, we've grown up with sex framed as something one person *gives* to another. That can create a sense of entitlement (mostly from men) where they don't think about the other person's needs, they're just seeking their own gratification. Before you get all #notallmen on me, I understand that there are men who do in fact care, but remember that the orgasm gap quite clearly shows us that not enough men do!

Nor have straight women generally been given the space to feel like they can be upfront. Women do not have the same privilege to be as demanding in the bedroom because we have been socialised to be givers, pleasers, and submissive in all areas of our lives. We're so used to putting the needs of others first, particularly those of men who are our sexual or romantic interests. So, if you're a cishet man and you're reading this, use your awareness and allow your sexual partner to freely express what she wants – really make her feel comfortable.

If we go into sex thinking only about what we can *get* then we are definitely not going to find our areas of compatibility, because sex isn't a competition, where one person is the winner and the other person is the loser. Sex is something we do *together*. It's a collaboration. It's teamwork!

On the flip side of that, we can also go into sex feeling like we've got to offer something. When we fall into that trap of believing that sex is something we *give*, we can end up putting our partner's needs first. Of course, there's nothing wrong with wanting to level up. Feeling like a throat goat can be sexy as hell. But we need to make sure it's coming from an authentic place and we're not just doing it to please and impress our partners at the expense of our own enjoyment.

The same applies to performing. I've read lots of times that 'sex shouldn't be a performance', but I don't actually think there's anything wrong with putting on a bit of a show during sex if it turns you on. I do! If you're naturally a bit of an exhibitionist then getting into the theatrics might genuinely feel good to you – as long as you're expressing yourself and not just imitating what you've seen in porn.

The times when 'performance' can have a negative impact on our sex lives are when we have an idea in our heads from porn of what 'hot sex' looks like and we feel like we've got to live up to that fantasy. So instead of focusing on our needs and our pleasure, we put on a performance, imitating the things we've seen because we think that's what our partner wants from us. That can even go as far as faking orgasms.

Look, I'm not going to pretend I've never done it. I have, many times, and don't you dare judge me, because I know many of you have, too. Why else would these otherwise very average cishet men walk around with so much sexual confidence? It can't just be me fucking them. Reasons I've done it might have been to massage his ego and maybe because I was, quite frankly, tired! Tired of the sex. A lot of the men I've had sex with have believed that they have made me climax and sometimes I've felt sorry for them, because some really have gone above and beyond to help me orgasm but it just didn't quite happen. There are so many reasons why we fake orgasms. Maybe we don't want to let our partner down or kill the mood, or we know it's what they want to hear. We don't want to hurt their feelings (although if your partner is more concerned about their ego than your genuine pleasure then, sis, you are not compatible). Maybe it's a case of not knowing what you want or how to explain it, in which case I refer you back to Chapters 5 and 6, which talk about getting to know your body and tapping into sexual pleasure with your partner. Or maybe we feel like what we need to reach orgasm is 'too much' to ask for and we don't want to admit that the things that *∗look∗* sexy to our partner don't actually do it for us.

During a house party I threw, my friend introduced me to this guy called Tayo. I don't remember how well we hit it off, but I knew I wanted to sleep with him. We swapped BlackBerry pins, spoke for all of two days, and the next day I was at his house. We had sex when his parents weren't home in the middle of the day and ... I faked it. Look, I was 19, I didn't have my toys with me, I was with some guy I didn't know all that well and I wasn't about to start giving him a sex-ed lesson in the middle of our hook-up and for whatever reason I didn't want to hurt his ego, so, yes, I faked my orgasm. I'm not proud as such, but looking back I get why I did that and I'm not ashamed either. Actually, I think what irritated me most was that word got back to me through the grapevine that he thought I was really noisy during sex. I was mortified! I was like, mate, I was doing you a favour! But the very same fake moaning I did to make him feel good had ended up being gossiped about and sniggered at. Lesson learned, I guess!

My advice now is that if you are faking it to protect the ego of some guy who isn't making you cum, you need to stop right now because you are never going to find your compatibility that way. You can't let him carry on thinking he's a sex god when he isn't. Not in this economy! But secondly, if you're constantly faking it, you're not giving yourself a chance to figure out what you *really* want.

I'm honest about my orgasms and pleasure today, but that's because I stopped returning to sexually disappointing men and only gave my energy to those who were patient, open to exploring and loved using toys on me in the bedroom. Again, compatibility is not about magically knowing what the other person wants or needs, it's about being able to connect with your partner to give *and* receive pleasure.

Another big thing that can limit compatibility is if we're being too rigid in our view of what sex is supposed to involve. If your favourite thing is getting your pussy eaten AFTER you've been fucked (because sometimes a girl wants to be the one who gets to cum and then roll over and fall asleep!) but your partner has it in his head that oral sex is **only** for foreplay then you've got a clear mismatch and you need to address it. Again, work up to asking for what you want. Encourage them to change positions, say you want to feel this kind of touch and that kind of touch, or that you want them to cum in a certain place. Just work on incorporating these easy prompts into sex until it feels OK to tell them: 'I want to feel your mouth on my pussy again.'

I talked in Chapter 4: Sexual Identity about how most of us get taught a pretty basic and limited idea of sex and how this can lead to us having set expectations that might not actually work for us (see page 58). Basically, if you or your partner is following a 'script' in sex then you're going to really struggle to find your compatibility, because instead of treating each other as individuals and being curious about each other, you're treating sex like a tick-box exercise. Five minutes of foreplay done, then twenty minutes of penetration is not good sex. It's shit sex, to be honest.

And when was the last time a tick-box survey made you cum? One of the key things we can do, then, to work out if we're sexually compatible is to ditch these scripts and go into each new sexual encounter with a fresh outlook, open-minded about what you might do together. What your former sexual partner enjoyed isn't guaranteed to be what your new one likes.

How to find out if you're compatible

Sometimes you can figure out whether you're sexually compatible quite easily. If you're flirting, sharing fantasies, having that 'sex before sex' I talked about in Chapter 6: What Kind of Sex Should We Be Having? (see page 120) and there's a lot of agreement (or at least enthusiasm and curiosity), and you both seem interested in the same things, it's a pretty good indicator that you're on the same page sexually. This is why I'm such a huge advocate for talking about sex. Studies have also shown that couples who talk openly about sex report higher levels of sexual satisfaction.[1] It really is the best way to find out if you're going to be a good match for each other in bed.

You might remember in Chapter 4: Sexual Identity I talked about sex menus and how they can be a good way to start thinking about what you're interested in and where your sexual boundaries are (see page 68). Well, needless to say they can also be a really good indicator of compatibility. There are lots of ways you could use one with a partner. You could both fill them in separately and then swap to see what you match up on, but that sounds a bit cold and clinical to me.

I know a girl who matched with a guy on an app and he offered to send her his sex menu *before they'd even met.* I mean, maybe that's gonna work for some people but this girl did not find it sexy at all and neither would I. I think a better way to do it would be to maybe go through the list together and talk about each thing. It doesn't have to be deadly serious. Being able to joke about sex and laugh about things you're *not* into is also a good way to establish compatibility.

If pen and paper isn't your thing, you could try sexual fantasy apps, which present you with various different sexual scenarios and fantasies and you can swipe depending on how interesting or arousing they sound to you. You and your partner can sync your accounts and it'll show you which ones you match on. The good thing about this is it takes the pressure off the conversation and turns it into more of a game.

Speaking of games, you can also get sexy card games that help you talk dirty and ask each other questions about likes and dislikes in a fun, low-stakes way. You draw a card, which might say something like, 'I want you to cum all over my ...' and you have to finish the sentence. Or it might say, 'Do you prefer to be touched like this ... or like this ...?' and it's up to you to decide what kind of touch you use. Again, because it's a game it can really open up the opportunity to explore without feeling awkward. And if something doesn't work or you're not into it, it's not on either of you because you were just playing a game.

Similarly, you could try a set of sex dice. Often you'll have one dice that has actions and activities written on it, such as 'kiss', 'lick', 'massage', 'tease', and another dice that lists body parts. You take it in turns to roll the dice and whatever combination comes up, you have to do it to your partner. As always, make sure you get consent, but because the idea is coming from the dice, rather than from you, it makes it easier to have fun and not get too stressed about it.

If you're up for it, why not have a sex-toy shopping date night? Before or after dinner, go sex-toy shopping and ask your partner what they think of different toys and restraints. Ask questions to see what they'd be open to and what their boundaries are. No one's saying you have to like everything your partner is into, or that they need to love everything you enjoy, but there should be room for a lot of mutual likes.

Do our libidos match?

How often we want sex and what we need to get us in the mood can be a big part of whether or not we feel sexually compatible with our partners. I get so many messages from women saying that they don't think their sex drive matches up with their partner's and I agree, it really matters. Nobody wants to feel like they're begging for sex, and similarly, nobody wants to be pestered for sex when they're just trying to get some rest. After a while it can start to feel like maybe you're just not compatible.

But it's important to understand that 'sex drive' is not a fixed thing, even though we like to talk about it as if it is. Once again, this idea comes from turn-of-the-twentieth-century psychoanalyst Sigmund Freud. He wrote about libido as if it was a constant force,[2] like hunger or thirst, which kicks in as a response to a basic need, and that idea has stuck around for more than a century now. But in reality, it isn't like that at all. If we forgot to eat or drink for several weeks we would die, or at least get pretty ill. That's why we have hunger and thirst drives, letting us know when it's time for a snack or a cup of tea. If we go for a couple of weeks without sex, what happens? Nothing. OK, you might feel sexually frustrated, but if you're busy and have other things going on in your life, you might not even notice.

Libido can come and go depending on circumstances, moods, hormones, overall health and lifestyle. On a good day, when we've had plenty of sleep and work isn't stressing us out, we might be DTF, but feeling exhausted, anxious, depressed or just being very busy and having a lot on our minds can completely suffocate our libido, so we don't feel even slightly horny.

Life events can affect it, too. Loads of people reported feeling less horny during the pandemic lockdowns, for example.[3] And it's well documented that having a baby can lead to a drop in sex drive.[4] But again, none of these experiences are permanent. And for most of us, our libidos will rise and fall at different stages throughout our lives.

So just because you and your partner are experiencing different levels of desire *right now*, that doesn't mean it's always going to be this way. However, it's a good idea to talk about it to see if there is something specific that's affecting you, and whether that's something you can work around or if you might just need to wait it out.

A difference in sex drive could also be down to the fact that your libidos respond differently to different things. I explained the dual control model of sexual response in Chapter 4: Sexual Identity – you remember, the sexual 'brakes' and 'accelerators' (see page 64)? Basically, our level of desire depends on the balance between what's turning us on and what's turning us off at any time. Those things are different for everyone, so while a stressful day in the office might not inhibit *your* sex drive, your partner might find themselves needing a bit more time to unwind and get into the zone before they're up for sex. It doesn't necessarily mean you're incompatible, but it might mean you need to spend some time figuring out what your 'ons' and 'offs' are so you can help each other get in the mood.

Sometimes this stuff can actually be quite an important clue that someone isn't right for us. Let's say you've figured out that using a computer all day and then being on your phone in the evening puts the brakes on your libido (and if so, you're definitely not alone – a lot has been written about the possible links between screen time and sex drive in recent years,[5] and a 2017 study suggested that regular gaming can lead to a drop in libido in men).[6] What you probably need is for you and your partner to put your devices to one side so you guys can have some quality time together, whether it's talking, cooking and eating dinner, or just doing something *other than* looking at a screen. So if the person you're dating thinks a romantic night involves being curled up on the sofa with you, half watching a show, half scrolling on their phone (or, worse, they want you to go over and hang out while they play FIFA!), that's probably a decent sign that you're not that compatible. Especially if they're expecting you to go from sofa slob to sex bomb as soon as they put down the remote.

Now, I'm not saying there's no space for Netflix in a relationship (although, honestly, the FIFA thing is never OK), but if the person you're dating won't help you address the things that hit your brakes and accelerators, or just expects your sex drive to magically work the same way theirs does ... I'm gonna go ahead and say you might not be compatible.

Similarly, some of us need a bit of time and attention to get really horned up for sex and if a partner isn't prepared to put in that time, that can be a sign of a mismatch. I go on about the importance of foreplay and talking about sex before you get into the bedroom, but that's because it can be a really important part of how our sex drive works. See, people experience desire differently. Some of us have what's known as 'spontaneous desire', which is where you feel horny seemingly out of the blue. Just momentarily thinking about sex can be enough. But others are more likely to experience what Canadian psychiatrist Rosemary Basson labelled 'responsive desire'. She noted that for lots of people (and particularly women) horniness tends to amp up a bit later, once they've actually started getting down and dirty, as illustrated in the diagram below.[7]

Basically, a lot of people actually start out feeling kind of neutral about sex. But if they're open to engaging with sexual stimuli, whether that's porn or sexting or listening to audio erotica or talking dirty, or even getting physical with their partners, they find that they do start to feel sexually aroused and *then* the libido kicks in and it starts to feel less like a case of 'sure, I guess we could' and more like the 'absolutely gagging for it' feeling we associate with high sex drive.

Again, this is a totally normal and very common way to experience sex drive, especially if you're in a long-term relationship. It's not a sign of having a 'low' sex drive, and it doesn't necessarily mean you and your partner are incompatible, it just means your libidos work a bit differently. So as long as you can navigate that together there's no reason why you shouldn't be able to stir up that chemistry and act out all your wildest, filthiest fantasies. What *will*

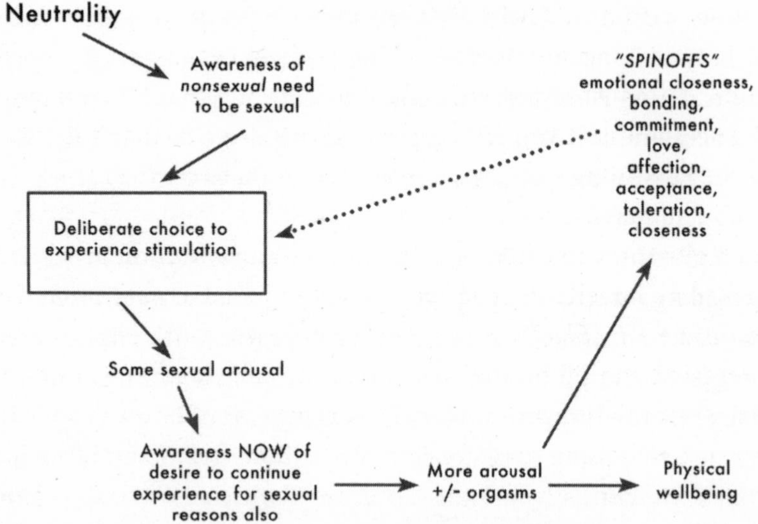

lead to incompatibility is if you and your partner aren't willing to engage with how each other's libidos work and just expect the sex to automatically happen without putting in any effort.

Speaking of long-term relationships, one reason they can start off really hot and then lose their spark is because of the novelty factor. It's a huge part of what turns us on – in all contexts, actually, not just sex. Humans have a very strong attraction to novelty; our brains are hard-wired to appreciate it and seek it out,[8] whether it's wearing new clothes, travelling to new places, checking out new bars and brunch spots, getting hyped for a new Cardi B album, changing our hair, meeting new sexual partners or just trying out new things in the bedroom. It's actually a survival skill. If we can't handle novelty, we can't adapt and cope with change. But most of the time it's something we associate with pleasure. Of course, like everything, it's a spectrum. Some of us thrive on familiarity and only need a little bit of novelty in our lives to be content. Others have a much higher need for novelty. You know your hypebeast friends? Or the ones who are constantly trying to drag you out to some new bar or club? Or who genuinely love dating and seem to have a new partner every month? I'm not saying there's anything wrong with this (although research shows *very* high levels of novelty-seeking are associated with risky behaviour and addiction),[9,10] I'm just saying we're all different.

The point is, if you felt like you were really sexually compatible in the beginning but things have started to drop off a bit – maybe you're not having sex as much as you used to or maybe things have got a bit samey in the bedroom – it might just be because you need a bit more novelty in your relationship. I'm not saying you have to go full-on *Fifty Shades of Grey* (although it's not a bad idea if you're interested and I'll be sharing some tips on how to introduce kink into your relationship in Chapter 13: Kinks, Fetishes and BDSM), but just switching up your date-night routine could help you feel that excitement again and get you both in the mood to be sexually creative.

How much sex is enough?

You tell me! If we've learned anything in this book it's that our sexual needs are all different. What one person considers plenty of sex might feel like a veritable desert to someone else. And just like libido, the amount of sex we want can change over time and with our circumstances. I don't think any of us needs a scientific study to tell us that we tend to have more sex at the start of a new relationship. Like, *at every opportunity*, am I right? And sometimes when there isn't really a good opportunity, too. If you've ever dragged the person you're dating into the toilets at a party or tried to get it on with them in a side street on the way home you'll know the kind of energy I'm talking about!

This is partly down to the novelty factor I mentioned earlier. But as time goes on and we've been dating a while, we tend to settle into a bit more of a pattern. The most recent large-scale survey of sex lives in the UK shows that the average person has sex a little bit less than once a week (or approximately three times a month).[11]

Whether this feels like enough to be fulfilling depends on you. Research shows that around 50 per cent of women say they'd like to have more sex than they are currently having,[12] and that definitely tallies with what *I* hear from the women I interact with daily.

If you are in a relationship and the amount of sex you're having doesn't feel like enough for you, it might be down to your sex drives working differently. As discussed earlier, there are lots of ways you can navigate this. But it might be because the sex you *are* having isn't fulfilling you so you're craving more. The problem is, you might not be craving more in terms of quantity but in terms of quality. So when it comes to figuring out whether the amount of sex you're having is enough for you, you need to ask yourself this question: *what is it you want out of sex that you think having more would provide?*

If the answer is sexual pleasure and orgasms then it might be that you can get that through masturbation. Maybe it's time to treat yourself to a new sex toy? If the answer is about being intimate with your partner then maybe there are other ways you could do that, too. But if the answer is that you're looking for more excitement, more novelty, more adventure, then it's not the frequency you need to address, it's the sex itself.

How to initiate sex

Initiating sex as a straight cishet woman can sometimes feel a bit intimidating if you're not used to it. It can be daunting, especially when we live in a world that says men are meant to take the lead in the bedroom, but that's not true! In fact, studies have shown that women are initiating sex more than ever before.[13] However, it doesn't change the fact that I still have many women ask me how to do so and I've heard some men complain that their girlfriends don't do it at all. Initiating sex with your lover can be a turn on for them. It's also a reminder of your attraction for each other. Men enjoy being desired, too, so below are some tips to help you with initiating intimacy.

Before seeing your partner, start by doing something on your own that boosts your confidence and makes you feel sexy af. This could be playing your favourite music video that lets you tap into a more seductive side of yourself as you dance in front of a mirror. Mine would be 'Ego' by Beyoncé; the lyrics and the video exude sex appeal, and after a glass of wine I'll be able to convince you I know the choreography (I don't). Try wearing something that you find hot – it can be lingerie or a sexy loungewear set: think crop tops and shorts that show off your ass. Whatever makes you feel sexy helps turn up the temperature, so wear it!

It's also vital that you pay attention to the situation by reading the room before trying to initiate sex. If your partner has just got some bad news, that's not the moment to try sucking their dick. Everybody is more in the mood when they're relaxed, like when they're watching a movie they've seen a hundred times – it's called Netflix and chill for a reason! Suitable moments might be when you're having a light and funny conversation, after a date night, during a shower together, when you're cuddling in bed – do you get the idea?

If you're in the bedroom and they're in the front room, send a risqué, flirty, fun text. It could be as simple as 'I'm horny', 'Come to the bedroom, I have a surprise for you' or 'I learned this new trick with my mouth, wanna see it?' You might just want to send some eggplant, water drip and peach emojis with a purple devil smiling. Text what makes you comfortable but also makes it clear that you're ready to get nasty.

In different situations you can offer or ask for a massage. Be playful with your partner. Make strong eye contact as you take their hands to softly caress parts of your body, like on the side of your breast or inside your thighs. And kissing! A good kissing session that you have started is sometimes all you need to let your partner know that YOU desire them and want to have sex.

These methods are not only initiating sex; they are also a form of foreplay that can help add a level of newness to your sexual relationship, especially if you hardly ever do the initiating. It's also vital to remember to switch it up and cater to the style you know your partner would really enjoy. I'm most likely to send a dirty text to my boyfriend if he's at work to prepare him for what's to come once he's home. I also know he enjoys my innuendos, as well as my direct approach in person, so test out different ways to initiate with your partner and see what they respond to best.

Speaking of dirty texting, sexting is a steamy way to tease and explore with your sexual partner. It allows you to fantasise about each other when you're not together and keeps them on their toes. It can be as sensual or graphically dirty as you like, but it's usually best to start off soft. Try, 'I'm thinking about what I'd love to do to you if you were with me right now.' Or refer back to a moment you've shared with: 'I can't wait to feel your hard-on again.' Check out my guide to dirty talking below for more tips on this. Don't take too long to reply and try to keep it hot and sexy!

Sexting is fun, especially when the other person is just as into it as you – there's nothing worse than dirty texting with someone who's giving it 30 per cent energy while you're giving it 100 per cent as you talk about what positions you'd like to be bent into. I guess sexting compatibility might be a thing, too!

Of course, sometimes words on a screen might not be enough. You might really want to show off your new crotchless knickers or that racy new balconet bra that makes your tits looking amazing! I get it, I get it, you want to give them something they can't forget and is worth over a thousand words, but again, you must ask for permission to share any sort of nudes. If you do want to send nudes and really trust the person (really, really trust them) go for it. See Chapter 6: What Kind of Sex Should We Be Having? for some tips on how to do this (see page 148).

Phone sex is another way to add some spice to your sex routine – again, take a look at my guide to dirty talking below to get you started. You want the conversation to be as sexually descriptive and pleasurable for both of you. The aim might be to allow your partner to fantasise or join you as you masturbate, so you might need your sex toy. Phone sex doesn't always have to lead to orgasms, but if it does then extra kudos! Sex over the phone can be the 'sex before sex' on a filthier level, which you enjoy because you're simply horny or want to some sexual attention.

Not everyone is into phone sex, and some people are just afraid they'll just suck at it, but relaxing and practising with someone who makes you feel comfortable can really help. It's also best not to just dive in the deep end, but to allow the conversation to naturally progress into it, and once you get used to that, who knows? You might want to try sex video calling ...

The Big O guide to dirty talk

Consent is always mandatory so find out if they're into dirty talk or if they'd like to try it first. An example: 'I've had some dirty thoughts about you. Can I share them with you?'

Before sex, you might want to prepare them for what you're like between the sheets and say something along the lines of: 'When getting down and dirty I do enjoy saying a lot of sexual things. What about you?' Start off soft and playful, describing what you'd want to do to them or what you're currently doing to yourself: 'Can I tell you what part of my body I'm playing with?' Alternatively, you can flip it and ask them what body part they'd like to feel if they were with you right then. Ask questions about what they'd like to tick off their sex bucket list, their wildest sexual fantasies, their kinks, their favourite porn category.

Tease your partner with your words: 'I can't wait to watch you eat it again.' Bounce off what they respond with and ask more questions, allowing them to fantasise and get adventurous: 'What are you going to do to me when we fuck again?' Tailor the questions to your situation, so if you haven't had sex yet, try 'I can't wait to watch my hands wrapped around your dick,' or 'I'm going to have so much fun with your dick sliding in and out of my ...'

This would also be a good time to share what you like and dislike being said during intimacy, such as, 'It would really turn me on if you whispered in my ears how my pussy feels when you're inside of me,' or, 'I want you to call me a slut in the bedroom.'

You could also mention your dislikes, such as: 'I love dirty talk but, please don't call me a bitch; it completely shuts me down,' or, 'I don't mind a bit of soft dirty talk but please don't go too far.' You can mention this during sex – 'Don't say that, tell me how I feel instead' – or after sex: 'When we have sex next can you please not call me a slut? I don't like it.'

It's important to note that some women enjoy being called degrading names in the bedroom. Some also have a praise kink, which I describe in Chapter 12 (see page 301). Fuck, I'm one of them! I take pleasure in being referred to by several filthy names, as well as soft, sweet things, but not all women do and have no idea how to combat that issue. We all have things that work for us and it's important to find out what those things are so our boundaries don't get crossed.

Below are some ideas to help you with dirty talking during sex. Use what works for you by experimenting and adding your own personal touch and choice of words.

Soft

I love it when you touch me here.

Use the head of your dick to rub on my clitoris gently.

Tell me how I feel.

Is it wet enough for you?

Kiss me on my neck as you're inside of me.

Play with my nipples.
Kiss me more.
Finger me slowly.
You make me so wet.
Use the vibrator to play with my clitoris.
Do you like it?
Rub some more lube on my pussy.
Do you want me to keep going?

Medium

I like it when you look at me when you're deep inside of me.
Suck on my clit and finger me slowly.
I want every inch of you.
What about me turns you on?
Suck and lick my clitoris.
I want to ride your face.
Lightly slap my ass.
Keep fucking me like that.
I want to watch you play with yourself.

Hard

I want you to nut all over my breasts/ass.
Tell me a dirty fantasy while you're fucking me.
I love when you go deep, but now use your fingers to play with my clit.
Would you like me to swallow or spit?
I want to feel your tongue in my ass.
I'm going to suck every drop of nut out of you.
I want to be your slut.
I can't wait to taste myself on your dick.
Suck on my tits as you deep stroke me.

What if we're just not compatible?

So many of the dilemmas I get sent end with a version of this exact question. *What if we're just not sexually compatible?* What if you try absolutely everything and the sex is still only average? It's a tough one to answer because on the one hand, I stand by everything I've said in this chapter. Usually there's a reason why you're not managing to connect intimately, and that reason can be addressed. But on the other hand, if you've been trying and trying and it's still not happening, you've got to ask yourself if it's worth it.

Maybe it is! Maybe you feel like you're really compatible in other ways and so you want to persevere. Some boxes are bigger than others when it comes to overall compatibility, and if sex isn't the biggest box, that's fine! Maybe there are some areas of sex you feel like you're compatible in but not others, and you're willing to make this compromise. Maybe you've decided that, on balance, the sex isn't that big a deal.

If it *is* a big deal, though, what then?

I'd love to tell you there's a way to find your sexual compatibility with everyone, but you know what? Sometimes it just isn't there to be found. Or maybe it *could* be found if you really tried, but, honestly, can you be arsed? Why not just find someone who you are compatible with? Do you really want to be giving away your best years of fucking to a partner who you aren't clicking with and who isn't stepping it up? Don't get me wrong, I am hoping a lot of men will read this book and educate themselves as they should, but I have to face the reality that the majority of my audience are straight and bi women and sometimes I do wonder why this shit is always on us. Why is it always down to us to learn about our sexuality, understand our libido and get good at communicating? Meanwhile guys just get to sit about, exist and wait to try out the finished product? Nah. It is not all on you to make the chemistry happen. So unless he's also going to put in the effort, it might be time to call it a day.

Oloni's tips for how to speak up and improve compatibility issues

- Practise by yourself – try saying things out loud in the mirror. Hearing your own voice, even if you're only talking to yourself, can help you get used to the idea of saying it to another person.
- Use this book to start a conversation! One of the best ways to start speaking up about what you're interested in is to take yourself and your partner out of the equation for a minute and just talk about the subject of sex. Saying, 'Hey, I read this in Oloni's book,' or 'I heard this on a podcast,' feels way less scary and gives you a chance to ask them what they think about it in a more neutral way.
- Turn it into a game. Obviously you can do this literally with the card games or sex dice mentioned earlier (see page 242), but you can also just take it in turns to tell each other a horny fantasy on the promise that you're gonna listen and learn and not judge. The talking itself can be great foreplay and you'll soon start to pick up on the areas where your fantasies overlap.
- Role-play. If you're craving to sit on his face but can't bring yourself to ask, how about a little role-play? It can be much easier to ask for things and explore new sexual territory if you're in character. You don't have to go all out with costumes (unless you want to!). You can just say, 'Hey, baby, what if we played a game where I'm in charge tonight?' and then use your dominant alt to bust out those moves you've been too nervous to try. Don't forget consent, though. Even if you both agree to the role, you still need to check in to make sure everyone's OK with what's happening.

- Take it out of the bedroom. We are extra vulnerable when we're having sex so if speaking up about what you want feels too difficult in the moment, find another time to start the conversation when things feel less loaded.
- Make a habit of it. If you get used to doing something regularly, it will start to feel like second nature and you won't even think twice about it. For example, studies show that people who use condoms regularly are no less likely to remember to use them when drunk.[14] Why? Because it's just a habit. It's not something they really have to think about consciously; they just do it. You can do this for communication, too – if you make a habit of asking every new partner, 'How do you like to be touched?' or telling them, 'Let me show you how I like to be touched,' it will soon stop feeling awkward and just become part of sex.

CHAPTER 11

Casual Sex

'I always tell the girls never take it seriously, if you never take it seriously you never get hurt, if you never get hurt you always have fun, and if you ever get lonely just go to the record store and visit your friends.'

Penny Lane, *Almost Famous*

Growing up, I was taught that sex was something you *only* did within the context of marriage. And even then, you weren't really supposed to have fun. Sex, according to my parents' understanding of Christianity, was for procreation. That was it. The idea that people might have sex for ... **gasps** ... pleasure was basically non-existent.

So you can imagine how mind-blowing it was for teenage me to discover shows like *Sex and the City* and *Girlfriends* in the late Nineties and early Noughties, which presented a very different picture. Contrary to what my parents had led me to believe, people absolutely *were* having sex for pleasure, and they were absolutely *not* married to their partners. Half the time, they weren't even in committed relationships with them. What's more, they didn't seem like they were being punished for this behaviour, either by society or their community.

There's a lot that's problematic about *SATC* when you watch it now, and the characters in *Girlfriends* weren't always totally supportive of each other's sexcapades, but I can't deny the impact the shows, their themes and storylines had on me at that age. In fact, *Girlfriends* is the first place I ever heard the term 'sexually liberated' and I won't lie, it spoke to me!

Turns out you could not only have casual sex, you could have a *really good time* doing it! This was big news.

Over the years I've had various experiences of casual sex and don't get me wrong, they were not all good! I'm not going to sit here and tell you every single casual hook-up I've had has been amazing. But when casual sex is done right, it can be fun, pleasurable, mutually appreciative, respectful, exciting, exhilarating and even life-affirming. The problem is, a lot of people are *not* doing it right.

One of the reasons people get casual sex wrong is because they're still buying into the myths around it. OK, maybe you don't *actually* believe that sex outside of marriage is a sin, but I think deep down a lot of people do see casual sex as a 'lesser' form of sex. They see it as a low-grade version, a consolation prize, the thing you accept when you can't get the Real Thing, which is a relationship.

Of course, I completely agree that settling for casual sex with someone you'd really like to be in a relationship with is a bad situation. We've all been there. That shit definitely feels like a consolation prize. But I also think a lot of us have been socialised to believe we *should* want a relationship with everyone we fuck, and that can trick us into thinking that casual arrangements such as hook-ups or friends-with-benefits are a failure of some sort.

It makes sense. I told you at the start that my mum's three goals for me growing up were that I learned to cook, went to university and found a husband. So *of course* there was a part of me that felt like that was the aim of any romantic or sexual encounter. And I think deep down a lot of us are doing the same thing. Consciously or unconsciously, we're thinking we need to try to maximise every opportunity, believing that we should be trying to turn every interaction into a relationship. And that's the part I have a problem with.

Because casual relationships can be valuable, too! Let's think about it in terms of friends. You have your best friends, the girls you're closest to, the ones who know *everything*, from your deepest secrets to how many vibrators you have stashed away (OK, I admit, most people in the UK know that fact about me!). You trust them with your life, with your money, even with your man. But then you've also got people like your work colleagues. Now, these can be great relationships. You have good conversations; you get lunch sometimes, and drinks; you can make each other laugh. But 'Olivia from work' is not the one who's going to come over to get drunk and high with you after a break-up or be brutally honest with you when you're spiralling out over some guy. And that's OK. It's a different kind of relationship. You might not have the same emotional intimacy with Olivia as you do with your best friends, but that doesn't mean you don't have mutual respect and genuine affection for each other.

The same can be true of casual sex. Just because it's not a romantic relationship doesn't mean it doesn't count. It's still a relationship, it's just a different sort of relationship. It might be a friendship where you spend time together and get to know a bit about each other's lives (and I'll talk a bit more about how to manage friends-with-benefits in a moment), or it might just be two people who have a laugh and some hot sex but otherwise don't really hang out much. It could just be a one-time hook-up or an occasional booty call – it's still a social interaction with another human with the potential to make us feel good, and that has value!

We've been taught that relationships are all or nothing, but I'm here to tell you that's bullshit. It's not a choice between true love and not giving a fuck. There's so much in between that can bring a lot of fun and pleasure, if we give ourselves permission to enjoy it for what it is.

The other big barrier to embracing casual sex is that it's still seen by a lot of people as trashy. The people who have it are viewed as cheap or slutty. At least, that's how it is for women. As usual, men are not held to the same standards. It's completely fine for men to go out and have as much casual sex as they like, and I'll come back to that later. But the point I want to make is that if you're going into casual sex and treating it (or your partner) as something that doesn't matter, something lesser, if you have shame around it or have been made to feel that it devalues you, then I guarantee you are not going to have a good time.

And if you're not having a good time, you are missing the entire point of casual sex.

The joy of casual sex

Now that we've established that 'casual' does not mean 'inferior' (and I hope we do all agree on that now!), we can talk a bit about what's *so fucking good* about casual sex. Because if we can let go of all the stigma around it and all the bullshit we've internalised, there are so many genuine benefits to having a casual partner.

The beauty of casual sex is that you can Really. Just. Concentrate. On. The. Sex. You don't have to worry about all the relationship admin, you can just focus on getting as much fun and filth out of it as possible.

For a lot of people, casual sex can also be an opportunity to be a bit different, to unleash a bit of nastiness. Not that you can't be nasty in a relationship, but let's be honest, when you're with someone for a long time and having a lot of regular sex with them, most of that sex is going to be pretty vanilla. And that's no shade on relationship sex, because that can be really, really good in its own way. When you're in a relationship, you have the opportunity to get really in sync with one another, to get to know all the other's likes and dislikes and the little tricks that are guaranteed to turn them on. You can develop a whole language and understanding, and there are times when you *just know* that something is going to press your partner's buttons, and that can be beautiful. But sometimes we can get a bit reliant on that knowledge ... we can get a bit complacent ... look, you know what I'm saying! Don't make me use the word 'lazy'! I'm not trying to imply that. I just mean that we don't always go all out.

Casual sex, on the other hand, feels like more of a chance to get creative, to throw everything we have at the encounter. Apart from anything else, we don't know for sure if it's going to happen again. Even if it's happening regularly, there's no guarantee it's going to last, so we might as well make the most of it. If I'm having casual sex with you, that's our time to get nasty!

And I know I'm not the only person to feel this way. Dr Karen Gurney talks about this in *her* book *Mind the Gap: The Truth About Desire and How to Futureproof Your Sex Life.* She points out that long-term relationships can sometimes feel constraining. If you want to bust out some new moves or try out a different persona during sex (let's say you're normally pretty submissive but one night you're just feeling really dominant and you want to take the lead), that can feel awkward with a partner who knows you really well. They might be taken aback, they might make you feel weird for acting unlike your usual self or even wonder where you got your new ideas from. But in a casual situation, you're basically a blank slate. You can be whoever you want because that person doesn't know you in the same way. They don't have any particular expectations of you. And this, says Dr Gurney, 'can allow us to feel less self-conscious ... this freedom can allow a greater variety in expression our sexual selves'.[1]

Obviously that's not true for everyone. Lots of people feel freer to express themselves when they're in a secure relationship. But casual sex can be really fucking liberating if you lean into its benefits.

Unfortunately, there are still a lot of things we're getting wrong.

Numbers mean nothing

For a lot of people, casual sex can feel like a bit of a numbers game. I think a lot of women have been led to believe that their 'body count' really matters and they worry that having a lot of casual sex is going to rack up that score. Now, first of all, ladies, if it really bothers you, remember *you can just lie!* Now, I know some would disagree with that statement, so before you screenshot that section to me in a tweet that I'll ignore, let me explain.

You may think that telling people to lie is the opposite of being sex-positive, and I understand why. I've had women and men argue that if we're truly meant to take pride in sexual liberation why on earth would we lie? The answer is simple: survival. I agree, we shouldn't *have* to lie. Believe me, I'd love it if we could live in a world where men and women didn't weaponise the sexual experiences of other women, but sadly that's not the reality.

Let's take it back to my first real understanding of slut-shaming. I remember at secondary school in Year 11 when rumour got around that this girl in our year had given head in the boys' toilets. From then on the boy in question was seen as a kind of hero, while she always hung her head down in shame. I remember how the other boys in our year would look for any opportunity to taunt her. They'd worm the word 'head' into a conversation ever so loudly when speaking around or to her, to deliberately cause embarrassment and shame. I'm sure we all know of similar stories. And even now, as an adult, I think many people still have the same mentality today, just in older and unevolved minds.

I create content where I constantly encourage and teach women how to have sex for themselves, by decentring men and exploring their sexuality. If you've followed me for long enough on Twitter, you'll have noticed the insults I'm usually met with. 'She's teaching women to be a slut', 'She doesn't want women to respect themselves' – sadly, this is the mentality of a lot of people. If I had a shot for every time I saw or heard a person compare a woman to an object when discussing why she shouldn't sleep with more than three men ... well, I'd probably be passed out drunk right now, instead of writing this chapter.

Women's reputations have been ruined because they dared to have consensual sex. Women have been coerced into sex because a rumour got around that she was 'easy'. So I'll say it again: if YOU want to, you can lie.

In a world where women can actually be killed for not being a virgin, it makes sense that some would want to withhold the truth about their sexual history, for the sake of peace and safety. We forget that the honesty people so desperately want from women about their past is rooted in privilege at times. A man will not have his reputation tarnished if he's thought to have slept with several women; instead, he's praised. True, for many women who live in the West, the reality is not as harsh as for those living in more conservative parts of the world. But it's easy to scream about how important honesty is when you aren't dealing with the repercussions of a judgemental community.

I value honesty in sex and relationships. When you're talking about STIs, how many kids you have, whether or not you're sleeping with other people, I completely agree that honesty is important. However, if you are with a guy who thinks he needs to ask this question(which may be a red flag for many, but not everyone), what's the issue? Are you suddenly pretending you've never fibbed before?

(Also, can we take a moment here to talk about how **interesting** it is that men are hardly ever bothered about the bi experiences women have had?! The question is never about that, is it? This can be considered within the frame of biphobia because other women are not seen as a 'threat'. It's just another example of how misogynistic the entire concept is. If a guy says 'women don't count', he's revealed his true colours.)

I'd love a world where we could be honest, and if I'm real the older I got the more I didn't feel the need to lie if the question of sexual partners came up in a random conversation. Even though I dislike the subject of 'body count' altogether, talking about it does at least show me the type of guy I'm dealing with. A judgemental prick? Or a man who understands that women like sex, too?

But let's take a moment to remember that these tropes can have a negative impact on guys, too. I had a friend in university whose mates used to call him 'No tally', which meant that he wasn't sleeping with many women. And they shamed him for that. As a guy, he was supposed to be upping his body count, getting notches on his bedpost. At the time I didn't think much of it. I probably just assumed he couldn't get laid, but when I think about it now I wonder if he even wanted that. For men, there's this big pressure to be having loads of sex with loads of different people, and if you're not doing that people start to take the piss and question your masculinity. That's not good for guys' mental health any more than feeling the pressure to shut down your sexuality is good for women's mental health.

We don't all grow up being sex-positive; it takes time to learn lessons, discover and feel comfortable. If you're not at a point where you can talk about all the men and women you've had sex with, that's OK. Likewise, we can call ourselves 'sex-positive' but does it really mean anything if everyone else still has a set idea about sex and how it's supposed to go down? It can feel really hard to push back against these assumptions, but I think we have to if we want to live our best shame-free sex lives. We have to just keep reminding ourselves, our friends and our partners that these beliefs are just that: beliefs. And while we can't change everyone around us, we *can* change what we choose to believe.

Women aren't cut out for casual sex? Oh, please!

The other thing people get wrong all the time is buying into the idea that casual sex is natural for men and not for women. Something I hear a lot from guys is that there's a 'lock and key' situation. I did a talk at a university once and afterwards this guy said to me that it wasn't the same for men and women because men were like keys – they had the potential to fit in many locks – whereas women were like locks – only one key would work for them.

Also, this metaphor doesn't actually make sense. Most keys are cut to fit just one lock. Furthermore, it's possible to get multiple keys cut for the same lock (I have three house keys so .... I don't know what that's saying about my vagina). But it's an idea you hear a lot: that men are 'designed' to sleep around and women are just naturally more suited to monogamy. But guess what? There's pretty much no evidence for this whatsoever. People have tried and tried to prove that men are 'naturally' more promiscuous, and they just can't do it! In fact, what keeps showing up in the research is that both men and women are programmed to seek short-term mates *as well as* long-term bonded partners.[2]

People will also tell you that men are evolutionarily hard-wired to seek multiple partners, but they are missing a crucial fact. Yes, it's true that men can theoretically get a woman pregnant at any time, but women can only get pregnant once a month when they are fertile. Does it therefore make sense for her to only have one partner? Actually, no. It would make more sense for her to have as many different partners as possible during that time (not least because most men can't manage more than a few rounds!).

It isn't just me saying this! Anthropologists who study the way humans live and how we have formed societies over thousands of years agree that it is much more likely that our natural state is to be 'cooperative breeders'.[3] This means we developed to live and raise children, not in ones and twos, but in larger social groups – collectively. This doesn't sound too shocking, does it? Admittedly in London where I live, and in the UK generally, most people still live in family units. But we don't have to stretch our imagination too far to think of examples where, to a greater or lesser extent, we can find people living in communities, sharing resources and looking after each other's kids. But here's the interesting part: there's also evidence that this kind of social set-up would have included 'multiple mating' – or what society calls sleeping around! In her book *Untrue: Why Nearly Everything We Believe About Women, Lust, and Infidelity Is Wrong and How the New Science Can Set Us Free,* anthropologist Wednesday Martin writes that 'multiple mating established and reinforced social bonds, so that there were low levels of conflict'.

Yeah, you read that correctly. Fucking around can actually make our lives better!

But only if we approach it with a 'cooperative' attitude, and all too often that's the bit people get wrong. It's not uncommon at all to hear men talking disrespectfully about the women they've had casual sex with, treating them as conquests instead of equal partners. I always find myself thinking of that Future track 'My Collection'. Do you know the one I mean? In it, he goes, 'Any time I got you, girl you my possession / Even if I hit you once, you part of my collection.'

I love hip-hop and I won't pretend I haven't danced to that track, or that I don't sometimes enjoy those kinds of lyrics (even though I know full well it's slut-shaming). But this line kind of got to me when I first heard it. I couldn't stop thinking about it, and it made me think that that's actually how a lot of men think. They believe that once they've fucked you, your value goes down. Now I know you know that's not true. Even if you're a guy reading this, I'm pretty sure you don't *really* believe that. I mean, even the fact that you picked up this book tells me you've got some questions about this whole thing, right?! OK, good. Well, I have some questions for you:

What I want to know is, why do guys *want* to be someone who taints their sexual partners? Why do they *want* to be someone who uses people? Do you enjoy being seen as the bad guy among your friends? And if so, why? Why do you consider it an achievement to be the person who cares the least in a sexual interaction? Why, in a world where God knows we have enough problems, do you see being a dick as a good thing?

There are times in this book when I feel like I'm being pessimistic and really down on men. I don't mean to be. I just want to make sure I'm not making it sound like this shit is easy and that if you can't make it work that's on you. Navigating this stuff is hard and on the one hand I want to be like, 'Free it up, ladies!' But on the other hand I feel like we need to talk about this side of it. It's complicated. If the things I've been talking about here are what put you off casual sex, I get that. I'll never tell a woman what to do with her body or tell a guy what to do with his body, but if you *do* want casual sex to be a part of your life then I think you have every right to try to make it work for you.

The hoe phase

I think the term 'hoe phase' just exists to make ourselves feel better about the slutty choices we're about to indulge in. You see, in my opinion there is no such thing as a 'hoe phase'; it's more of a 'I want to temporarily unsubscribe from society's standards on where my pussy ends up' phase and, hey, there's nothing wrong with that. Free it up; don't free it up. What's important is how you feel when you're having these experiences and why you're doing it.

I think a lot of women I grew up with had this phase because they wanted new sexual experiences and enjoyed the rush of random hook-ups and sex with no strings attached. Casual sex empowers women to have agency over their sexual decisions in a society that dictates them for us before we even get a say. It can help us figure out how we enjoy sex and what gets us off during sex, and it can be pretty fucking exciting.

I think about some of the hoe phases I've had and the reasons I've had them have been various, but the main one was usually because I enjoyed sexual attention from people I was really attracted to. Knowing that I could sleep with someone I've experienced sexual tension with, without having to deal with the responsibility of being in a relationship or dating, is in itself exciting. Instead you can just enjoy the moment and the random scenarios that might be involved.

There was a time I hooked up with a guy who'd taken me out to dinner. All I thought was, 'This guy's really taking me out on a date and is trying to take me home, when I want to get laid.' I was being treated like a lady, when I wanted to be a whore. This was the second date too, so at this point I'd had enough and made a move and told him to find somewhere that wasn't too obvious so we could just sit and 'talk' more. He found an empty car park and one thing lead to another (like I'd planned), and before I knew it I was blowing him off in the back of his car and we had sex. I think what made it a very memorable hoe phase for me was that the following day, a guy who was about to become my actual friend with benefits messaged me to hang out and we went for a drive, then he ended up in the exact same empty car park spot where I'd had sex the night before, and again, one thing led to another. You'd have thought these men knew each other, but they didn't. I'll be honest, the idea alone, of knowing what I'd got up to the night before, made the experience worthy of being in a hoe thread on Twitter – and I'd do it again!

Casual doesn't have to mean you don't care

One of the best experiences of casual sex I've ever had was with a guy I'd known as a teenager (in fact, I had a childhood crush on him!) but who I didn't end up hooking up with until I was in my late twenties. We'd been friends on Facebook all that time and I can't really remember how it came about but we were chatting about something and the conversation led to us deciding to go on a date. From the start he was really upfront with me about what he wanted. I knew he had a busy job, he worked long hours, and so I simply asked him from the off, 'Do you want something or do you just want it to be casual?' He said he just wanted it to be casual and I was fine with that.

Now, the first thing to tell you is that the sex was great! But what made it such a good friends-with-benefits experience was the fact that we were able to have proper conversations – you know, like actual friends! And our interactions weren't limited to 'U up?' We'd go out for drinks and dinner and have genuine chats about our lives and friends and jobs. Neither of us wanted things to get romantic, we didn't want a relationship, but that didn't mean we needed to behave like we didn't give a fuck about each other.

Now, he wasn't perfect – just in case I'm making this sound too good to be true. There was one time when I brought out my wand toy during a session and he moaned about it. But in general he was very open-minded. He was also respectful and treated the sex as something we had equal responsibility for. One time I needed the morning-after pill and he sent me the money for it, no problem. He trusted me, I trusted him and, yeah, we cared about each other ... as friends.

Caring about someone doesn't necessarily mean you wanna be with that person. It just tells me you're a good person. You're good to your friends and you don't want to be in a relationship with them. It's really not rocket science when you think about it, but so many people get strung out about the idea of 'catching feelings'. Well, I've got news for you: if you *like* the person you're sleeping with, then you already have feelings. Even if you just have a crush, if there's lust between you, that's a feeling! And it's a really nice feeling. Why would we want to avoid that? That's what I don't understand.

No matter how casual the relationship, there's always going to be feelings involved. Does that mean you want to start a family with them tomorrow? No, it doesn't.

Picking the right casual partner

OK, I will acknowledge that this is the hard part. Yeah, I know I just told you about my friend with benefits, but trust me, I have also had my share of unpleasant experiences.

Often, when it comes to casual sex, it feels like guys are here for it but they're not really. They want you to do it, but they also want to shame you for doing it. They want you to play the game with them (well, of course they do! Who are they going to play it with otherwise?), but they don't want to respect you for being part of it.

I've been there. I've been shocked at times by guys who've acted like there's mutual respect between us and then afterwards they've revealed their true colours. I've even had moments in the past when I've said I think casual sex is a scam because the playing field just isn't level. For all the ways casual sex can be good, equal, caring and respectful, you are always going to meet people who don't want to play it that way.

I've tried flipping it. I've tried playing them at their own game. I've fucked guys and then kicked them out. But in the end I realised that something was still lacking, and that thing was mutual respect.

I don't know what we do about that attitude. All we can do is establish our own casual-sex etiquette and stick to it and try to rise above it with those guys. The best way to start doing that is by talking. We need to be having open and honest conversations with our sexual partners about what we want and what they want, both in bed, but also from the relationship. And if that's something they're resistant to, if they make a fuss or try to avoid those chats, that's a pretty sure sign they're not going to be a good casual partner.

Finally, and most importantly, you have to try to find yourself someone who is not just in it for themselves. Sex – whether it's in a relationship or not – is something you do together, and I think so much of the bad casual sex people have comes down to the guy (I'm not saying this doesn't happen with women but, let's be honest, it's usually guys) treating it like an opportunity for his dick to have a nice time without really thinking about what you're getting out of it. The right casual partner is going to care about *your* pleasure as much as their own. Which brings me to my next point ...

Make sure you're getting yours

I get women talking to me all the time about their sexual experiences, and I love those messages. Believe me, I wanna hear *all* the ins and outs of how great their sex was. But it happens all the time that I'll ask, 'Oh, did he go down on you?' and she'll say no but then five minutes later I'm hearing that she went down on him! And I'm thinking, 'Hold on, is it not supposed to be mutually beneficial?'

Of course, this doesn't just happen in hook-ups. The disparity between women giving blowjobs and getting their pussies eaten exists in all kinds of straight sexual encounters and is a big contributor to the orgasm gap.[4] But it's fair to say that it's even worse in casual relationships.

When she was researching her book *Girls & Sex*, journalist Peggy Orenstein found that giving blowjobs was considered a 'standard' part of a hook-up for most girls and young women.[5] But when it came to them receiving oral sex ... nah. It wasn't happening.

Obviously oral sex isn't the *only* way to get pleasure during sex (and I also acknowledge that some people aren't into it at all), but it is one of the key ways that people with vulvas say they can reliably orgasm.[6] No wonder then that the orgasm gap is so much bigger in casual sex.[7]

The problem is, many people don't put the same thought into casual sex as they put into relationship sex. They just fall into bed with someone (often while drunk or high) and hope it'll work out as good as it seemed in their imagination. And you know what? Sometimes that's OK. Sometimes the spontaneity and the pleasure of getting someone you fancy naked is enough. But if you are regularly coming out of casual sex without having got yours, it's time to rethink your approach.

Whether it's oral sex, a specific kind of finger action or your favourite toy, you need to be bringing those sexual preferences to your casual encounters. Once again, the best way this can be achieved is by *communicating* with your partner. Find someone who's genuinely open to having conversations about what gets you off and who actually wants you to have a good time. And don't forget, the talking doesn't have to be the boring part ... turn your communication into sexting, foreplay, flirting and dirty talk, and you're actually *adding* to the pleasure of the interaction.

Carrying condoms and talking tests

There is one aspect of communication that is a little bit hard to turn into dirty talk, and that's when you're talking about sexual health. But that doesn't mean it has to kill the mood. Somebody once said to me that they find the moment when someone says, 'Have you got a condom?' really hot because it's suddenly like, 'Oh, it's ON!'

But you also don't have to make a big deal out of it. If you want to know when someone last got tested for STIs my advice is to just ask the question and own it. All you're revealing is that you're someone who cares about her health and her partner's health. Treat it like a basic part of the hook-up admin, like calling an Uber! I actually have a friend who has a message saved in her Notes app that she just copies and pastes to all new partners before meeting up with them.

Obviously it's harder to do this if you're hooking up with someone you met IRL or on a night out. But you can still be upfront about contraception. I was once out in a bar when I saw a woman trip and drop her bag on the floor. Among other things, a packet of condoms came spilling out. A lot of women would be embarrassed by that, and a lot of people would probably shame that woman (or at the very least take the piss out of her), but my immediate reaction was one of admiration. 'Oh my gosh,' I thought. 'That's very sexually mature. This is clearly a woman who takes her sexual health seriously.'

I want women to have condoms in their bag and feel proud of it. And I want the people they sleep with to acknowledge that as a sign of someone who cares and is responsible. Asking up front about when someone last got tested and making sure you discuss what birth control you're using is an essential part of how we do casual sex well. I'm sure I don't need to say this again, but if the person you're thinking about hooking up with is put off by you taking control of your sexual health, or asking those questions, that person is not gonna be a good casual sex partner.

You do you

Enjoying hook-ups, casual sex and flings is something I've always encouraged women to do with wisdom. Whether this means having open conversations to gauge the personality of the person you want to sleep with or just trying to avoid sleeping with all three guys from the same group of friends (personally this is a drama I try to avoid, but if you really couldn't give a fuck, then don't let me stop you). Do you, and do it well, sis!

For example, I'm always sent dilemmas from women who want to sleep with an ex, as if we've suddenly run out of men and women in the world. And I used to think there wasn't anything wrong with exes hooking up. I mean, I get it! There's nothing better than sleeping with someone who knows their way around your body. You get to skip the teaching part. But these days I have to admit that in some cases it isn't the healthiest choice. If you broke up on bad terms and haven't actually healed, the hormones might just distort your or their feelings about the relationship. The truth is, sex *can* complicate things and make you mistakenly romanticise feelings you're meant to be letting go of. If you understand that and you're ready to deal with the emotional fallout then by all means go for it. You don't need my permission. But if you know deep down that things are gonna get messy then, girl, stay away.

The truth is, casual sex is not for everyone. When we stumble into it blindly without asking the right questions or checking in with ourselves and our partners, it *can* lead to people getting hurt. And it *can* lead to catching feelings that are not reciprocated. It can even lead to you having a relationship when you didn't expect it! That's happened to me before; I've been having casual sex and suddenly I've turned around and gone, 'Wait, how did we get here?'

It's so important to understand how to have sex for yourself. What I don't want is for you to be doing it because you think it'll keep the person you're intimate with around. On the flip side, I don't want you to be avoiding it out of concern that you don't want the number of people you've slept with to get any higher.

Before you go into a casual encounter, you need to establish *your* relationship with sex first. What does it mean to you? What do you want it to mean? What does a healthy casual sex life look like to you? Every type of sex you have should include respect, a basic understanding and discussion of contraception options, well-established boundaries and healthy conversations about what you're both looking for.

I've said all the way through this chapter that if casual sex is not your thing, you don't need to force it. But if you do want to explore your urges, you should be able to, and you shouldn't feel any shame around that.

CHAPTER 12

Sexual Health

Let's imagine that a man has sex with a different woman every single day of the year and, assuming that the stars are aligned, he successfully impregnates each woman ... that's 365 babies created (and potentially a whole plethora of diseases spread around). Surely someone should stop that man and the havoc he and his penis are wreaking?

Well, happily, that's what contraception is for. Except ... why then is the overwhelming majority of contraception geared towards women? After all, a woman can realistically only go to full-term pregnancy once a year. Compare that to our potential super-breeder above and you have to wonder how it became *our* responsibility to keep tabs on the baby-making.

I'd love to say this was an original thought, but I have never met another woman who hasn't thought the exact same thing. The world of sex is so biased in favour men, their pleasure, their wants and needs, their comfort, that even though male contraception would be much more beneficial for humanity, it is left to women to deal with it. You know as well as I do that it's not fair, but here we are. And we still need to protect ourselves and our sexual health, so I'm afraid, ladies, that we have to work with what we've got.

Ladies, have you ever caught an STI? DM me, I want to know your story!

STI Twitter thread*

27, Oregon, USA

Hi Oloni,

I was in a relationship this past summer where I ended up with chlamydia .... twice! We only dated for four months, I knew it wouldn't last, but I made it clear I wasn't comfortable continuing to sleep with him if he was sleeping with other people. That was just what I needed to feel comfortable and safe. He told me multiple times he would get tested but he never did. It was a pattern of his to offer to do something and then never do it. My vag started getting itchy so I got tested just to be safe and sure enough I had chlamydia. I called him sobbing and he promised up and down it was from a previous relationship and he wasn't sleeping with anyone else. I got the antibiotics and eventually forgave him (I'm not here to shame anybody). He PROMISED to get tested, even sent me the appointment confirmation. Not long after, my co-worker caught him with another woman and I obviously dumped him immediately. But then a few weeks later, I'm itchy again. So I get tested again and sure enough, I have

* Not all the views expressed in the Twitter threads reflect my opinion as the author of this book, but it is important to me to share other perspectives and experiences of peoples' sexual expression and relationships.

chlamydia. Again! I got him the antibiotics (again) because it seemed like the right thing to do for whoever he sticks his nasty, lazy dick in next. I don't even care about the cheating anymore, but the fact that someone I trusted with my body and my health and my feelings could ever treat me so recklessly, I'll never get over that.

21, Luton, UK

Hi Oloni,

I just told my boyfriend that when he goes to Ibiza I always get tested after we have sex upon his return. He's actually deeply offended by this and just left the room. I don't distrust him necessarily, I'm just being precautious as I believe every woman should be. Nonetheless it seems to have affected him quite a lot. Obviously I'm not trying to have Twitter talking about my relationship so consider this an anonymous message but I think the conversation around STD-checking while in a long-term relationship is defo an important one to have!!

26, Birmingham, UK

Finally I can participate properly!! I had a friend with benefits at uni who gave me chlamydia just before I went travelling. He sent a group text to me and four other girls! 🙁🙁

When I got back we decided to carry on fucking (dumb, I know, but the D was good) and this man gave me chlamydia AGAIN. This geezer couldn't even take antibiotics properly.

27, London, UK

I definitely got PTSD from that tweet but I still had to reply … yes!! He was the first and only person I'd ever had sex with. I was in love but I ended it after several years because of red flags I was noticing and I had to put myself first. I went to the clinic months later for a routine check-up and found out I had chlamydia and had probably had it for well over 6–7 months. With absolutely no symptoms at all. To say I was shocked was an understatement! I found out that having chlamydia for such a long period of time without treatment is a risk in itself and can cause infertility. Let's just say it spread into my uterus and along came pelvic inflammatory disease which is where the real nightmare began! What I can say is: ladies, GET TESTED REGULARLY, even if you trust and wholeheartedly believe these men! DO IT FOR YOURSELF, I'm begging you!

25, London, UK

On a routine doctor's check-up I was offered an STI test and thought why not? I hadn't had one since before I got with my boyfriend of three years. It came back positive for gonorrhoea. I was in so much denial that he cheated on me that I convinced myself I must've got it another way or had it from before we got together and it just didn't show up on my previous test. I never told him because I was scared he would think *I* cheated. I did mention to him he should probably test as he's never been tested before. He kept saying he will at some point but I broke up with him a few months later so I don't know if he ever got round to it.

A brief history of contraception

Modern contraception, as we know it today, can be dated back to the nineteenth century. As far back as the late 1800s, newspapers would openly carry adverts for condoms, which were sometimes referred to as 'letters' or the 'French remedy'.[1] The most famous pioneer of birth control in the twentieth century was feminist Marie Stopes. Along with her husband, she opened up a Mothers' Clinic in North London in 1921. The clinic advised mothers on contraception and taught them how to use the cervical cap. This was a pivotal moment for contraception and led to more birth control clinics opening up in London and around the world. The Marie Stopes charity evolved to become a global organisation, which now provides reproductive healthcare across 37 countries worldwide.

Then, in the late 1940s, chemist Dr Carl Djerassi found a way to synthesise the fertility hormone progesterone, which, when taken by women, stopped them ovulating. The contraceptive pill was born![2] Of course, it took a bit longer before people were actually able to get their hands on a licensed drug. The pill was introduced in the UK on the NHS in 1961, but at first it was only for married women! The Family Planning Act in 1967 finally made it available to everyone.[3]

Needless to say, it was controversial. Contraception became a political tool used by both sides to debate moral values, the idea of family and how involved the state should be in our personal lives. To be honest, this still goes on today in politics and religion, especially when discussing abortion. To unpack the tightly wound but ultimately rather straightforward concept of allowing women to make decisions about what happens to their own body would require an entire book of its own.

I'm sure I don't need to point out to you that there is, as yet, no male version of the pill. Research into new male contraception has been going on since the 1970s, but still nothing. There are people who will tell you that controlling the male reproductive system is more complicated, and maybe it is, but if you ask me it's mostly down to a lack of interest by drug companies, a lack of funding and the unwillingness of male consumers to take such drugs.

Choosing the right contraception for you

Personally, my main form of contraception is condoms. I have dabbled in other forms in the past and for one reason or another I didn't get on with them. According to the Centers for Disease Control and Prevention, 64.9 per cent of women aged 15–49 in the United States are currently using a method of contraception.[4] It's important to try different forms of contraceptive to find what works for you. It will be very unlikely that your 16-year-old self and your 36-year-old self will have the same contraception needs when so many different things come into play: your lifestyle choices, sexual behaviours, menstrual cycle, medical history and so on are unique to you and will change over time, so your approach to contraception might need to adapt, too.

If you're a woman who has sex with men, I'm pretty sure that, like me, your first experience with contraception will have been the external or male condom. We are very briefly taught about it in sexual health classes as teenagers, and every coming-of-age film there is has a scene with a condom in it. They're given out for free in various places (unlike feminine hygiene products, which we are still fighting for!) and don't contain any hormones or cause any long-term side effects. Along with internal, or female, condoms and dental dams, these usually latex (but also available in latex-free polyisoprene) products are known as 'barrier' contraception. Barrier methods are the only form that can protect you from sexually transmitted infections like chlamydia, gonorrhoea, trichomoniasis and HIV. However, they do not protect you from STIs such as genitals warts and genital herpes, as these are contracted by skin-to-skin contact.

Regardless of your sexual practices, it's a really good idea to get tested regularly for STIs. For most people this will require a genital swab, a blood test and possibly a urine sample, although you may also be asked to do a throat or anal swab. When I first started having sex the only way to do this was to go to a drop-in session at my local sexual health clinic and sit for hours, waiting to be seen. This is obviously still an option and if you feel like you'd like to talk to someone about your sexual health or get advice it's definitely the best way. But in London and many other parts of the UK these days, you can have a discreet test kit sent to your home. It comes with full instructions and a form to fill in. You take your swabs and do a finger-prick blood test (honestly, it's no big deal) and then put it all back in the box, seal it up and send it off in the post. It really couldn't get any more convenient.

The most basic test kits just test for chlamydia and gonorrhoea, but I do recommend asking for an HIV test as well, even if you think you couldn't possibly be at risk. Rates of HIV among heterosexual people are now *higher* than among gay and bisexual men. In February 2022, it was reported that 49 per cent of all new diagnoses were in straight people, compared to 45 per cent in gay and bi men.[5] This statistic can be a bit misleading, as heterosexual people make up a far greater percentage of the total population than LGBTQ+ people, but it's still a good incentive for everyone, regardless of sexual orientation, to do more testing.

As we discussed in Chapter 2: Society, Stigma and Slut-shaming, the LGBTQ+ community has had to deal with the stigma of HIV for decades. But HIV does not discriminate, and despite what we may have heard or been told, there is no way of knowing if a sexual partner has HIV. Luckily, HIV treatment and prevention has come a long way, and with effective medication more and more people with HIV are living normal lives. Often, the virus can be treated to the point where it's undetectable in their blood and they can't even pass it on. This is known as U=U, which stands for 'undetectable = untransmittable'.

However, if you are sleeping with someone with HIV, you can also take pre-exposure prophylaxis (PrEP). This is a tablet containing antivirals that will block HIV if you do come into contact with it. There's also post-exposure prophylaxis (PEP), which is a combination of antivirals used after potentially being exposed to HIV (perhaps after a condom breaking, for example). It needs to be taken within 72 hours – the sooner after exposure, the better.

When it comes to birth control, the list of options is even longer. There are two main types of pill: the combined oral contraceptive pill (COCP) and the progesterone-only pill (POP). When I started having sex with my first boyfriend I went to my GP and asked to be started on the contraceptive pill. They prescribed me the COCP and I started taking it as instructed for 21 days, with a seven-day break for a withdrawal bleed (which is not a real period because you're not ovulating, but it mimics your period). Within a month, however, I started to notice that I was gaining weight and even convinced myself I'd started to develop stretch marks on my arms. Neither of these things were necessarily an issue in themselves, but for a very insecure and self-conscious 18-year-old this was my worst nightmare. I started looking into the pill to see if others had had similar experiences and of course as soon as I went online I started reading horror stories (which is why I never recommend googling health symptoms!). Looking back, I understand that a lot of these stories weren't true or were coincidental. For example, there's actually little evidence that hormonal contraceptives cause weight gain,[6] but that isn't to say that women don't experience side effects from them. The NHS website lists some of the more common side effects of the COCP as including headache, nausea, breast tenderness, high blood pressure and mood swings. It has also been linked to blood clots.[7] A pretty unpleasant list, however you look at it. No wonder increasing numbers of women are starting to move away from the pill and look at other forms of contraception.[8]

Along with the COCP, there's also the progesterone-only pill, implant, vaginal ring, contraceptive patch, diaphragm/caps, intrauterine system (IUS) or hormonal coil, depot injections, intrauterine device (IUD) or copper coil, sterilisation and the internal condom. Recent years have seen an uptick in the number of women choosing forms of long-acting, reversible contraception (LARCs) *other* than the pill. Around 40 per cent now opt for one of the following: the copper coil (IUD), the hormonal coil (IUS), the implant or contraceptive injection – that's double the percentage in 2007.[9] These methods can be good because they don't involve you having to remember to take a pill every day and are said to have fewer side effects. That doesn't mean they have no side effects at all, though, and as I said at the start, it's important to be open to trying different things until you figure out what works for you.

Another somewhat controversial form of contraception is the fertility awareness method. This is when a woman tracks her fertility, via an app or the old-fashioned pen-and-paper way, by looking for the signs and symptoms in her menstrual cycle that might indicate when she is and isn't fertile to prevent becoming pregnant. When done properly, it can be an effective method,[10] but it is definitely not foolproof. It requires a lot of vigilance and it's obviously not a great idea for all women, especially those with irregular, unpredictable cycles.

You may also have heard that research was being done into a form of injectable male contraception. Unfortunately, this is just one of the many examples of male contraception that has never made it to the market. Although it was showing positive outcomes in terms of preventing pregnancies, the trials were stopped due to concerns over side effects.[11] What were these worrying side effects, you ask? They included acne, headaches, mood swings and muscle aches. Sounds familiar? Almost identical to what women have been experiencing for the past half-century!

Let's look back at that long list of contraception methods that have been created for women. Now let's look at the list for men: external condom and sterilisation. That's it, just two forms of contraception compared to 11 for women ... and that's not even including emergency contraception.

Once, in my first year of university, my friend and I both had unprotected sex on the same day. Like the responsible adults we were – **ahem** – we decided to head to the pharmacy together the next morning. We spoke to the pharmacist and asked for a morning-after pill each but they only had one pill left in stock. That's when my friend and I started going back and forth pleading our own case to one another, giving reasons as to why one of us should take it instead of the other. In our increasing urgency to pitch our case, we were both coming up with the most ridiculous reasons. My personal favourite was when she tried to argue that because she had a boyfriend (and it just so happened that the man she had slept with the night before was not him!), getting pregnant would be way worse for her. Whew! University was a trying time for us all. Now you could argue that it was silly of us to stress out so much about who would take the 'only' morning-after pill. Surely we could just go back the next day for another one? But thanks to its colloquial name, emergency contraception is often mistakenly thought to only work if literally taken the *morning after* unprotected sex. Neither of us knew it at the time but depending on which brand of pill you take, you actually have 72–120 hours post-fuck to take oral emergency contraception. In the end, in the spirit of fairness, we agreed that neither of us would take it and instead we would keep looking until we found a pharmacy that had two in stock. What a day that was!

The two lines

When we discuss sex and contraception I find that we rarely talk about abortions. We know many people have had them (210,860 abortions took place in England and Wales in 2020, the highest number since records began),[12] but we're not speaking about it.

Sure, we talk about the rights from time to time – particularly when states like Texas pass laws by men who have absolutely no idea what we experience, and who think they have a right to dictate what happens to a body they do not own. But it's often that we talk about what women who need to have them actually go through.

The lack of conversation might come from fear, since women are often shamed for having an abortion, or it might come out of pain and grief. Some may not wish to discuss it due to what they had to do to get it, such as travelling far and wide, or undergoing an unsafe procedure in a back-alley clinic. Or perhaps it's because we're worried that someone will mention an old myth that makes us regret sharing what we've been through, such as, 'Did you know that an abortion can affect your chances of getting pregnant again?' (Which just isn't true, by the way!) But like all stigmas, one of the best ways to dismantle it is to shine a light on it and talk about it.

I was in my mid-twenties and had just had one of the biggest arguments with my then on/off boyfriend. We had one of those scary arguments you watch in *EastEnders* outside his house, me calling him all sorts of names and him doing the same. Looking back, I can't even remember what we were arguing about, but what I do remember is thinking that would be the last time we ever spoke, and if it was, how would I tell him about something I wasn't 100 per cent sure of, which was at the back of my mind? Something which could potentially change both our lives. But what was I going to do? Tell him in the middle of an argument when tensions were high?

Not using contraception properly in my mid-twenties meant I had to go through one of the toughest experiences of my life. It meant having to communicate with someone I didn't wish to speak to. How do you pick up the phone and say, 'Hey, I know we hate each other, but you might need a second job'?

Once I got home and was sure of the situation, I called him and there was no answer. He probably thought I was calling to shout some more and, had I not been trembling in fear, he would have been right. So instead, I sent a photo and within seconds got a call back. Even with how mad we were at each other, we set our differences aside to have that uncomfortable conversation.

He saw me immediately and comforted me. I was scared but knew I just wasn't ready to give up my life to have a child. I dreamed of so much. I had a vision board – and this? This was never on it. Him and I knew we weren't ready; we weren't stable as romantic partners, never mind as providers for a dependent human.

I was happy with my decision to have an abortion, but I still cried. I cried because I felt as though I had failed myself. I'm a sex educator, after all. I knew how conception happens and yet I hadn't taken adequate preventative measures. I had days when I was OK and days when I was sad and was looked after by my ex. I have never regretted my decision, but I must admit in all these years the one thing that hasn't changed is wondering if the baby would have been a boy or a girl. I'll never know, and that's OK.

It's OK to have an abortion and feel happy about it. It's OK to have an abortion and feel sad. It's also OK to have mixed feelings, to feel ambivalent, to feel conflicted. None of this makes your choice (and your right to choose) any less valid.

Vaginal health

Cleanliness is next to godliness (and I am all about being a sexual goddess), which is why coochie care in and out of the bedroom is so important. It's also part of sex positivity too. Taking care of all areas of your sexual health means saying, 'Aht aht, go wash your hands before you finger me,' or 'Baby, let's have a shower before we get into it,' to your lover. You and your vulva are delicate and deserve care, OK?

It's also making sure you clean your sex toys regularly and properly, using a mild soap or a dedicated sex-toy cleaner. We do not want that bacteria build-up, ladies. Our pussies will not thank us.

And it's making sure we avoid products that aren't kind to our vaginas. As I've said before, we're all different, so some ingredients might cause issues in some people and not others. But if you've identified something that makes you feel stingy, itchy or otherwise not quite right – avoid! Make sure you read the back of that lube bottle and know what is being slathered across any vulva or penis you might be interacting with.

Taking care of your vulva also includes peeing after sex, because some believe that flushes out germs and decreases the chances of getting an annoying urinary tract infection. It also means not ignoring the signs that feel like bacterial vaginosis, or thrush, and hoping it'll just miraculously go away on its own. By the way, all of this is extremely common, so never hesitate to get yourself down to the chemist or book a GP appointment to discuss your symptoms. Trust me, doctors, pharmacists and sexual health nurses see these issues daily.

Do not allow the pussy pressure of capitalism to force you into believing your vagina is meant to taste like Skittles and Starbursts or that you need to douche. You don't! Plus, all those bogus feminine hygiene products fuck up your pH balance and that really will put you at risk of getting an infection. A study from the University of Pittsburgh found that when women douched, they were actually *more* likely to get bacterial vaginosis or an irritation that could upset the vagina.[13]

Plain water is all you need to keep your vulva clean and happy. Use your fingers or a soft washcloth *at most* to get in between the folds of your labia and rinse. You do not need to clean inside your vagina with soap. We really are fearfully and wonderfully made, because our vaginas are self-cleaning organs that produce discharge full of good bacteria.

We've been told for so long that if our vulva doesn't taste or smell like something out of a sweet shop, there's something wrong with us, but that's just untrue. Vulvas are meant to taste and smell like vulvas. Do not let society fool you into believing you need extra products to feel healthy. I mean, if we're serious about encouraging people's genital parts to smell better, where are all the penis scrubs or dick cheese washes? Don't get me started!

Ending the stigma around STIs

Wanting to become fearless and progressive with sex positivity to me meant having ownership over my body and any sexual situation I was about to give consent to. I had to educate myself on the importance of asking people when they'd been tested last before sleeping with them so I could protect myself and others. These days, I hear people have these conversations more and more. However, when I was in university it wasn't quite so easy. I remember asking a guy when he'd had his last sexual health test and the response was not positive. 'What are you trying to say? Are you calling me dirty or something?' he demanded. I wanted the floor to swallow me. How did we go from laughing and flirting to him slowly sitting up on my bed with an unpleasant expression on his face in response to my question? I honestly thought I'd done something wrong. I even saw it from his point of view at the time. Maybe by asking the question I came across as though I thought he was quite sexually active and never protected himself. He was so irritated by the question he ended up leaving my house.

I sat like a fox at the end of the bed with my legs crossed, stunned, going over and over how I could have said it better. I'd done nothing wrong but had asked a responsible question he probably wasn't used to. I was made to feel as though I was the problem, but his reaction spoke volumes. He was triggered by my honesty and openness. He was not at all prepared to offer the same in return. After all, this was not a husband I'd known for 20 years, he was a classmate who'd had the liquid courage to finally speak to me at a drink-up. He wanted to have sex, but clearly couldn't cope emotionally with a light conversation about sexual health. I decided I'd probably had a lucky escape.

Luckily, I've never had to deal with that sort of reaction since, and I'm glad this bad experience didn't stop me from continuing to ask, because people are really out there fucking with no care or protection in the world. Being sex positive to me means caring about not only your pleasure, but your health as well. It's taking care of yourself sexually and making sure you do whatever you need to do to protect yourself and your sexual partners, whether past, present or future.

I still ask the majority of guys I have sex with when they were last tested and they mostly react positively and upfront. Wanting to know someone has been checked does not mean you are making an assumption about their sexual activities. Apart from anything else, having an STI does not equate to how sexually active you are. Just like it can take one sexual experience to get knocked up, it can also take just one time to catch something. There's also this misconception that having an STI makes you dirty, irresponsible or sexual deviant, when that just isn't true.

Humans have sex and along the way our genitals might possibly get sick – it's a part of life. We don't look at people funny when they have a cold, because colds are common. Well, whether you want to believe it or not, so are chlamydia and other STIs.

I mentioned that the guy who had an issue with me asking about his last STI test wasn't someone I was committed to, but please don't get it twisted. Being in a relationship is not a safety net from catching an infection. If it was, I wouldn't have a job and an inbox full of women wondering how they caught something in a monogamous relationship and second-guessing themselves. It's probably why I made sure that I got tested in relationships, because sadly you can't vouch for anyone's genitals but yours.

In fact, research shows that people in (supposedly) monogamous relationships are just as likely to catch STIs as people who are in consensually open relationships.[14] Why? Because people cheat. Sorry, but it's true. And not only that but people who cheat are also less likely to use condoms, get tested regularly for STIs or have honest discussions with their partners about sexual health concerns.[15]

Often when I'm sent dilemmas from women I'm told that their partners believe that the STI they caught might have been picked up from a toilet seat (yes, insane, I know), but it's important you understand that sexually transmitted infections can only been passed on through bodily fluids or skin-to-skin contact. It is highly unlikely that you can catch it from a toilet seat, old bed sheets, a bathtub or a shower head, or any other inanimate object. This is because the bacteria that cause things like chlamydia, gonorrhoea and syphilis can't live for long outside of our bodies.[16] Even viruses like HIV and hepatitis B need very specific conditions to survive outside of the body and your average toilet seat is not it.[17]

Now, obviously there are illnesses that can be caught from unhygienic toilets, but they are far more likely to result in a stomach bug than an STI. That's why your mother always told you to wash your hands after going to the loo!

So please, if you're in a relationship, no matter how serious it is, I encourage you to still get tested regularly and see it as getting checked as you would with any other routine health check-up. You don't need to itch, see a difference in your skin or pee before booking an appointment with a sexual health nurse (again, many STIs are asymptomatic) – just look at it as something you do every six to twelve months, like going to the dentist.

The importance of busting myths and dismantling stigma around sexual health isn't limited to STIs either. Shame around being sexually active and fear of being seen as a slut can put us in some stressful situations when it comes to birth control as well.

I know I've been sharing several stories from when I was in secondary school and university, but that's where I witnessed a lot of crazy shit that young girls went through, which, in hindsight, gives me an idea of how truly shitty our sex education was.

Maria and June* were tight, and always sat in front of me and my best friend during one of our lessons. Two hilarious white girls that could never be separated, they did everything together – bunked off school, got the same hairstyle, spoke to guys outside of school who really had no business talking to them.

Maria was the ballsier one. No surprise, then, that the day June needed the morning-after pill (MAP) from having unprotected sex the night before, it was Maria she asked to go into the pharmacy. They really were best friends, because Maria didn't bat an eyelid. Pretending to be June, she went inside the pharmacy and allowed herself to be led into that tiny private cubicle-like room that nonetheless obviously screams, 'I just had sex!' There she diligently answered all the tedious-yet-important questions the pharmacist usually asks. You know the ones: 'When was your last period?' 'Are you on any medication?' 'When did you last have sex?' 'Are you allergic to anything?'

But what neither June nor Maria realised when they concocted this scheme was that Maria would have to take the pill there and then in front of the pharmacist. She was handed the pill, along with a plastic white cup filled to the brim with water. Thinking quickly, she sipped the smallest amount she could manage and carefully and surreptitiously rested the pill on her tongue. She then hurriedly finished up with the pharmacist and ran outside where she met June around the corner. She instantly took the pill out of her own mouth and told her friend to open up so she could transfer it! She really had her back!

Now, of course I do not encourage you to do this. These were two young girls in the Noughties who were desperate and didn't have pharmacy apps in the middle of their palms. They couldn't order it online like we can today. I'm just using their story as an example of

* Names changed to protect privacy.

how dealing with your reproductive health can be made stressful and scary thanks to the stigma surrounding it.

Dealing with untreatable STIs

Most STIs such as chlamydia and gonorrhoea are easily treatable with antibiotics (if they're diagnosed in time!), but some are incurable. The obvious one we all know about is HIV/AIDS, which has killed 36.3 million worldwide since its discovery in 1983. But thanks to the medical advancements in its treatment, there are even more people *living* with HIV – at the end of 2020, the World Health Organization reported 37.7 million people living with HIV globally.[18]

Another one we've all heard of is herpes. Nearly 70 per cent of adults under 50 worldwide have either oral or genital herpes.[19] One in three of us will experience herpes symptoms at some point in our lives.[20]

A myth I've often heard is that being diagnosed with one of these means your sex and dating life is effectively over. Not true. You can have a totally normal life with an incurable STI.

Flare-ups of herpes (which can include itching, inflammation and painful sores) can be treated with an antiviral drug, but in many cases the symptoms will clear up on their own. For most people herpes tends to be a painful nuisance once or twice in their lives and after that they never really have to think about it. It's true that the virus will stay in your body for life but if you don't have any symptoms, the risk of transmission is low and it decreases over time.[21] So if you haven't had a flare-up in years, you're much less likely to give it to someone else. It's not impossible, but even so, I'm not sure it's worth all the stress we have around it.

Will you face some challenges? Maybe, but it's usually due to the stigma. And one of the best ways to break down stigma is to educate people. Luckily, I just debunked the stigma around HIV and herpes so you are now armed with information and can bust those facts out anytime you hear someone chatting shit about incurable STIs. We have to understand that if we want to be comfortable and free to truly enjoy sex, we have to let go of the stigma around STIs. All we do is spread misinformation and stop people seeking medical advice or attention out of shame.

There are some people who argue that it's not necessary to disclose your STI status if the STI in question is under control and there is no likelihood of you passing it on. Or if, in the case of herpes, it's really common anyway and causes no long-term health issues. I guess that's up to you, but personally I think you should always be honest about your status before you become sexually intimate with someone. You don't have to grovel about it or be ashamed; just explain the situation and let them know the steps you're taking to manage it and help them stay protected.

How to have open conversations about sexual health

When we push ourselves to have conversations about sexual health we help destigmatise the negative attitude that people have about it and help debunk the silly myths. If you aren't comfortable asking a partner about their last STI screen, my view is you shouldn't be having sex with them at all. Period. Here are some ways you can ask your sexual partner if they've been recently tested before getting down and dirty:

- 'I got tested a week ago and my results came back negative. When did you last have a sexual health test?
- 'I'm going to get an STI test soon, do you want to go together?'

Having a disclosure conversation can look something like this:

- 'I have something I want to share with you. I'm into you and I'd like to see where this can go, but I do want you to know that a few years ago, I found out that I have [name diagnosis here]. I've had treatment and I'm able to manage it so I can still have a very normal sex life, but obviously feel free to ask me any questions if you're concerned.'
- 'I've enjoyed the time we've spent together and I feel like we might get intimate one day, so I just want you to know that I have herpes. It's actually more common than most people are aware of and to be honest it really isn't a big deal, but I thought it better to mention it. Feel free to ask me anything about it.'

Don't present it in a negative light, as it looks like you've done something wrong. Remember, this infection or virus does not rule your life. You are deserving of pleasure and happiness.

If you're not having sex with that person, you don't need to disclose it, or you might want to. It's up to you! Again, people shouldn't feel ashamed about STIs, but instead allow themselves to feel comfortable enough to bring it up when it feels right in any situation, this helps destigmatise sexually transmitted infections.

Telling someone you're intimate with that they might have an STI/HIV after testing positive is important. In my opinion, withholding that information is selfish and quite dangerous. There are ways it can be done anonymously through the help of your clinic, if you don't want to attach your name to it.

Ladies... I want to hear your positive STI stories, DM me!

Positive STI Twitter thread*

I asked some women to share their experiences with me of when they told their sexual partner they had an STI, to help add perspective about the reality of this issue:

30, London, UK

Hey sis,

So after a really horrible and heartbreaking experience of telling the guy I dated before this one that my ex had given me herpes, I was really nervous to let the next guy know as I was feeling so rejected and alone. However, he was very sweet and understanding and it made the world of difference for my self-esteem.

He is someone who gets cold sores, so even though I suffered from the genital version, he made me feel comfortable by turning it into an 'us' thing, rather than a 'me' thing.

[She then shared a screenshot of their iMessage exchange with me.]

Honestly it lifted my spirits so much. People don't understand how low they can make someone feel with all

*Not all the views expressed in the Twitter threads reflect my opinion as the author of this book, but it is important to me to share other perspectives and experiences of peoples' sexual expression and relationships.

the dumb, immature stigma around STIs. I hit rock bottom at that time because it was the cherry on top of years of other sexual and emotional trauma.

Unfortunately I am no longer seeing this particular guy that was so nice to me about it, and the reason is actually because the previous trauma combined with the cheating, which lead to me getting VERY sick with this STI (my body completely shut down!) and then being rejected by the next person I tried to date, all left me in a bad state mentally and I really struggled to let my guard down with him to the point where I was unintentionally cold and unloving.

I'm still working on being able to open up again, so I really hope that the next person I choose to do so with is also as understanding and sweet as this guy was that I missed out on.

Lord knows my heart needs it!

25, Toronto, Canada

Hi Oloni,

I'd gotten tested and found out I had chlamydia – it was the first time I had contracted anything so I'd never had that talk before, nor had anyone had that talk with me. The guy I was seeing, we had just become exclusive, and I was really afraid he would react badly (even tho if he did it would have been a sure sign to run). But I had to do it lol. He was so kind about it though, we just laughed it off like 'it happens' and made sure we both went and got treated at the same time. The shittier side to all this was telling the people we were no longer seeing omg.

We are still together today, going on three years!

25, London, UK

Hi Oloni,

I started seeing a new guy but a few weeks into dating I did a STI test (I was getting repeat contraception from a sexual health clinic so they make you take a test) and found out I had chlamydia. Had absolutely no symptoms whatsoever but it turns out I'd caught it from my trash ex who I'd seen months before. The new guy was totally cool and understanding, said it was no big deal, and got some antibiotics the same day! Reminder to test regularly!!! X

25, Norwich, UK

Hi Oloni!

I tested positive with HSV2 last year (genital herpes) after I had a random cold sore down there after being with my boyfriend at the time for a year and decided to get checked. He knew he had herpes all along and didn't disclose so I was heartbroken.

I broke up with him and met someone else a few months after; we hit it off right away and I liked him a lot so I knew I had to disclose if I wanted things to continue. I was so scared it would put him off me, but the exact opposite happened. He was so kind and didn't mind at all as long as we used condoms, which was fine with me! Fast-forward to a year later: we are still together, don't use condoms anymore and I'm on anti-viral medication (he still hasn't had an outbreak either!). HSV is nothing to be ashamed about and I'm lucky I found someone who was educated and understanding.

24, NYC, USA

I got herpes a few months ago from a man I was seeing who lied about having it. When I found out I was so scared and I thought that my sex life was over. I figured no one would want to have sex with someone that has herpes. I was so scared to tell people but I finally did and people have been super nice (but also I'm not sure if it's cuz men are sexually irresponsible and want to fuck no matter what!). I told one guy I had been dating and he said he had fucked with a girl with it before and he was down to fuck no condom. Then this weekend I told a one-night stand before we fucked and he said he didn't know what it was! I explained and he was still down (with condom)! Having herpes is not as bad as I thought; everyone is super understanding.

CHAPTER 13

Kinks, Fetishes and BDSM

When we think of kink, most of us probably think of whips, handcuffs and blindfolds, even if we know this is an outdated cliché!

The letters BDSM stand for bondage, discipline, domination, submission, sadism and masochism. These are generally considered to be some of the 'main' kinks as far as sexual activities go, although the term 'kink' is a bit broader and can apply to any unconventional sexual behaviour or preference. For example, people who enjoy watching their partners having sex with someone else might be getting off on a feeling of humiliation (which would make it a kind of submission and/or masochism and thus fall under the BDSM umbrella) or it might be more of a voyeuristic thing. They might just *really* love watching people have sex and find it even hotter when it's their own partner.

Then there's fetishes. A fetish is an unusually strong sexual attraction to a particular object, item of clothing or part of the body. Some common ones we tend to think of are foot fetishes, leather and latex fetishes, and used underwear fetishes, but almost anything can be fetishised! In the 'looner' community (that's people with a balloon fetish), for example, sexual satisfaction is derived from popping balloons.

It's also not unusual to hear people use the terms 'kink' and 'fetish' interchangeably, such as, 'I have an armpit kink,' or 'I have a real kink for body piercings.' And again, there can be crossover between fetishes and BDSM. A man who's into wearing women's knickers might enjoy the feeling of submission (for example, if he's been ordered to wear them by his partner), the taboo of defying gender norms or the sensation of the fabric. In lots of cases it might be a combination of all three.

Despite the fact that kinks tend to refer to sexual behaviours outside the norm, being interested in or practising kink is actually pretty common. A 2017 study found that almost half the population had engaged in a BDSM activity at least once.[1] And in his 2018 book *Tell Me What You Want,* social psychologist Justin Lehmiller surveyed over 4,000 people and found that over 90 per cent of women and more than 80 per cent of men had fantasised about BDSM in some form.[2]

So if you've ever daydreamed about being tied to the bed, having sex in public or getting gang-banged then, girl, you're not alone.

How to figure out what you're into

When it comes to kink, the possibilities are, if not endless then really, really extensive. If you can dream it and it's consensual then, in theory, you can do it. In some cases you might have to use your imagination a little bit. For example, the tentacle dildos and ovipositors (specially designed dildos that 'lay' gelatin eggs inside you to recreate the fantasy of being impregnated by aliens – yes, that's a real thing) you can buy online are made of silicone. There's no alien attached, and they don't come with a spaceship so if you're wanting to act out a whole 'alien abduction' fantasy then you're going to have to get creative.

But how does someone realise they're into this in the first place? And how can we start to understand what we might like? For some of us, it might be obvious. We might have sexual fantasies we find ourselves returning to when we're masturbating or porn genres we just can't get enough of. But for others, it might be more about paying attention to the dynamics or feelings that make them feel excited.

I'll be honest with you, I'm pretty vanilla. I love me some spit play, I'm into dirty talk and dressing up for role play, but in the grand scheme of BDSM, I wouldn't say my tastes are that hardcore. Oh! I also have a slight praise kink, also referred to as affirmation play. This is when your partner communicates in the bedroom by praising you in a really hot and dominant way. Think 'Good girl' or 'You're so pretty when you're taking all this dick.' It's all about giving and getting sexual compliments that excite and turn you on, and I love it.

When it comes to BDSM I wanted to talk to someone who really knows the kink scene inside out and has first-hand experience at the outer fringes of what people get off on, so I scheduled a call with Jet Setting Jasmine. Jasmine is a professional dominatrix and master fetish trainer as well as being a licensed therapist. Along with her partner, King Noire, she's also the co-owner of porn production company Royal Fetish Films and has over 20 years' experience as an adult performer. With a CV like this I was fascinated to hear how and when she first realised she was kinky.

'I definitely didn't have the word "kinky" or "dominatrix", or "fetishy", or any of this kind of language. I think, at the time, the words that were being used were like "nasty",' she says. But she did know she was different somehow. She recalls enjoying making the boys she was at school with feel uncomfortable and embarrassed. And for reasons she didn't quite understand at the time, many actually responded really well to this.

'I'd be walking on the basketball court and the guys would be sitting in the bleachers watching the girls play or waiting for it to be their turn to practise. And they had those basketball shorts that used to hang kind of low. And if you look up the bleachers, you could see in their shorts. So that was my first opportunity of penis humiliation and voyeurism. I would look up, and then I'd make eye contact with him, and I'd look again, and then I'd quit,' she remembers. 'Honestly, I really couldn't see anything clearly, but I would make them uncomfortable and vulnerable just with the *idea* of me looking and judging.'

She now understands this as a form of psychological domination. She's not exactly proud of it. She gets that it wasn't really OK to behave like, but it was the reality of her experience at the time. Back then, as a teenager, she just knew she liked making boys feel awkward, whether that was on the basketball court or in the bedroom. 'I would get into these pretty close calls with a lot of boys where I enjoyed edging them. So I would get them hot and bothered and then I would say, "Oh, OK, let's go back to school now," or I'd tell them to take me home,' she says.

Looking back, she marvels at how risky that behaviour was. No partner ever got angry or tried to force things with her, but knowing what she knows now about rape culture and how society normalises the idea that men are entitled to sex, she admits it wasn't very sensible. With hindsight, she also acknowledges *their* lack of consent to being edged and dominated in this way. But nevertheless, it was the beginning of her understanding of her kinks.

'That was where I found my satisfaction at a really young age – it was bringing these guys to a point and then exercising my power to say "no", and to edge them. And, you know, they would say things like, "Oh, you're going to give me blue balls," and I was like, "Great. I love the colour blue!"'

Paying attention to which parts of our sexual or romantic interactions give us that kind of thrill can help us figure out what kind of BDSM we might be into. Even outside of this, there might be aspects of a film, TV show or book, or even pictures, that captivate us just that little bit more than usual.

I enjoy an intense level of dirty talk, but I only truly realised this by accident through an ex. He'd told me off during a disagreement and even though we were arguing, something about his tone at that moment stayed with me. During sex one evening I asked him to talk to me the same way he had during our back and forth, and now I was obviously turned on by it. In this situation, I was clearly taking on a submissive role, and allowing him to take on the role of the dom. I encouraged him and gave him consent to move from telling me off to calling me degrading words that I wouldn't want to hear outside of sex.

One of the things people get wrong a lot is believing that all kinks are inherently sexual in nature, that they only exist in the bedroom, as a source of sexual arousal and a way to help us achieve orgasm. For many people, the pleasure or excitement or satisfaction they feel from practising kink is kind of ... well, platonic. There are also people who live out their dominant and submissive roles in everyday life. This is often referred to as a 'lifestyle kink'.

'This is where your primary intimate relationship involves a dynamic of a dominant and a submissive, or dominant and a switch – you know, any of the acronyms within BDSM,' explains Jasmine. 'Your fetishes are not something that you do on vacation only, or for Valentine's Day; they really are an integral part of the way that you relate to your partners.'

She tells me a story about someone who grew up in a family where their parents were in a BDSM lifestyle, specifically one that involved age play. This usually takes the form of one partner adopting a child-like role (often known as a 'little'), with the other person taking on a parental role (the 'Daddy' or 'Mummy' dominant). To a lot of people this probably sounds really fucking weird, especially given that they also had *real* kids. But you have to understand that it wasn't really about sex; it was more about how this couple chose to show affection and care for one another.

'It was very normal [to them],' says Jasmine. 'Their dad would tuck their mum in at night and read her a story, after he did the same for the children; or, after the mum did it for the children, the dad would do it for her. And then there were some other attributes that he would allow her to be a "little" in, or [he would] encourage that role of being a "little" as part of the family dynamic.'

She points out that actually a lot of couples enjoy performing their gender roles in ways which some of us might find regressive or twee, and that sometimes a kink can simply be an extension of this.

I know this is probably going to be really hard to get your head around because I think as a society we just automatically assume any niche interest must be a sex thing. But actually, we might be better off viewing these kinds of relationships as two people who share an unusual hobby. Of course, that's not to say the two can't coexist. There are plenty of people who practise kink as a lifestyle for whom it also forms part of their sex lives, but it's worth knowing that it doesn't have to be this way.

What do our kinks say about us?

Kinks and fetishes used to be associated with perversion or were held up as evidence that someone was psychologically damaged in some way. I've mentioned the *Diagnostic and Statistical Manual* (the *DSM*) already in Chapter 4: Sexual Identity (see page 60), which is a text used to classify and diagnose mental health disorders. Until 1994, the *DSM-3* (as it then was), actually categorised being into BDSM as a mental illness. It wasn't until 2013 when the *DSM-5* was published that the language linking kink with pathology was finally removed from this influential handbook.

We now understand that having a kink or a fetish is not a sign of a disorder (although I still see far too many people on social media claiming it is). I'm going to come back to kink-shaming at the end of this chapter, but for now I want to discuss what our kinks *do* say about us.

As usual with sex, it's pretty individual. Justin Lehmiller, whose book I mentioned earlier, is a social psychologist and sex researcher at the Kinsey Institute in the US. He notes that people can have the same kinky fantasy for a wide variety of different reasons. For some people, a kinky scenario offers an escape from reality – you can pretend to be someone you're not, take on characteristics you don't normally have in your day-to-day life. For others it might be a rebellion against the things you were taught growing up, particularly if those things were oppressive in some way. Right-wing Republicans, for example (Lehmiller's research was conducted exclusively in the United States), who tend to be brought up with the message that sex is only permissible inside a monogamous marriage, with many advocating abstinence-only sex education, are more likely than Democrats to fantasise about orgies, infidelity, swinging and cuckolding (where you watch your partner having sex with someone else). The implication is that because Democrats have slightly more progressive views about sex and relationships, these things are less likely to become a kink for them.[3]

If something is taboo, it is more likely to become a kink for us. You only have to look back to the surge in 'coronavirus porn' at the start of the COVID-19 pandemic. Common themes included people breaking quarantine to have sex outside and people getting caught breaking quarantine by the authorities, as well as various dynamics between patients and medics. Madita Oeming, a porn scholar and lecturer at Paderborn University in Germany, explained at the time that it made complete sense to use our sexual creativity to play with our fears and feelings about the pandemic. 'The current situation lends itself perfectly to being fetishized,' Oeming told *Forbes* in April 2020. 'In general, anything that is dangerous has the potential to be titillating, just like anything that is forbidden.'[4]

When it comes to fetishes, most experts believe it's tied to a specific experience you had either in childhood or in your teenage years. I remember hearing the story of a guy who developed a fetish for feet after he witnessed his favourite teacher taking her shoes off under the desk during lessons. People start to associate the thing (in this case feet) with the feeling (calm, contentment, admiration, attraction) and over time this develops into a fetish.

But it's not always that straightforward. Sometimes there's a whole bunch of different things going on that may or may not contribute to our desire for certain activities and scenarios.

When I asked Jasmine about this, she gave the example of a tickling fetish. 'I find this one really fascinating because as I meet different clients that have this tickling kink, [I see huge differences in] where they like to tickle, how they like to tickle, what they like to tickle with,' she says. 'So I love exploring that particular kink. Not participating in it, but exploring what people are after. What is it that they like? Is it that they like to see the body convulsing? Some do. Some like to see the body tied down and they like to hear the laughter. Some like to see the feet contract or the hands contract. It's so particular.'

And for those with a kink for being tickled, the motivations can be just as diverse. For some, it's about the loss of control. 'It involves your body involuntarily doing its own thing,' says Jasmine. '[We can also] look at tickling as a way of bondage in a totally different form. Because when you tickle me, I can't do anything. I can't think, I can't move.'

Sometimes the arousal doesn't even come from the activity itself but from the feelings surrounding the activity. Jasmine tells me about an occasion in which she was asked to participate in a custom porn film involving belly-punching. Why on earth did people want to watch someone being punched in the belly, she wondered? And what possible sexual gratification was there from being on the receiving end of a belly-punch? The answer, she discovered, was not that people enjoyed the punching itself especially, but they got off on the heightened adrenalin around such an extreme activity.

'There are two things happening,' she explains. 'The person that's watching it is enjoying that anticipation of fear. It's like some of us that watch horror movies, we may not get sexually turned on, but we get really entertained and it changes our body chemistry. So with the belly-punching, the person watching was enjoying the fear and anticipation. And as someone who was getting punched, what I actually liked about it was also the anticipation; it was like, "OK, it's coming," and then tensing up your body.

'It wouldn't be on my personal list of things to do,' she admits. 'But it wouldn't be a hard *Hell no!* [which] I thought it was going to be. And of course, it's negotiated, right? I'm not just like, "Sure, knock the wind out of me." There's a build-up to it.'

So what do our kinks say about us? The broad answer is that it depends. It could be down to one specific thing, or it could be a combination. There's no way of knowing whether the third of American men who say they've fantasised about lactation have a 'mummy fetish', want to engage in adult nursing or simply find the sight of full, leaking breasts sensual.[5] Let's not forget that in lots of cultures public breastfeeding is taboo, so again it could just be that something you're not supposed to see becomes arousing for you.

As I said, the whole idea of 'not supposed to' can be a powerful aphrodisiac. Which leads me on to the next question I get asked all the time ...

Can I be kinky and a feminist?

Yes. OK? Next!

Nah, I'm kidding. I just hear this a lot, or something like it. If I'm not fielding messages from people on social media who are worried that their submissive fantasies mean they've got internalised misogynistic views, I'm reading questionable takes about how it's 'psychopathic' to be into sexual degradation.

Look, I understand. You'd never in a million years let a man tell you what to do in your day-to-day life, so it's confusing to realise that it turns you on to fantasise about it in the bedroom. If your partner was physically abusive to you IRL, I'd tell you to get the fuck out of there. So why is it suddenly OK just because he's using a pink leather sex whip?

It comes down to two things: context and consent.

Even though sex is a part of our everyday lives, it's not the everyday world. We enjoy things in sex that we wouldn't want to do at work or while shopping in a store. It's a different context. So it doesn't have to follow the same rules. So, yes, you can enjoy being called a 'dirty slut' during sex; it definitely does not mean you want to have that insult yelled at you in the street.

It's also important to remember that recreational sex is a form of play (there's a reason we call them sex 'toys' after all!). It's a time for adults to play ... with ideas, with feelings, with roles, with sensations. And just like a child's playtime, it's largely imaginary! We're pretending. During sex we can try on different roles – we can play at being the leader, the authoritarian, the bossy brat, the innocent – and see how they make us feel. It doesn't mean we want to be or do those things in real life.

'Those words would be humiliating and degrading outside of that sexual space,' explains Jasmine. 'But for whatever reason, [in the context of sex] it allows you to relinquish control, it allows you to behave in a particular way that you wouldn't naturally feel comfortable with unless you were role-playing as said "slut" or "whore".' What I do say, though, is this: that person has to initiate that play.

'If I get into a sexy situation with a man that I don't know, and he just comes straight off the bat, like, "You fucking dirty, filthy whore," [that's not OK]. That has to be something that we negotiate, and we understand the context.'

Jasmine draws parallels with race play, admitting that as a Black woman she instinctively finds the idea problematic, but she tries to look at it on a case-by-case basis. As a dominatrix, she sometimes has white male clients who come to her asking to be humiliated. 'They want to be told that they can't satisfy me, that their penis is too small, that they're not good enough – those type of things,' she says.

The problem with this kink is that it's rooted in the idea of her being racialised as hypersexual, or insatiable – something I already talked about with Yasmin Benoit in Chapter 2: Society, Stigma and Slut-shaming (see page 41). Just as I can see why some people might struggle with the idea that a woman wants to feel degraded during sex, Jasmine can see why someone might be disgusted by the thought of getting into a dynamic that draws on real-world racist tropes. She tends to make a judgement based on how well she knows the client, what kind of person they are in real life and, to some extent, her gut feeling about the situation.

'Sometimes the things that they want to hear are not even true, in my opinion. I'm like, "Your penis is ... fine!"' she laughs. 'But that is where their turn-on comes from. And so I choose not to take that away from them. But it has to be very fantasy-based. If there are certain things [where] I feel like, "Oh my gosh, this is rooted in a really unhealthy place," then I opt out for that, because it doesn't make me feel good to feed something that is incredibly unhealthy. A fetish is about objectifying something and getting sexual gratification. So if someone says they [specifically] love fucking Black women, it's like, "Hmmm, that's a fetish." You have taken a human being and objectified them to a thing that you enjoy for sexual gratification.'

It's up to individuals where they draw the line in their own sex lives, but Jasmine is keen to stress that in any situation where the kink is drawing on real-world power discrepancies, there needs to be a very clear negotiation of the boundaries. 'I do think the person who has been oppressed by those terms, oppressed by that ideology, is the one [who] needs to be requesting, initiating, negotiating, setting those firm boundaries,' she says. 'And then, also, there needs to be a clear distinction of where this starts and stops.'

As I mentioned earlier, BDSM can also be a form of escapism. For a lot of people, being submissive is about being able to experience a feeling of vulnerability (sometimes quite intense vulnerability) but in a completely safe space with someone you trust. If you think about it, that's actually not something women get to do very often.

We have to be on our guard all the time. We have to be on alert because in the real world we know only too well that there are people who would exploit us. Being sexually submissive with someone who you know is 100 per cent committed to looking after you and giving you pleasure actually offers a break from that, a chance to truly let go. No wonder it's a huge fantasy for people!

And being submissive is not actually about giving up your agency. Just by communicating that you want to be submissive, you've already exercised your agency. You've consented. And that's the other key difference. Why is being spat on during sex different to being spat on in a café? Because you didn't *consent* to having some guy's saliva dripping down you while you're just trying to enjoy your brunch. Sometimes, it really is that simple.

As I've been saying to you all the way through this book, understanding what you like and knowing how to get it is *empowering*. Far from having internalised misogyny, you're actually *using* your sexual agency. And that applies to everything from being eaten out for a full half-hour to being tied up and made to beg for your orgasm. Whether you're dominant or submissive, vanilla or kinky, owning and communicating what your partner needs to do to drive you wild is you using your pussy power, and I am here for it.

How to introduce kink into your relationship

You know what I'm going to say, right? Yep, you guessed: you have to talk about it. As with anything you want to introduce into your sex life, it has to start with communication.

As a master fetish trainer, Jet Setting Jasmine works with a lot of people who want to introduce kink or fetishes into their relationship but aren't sure how. A lot of the time it's not even shame or fear that's holding them back, it's simply the fact that they've never said it out loud before. This is one reason why, in Chapter 10: Sexual

Compatibility, I mentioned rehearsing in front of the mirror (see page 249). Yeah, you might feel a bit silly telling your reflection, 'I want you to suck my toes,' but nobody's ever going to know (just make sure your flatmate is out while you're practising) and it might just help you say it out loud later on when it matters.

'Sometimes it really is just the difficulty of saying something that is new to someone that you're intimate or wanting to be intimate with,' agrees Jasmine. 'What are [the] other ways that we can communicate this? We could send them a podcast; we could send them a screenshot of this page in your book. I also like to use porn clips. I send them to my partner, because I don't always know how to describe it, and so I'll send him something like, "I think that this is hot."'

This is a really good way of letting someone know you're into something without putting pressure on them to immediately say yes. But if they do respond positively, you can take the conversation from there and ask them which bits they like and what role they'd like to take in it. 'We have this third-party medium we can use without having to go, "OK, but I want to hold my leg up like this, and then I want you to do it like that," you know? That feels so technical,' says Jasmine. 'We can also use some other media, like Cardi B saying, "Spit in my mouth." I could send you that and be like, "Hey, what do you think about this line?" without ever having to say, "Oloni, can you spit in my mouth, please?"'

I agree. Communication doesn't just happen when we're in bed together (although it does also need to happen there). You can also do this via text, or, when a kink comes up on TV, you could say, 'That looks interesting. Would you ever want to try that?' You can copy the link to a kink you've read about in one of my Twitter threads and message it to your partner or mention it during some light-hearted banter. You can even build it into foreplay, asking your partner to name a kink or fantasy they'd like to explore one day and agree to discuss it again after sex.

However you decide to do it, go slow. Just because you've watched someone getting their nipples electrocuted in porn and found it hot doesn't mean you should rush out and buy a cattle prod (I'm obviously kidding, and anyway you should only ever use products designed for use on the human body – there are a number of companies that make safe electrical stimulation products). If it's the sensation you're drawn to, you could start out by asking your partner to use their hands to squeeze and pinch the nipples, before moving on to buying some nipple clamps. Pinwheels and vampire gloves also deliver 'spiky' sensations. If it's the 'tech' aspect you like, you could try using your existing sex toys (have you ever put your clit sucker on your nipples?), while an attraction to the procedural dynamic could be achieved with a bit of medical role play.

And it's also worth remembering that kink doesn't have to be hard. When we think of kink, a lot of us think of spanking and hair-pulling, black leather and latex, metal cuffs and chains. And this makes sense. The popular image of the BDSM 'dungeon' is a room for punishment, pain and discomfort.

'The only thing we see, maybe in porn, or in some type of action movie, is where the woman is a dominatrix or something. She's all in leather, and it's always a white woman,' agrees Jasmine. 'She's got to be covered in leather from head-to-toe, and she doesn't have a compassionate bone in her body.'

She's not wrong either; think of the mainstream shows and movies about BDSM! That hardcore leather-clad vibe is definitely one side of it, and something that lots of people are into, but it's not the only side. A lot of what people find hot about dominance and submission is the psychological stuff, the *feeling* of obeying somebody or of being in charge. And that dynamic can play out in many ways, including softer, more sensual ways.

Submitting to someone who's going to engage in a really long, drawn-out tease until you're begging them to fuck you, for example, can actually be really romantic and intense. You don't have to be tied up (although you can get soft silky rope that feels really nice against the skin) to submit, and agreeing to do so *without* any restraints can be just as powerful as it becomes all about the dynamic between you. You might use soft touch, with hands, or feathers, or silk scarves. You might even just use words. Having someone almost touch you but not quite, while talking dirty to you all the time, can be an incredible way to build arousal and have you squirming around in pleasurable agony.

And, as Jasmine has discovered over the last few years, there are many ways to do BDSM virtually or in a long-distance relationship that don't even involve you being in the same room as your partner. During the lockdown and social-distancing restrictions, she had to give up a lot of her in-person sessions with clients or personal submissives. Instead, she's learned a lot about how to give orders to someone to do self-domination and spin a subtle web of psychological control over somebody from afar (with their consent, of course).

'[It could be] through control of people's finances, control of people's food intake, what they wear,' she says. 'And all without ever laying a finger on them.' I've heard other stories of creative BDSM during the pandemic too, such as a dominant who had his submissive partner put elastic bands around her thighs and, upon his orders, ping them hard against herself while he watched on Zoom.

There are other benefits to trying it out virtually or non-physically too. It can help build up trust and allows you and your partner to play around with the feelings that come from being dominant or submissive before you get into the physical stuff. And getting to grips with how kink (and sex more generally) makes you feel – emotionally as well as physically – is a huge part of healthy consent.

Boundaries, safe words and consent

Consent is the cornerstone of kink. At its heart, most kink is a power exchange. You're giving and relinquishing power so it's absolutely crucial that you play with someone you trust. If you're the one giving up power (for example, in a submissive scene), you're trusting your partner to use that power responsibly. But also, if you're the one wielding power, you're trusting your partner to be honest with you about how it feels and what they're comfortable with.

So where do we start? I've already discussed consent in depth in Chapter 7, but there are a few things that are key to BDSM specifically and I'm going to talk you through those in a moment, with some help and insight from Jasmine. But first I want to address the elephant in the room. Because for all the DMs I get from women happily sharing their nastiest fantasies with me, I also regularly hear from people who don't believe that kinky sex could ever be consensual, that's it's violence and it's wrong.

While I don't agree, I can understand why some people feel this way. And I think this belief partly comes from the coverage we've seen of horrible sexual violence where the offenders have tried to pass it off as BDSM. It's a really tricky subject and, I'll be honest, it's not one I feel very enthusiastic about wading into because I know it's so triggering for people, but I think there are a few things we need to clear up here.

⚠ **Content Warning: Sexual violence.**

There has been a lot of debate in the media in the last few years about rough sex. The subject came to the fore because an increasing number of men were defending themselves against murder and domestic abuse charges by arguing that the victim consented to the violence. Legally, it has never been deemed possible to consent to serious bodily harm, but in practice, campaigners argued, sexual violence cases were often dismissed by police and the Crown Prosecution Service as 'rough sex'.[6]

When cases did make it to court, juries were regularly being told that the death was an accident, the result of 'sex games gone wrong'. When British backpacker Grace Millane was killed in New Zealand in 2018, her murderer tried to use the fact that she was into BDSM as a defence (he was eventually convicted and given a life sentence).[7]

In the horrifying case of Natalie Connolly, her partner John Broadhurst actually went as far as to claim that the 40 separate injuries she sustained (including serious internal trauma, a fractured eye socket and facial wounds) before he left her drunk and bleeding at the bottom of the stairs were 'within the boundaries of her masochistic desires'.[8]

Clearly this is total bullshit. Even if these women *were* into BDSM, why the fuck were their partners not checking in with them? Essentially what these men are saying is that the person on the receiving end is the one responsible for how it goes down. No way! How could it ever be one person's responsibility? Sex is something we do *together*, guys. If you are having sex with someone (any kind of sex TBH, not just kinky sex), it is just as much your responsibility to make sure your partner's enjoying themselves and that you're playing within your agreed boundaries. And nobody agrees to being left to die at the foot of the stairs.

Still, these lines of argument have kept coming up in the courts, to the point where it became known as the 'rough sex defence', and in 2021 the UK Government passed a new Domestic Abuse Act, which aims to close the loophole that allowed abusers to make this claim. The bill seeks to 'clarify by restating in statute law the general proposition that a person may not consent to the infliction of serious harm and, by extension, is unable to consent to their own death'.[9]

But the subject of BDSM and rough sex in particular remains controversial. That's understandable. But it's really important to remember that what happened in these tragic cases *was not BDSM.* How do I know? Because people who engage in consensual kink do not do so with abandon. There needs to be careful discussion of everybody's boundaries, there should be ongoing check-ins to make sure you're both having a good time and you should be paying very close attention to each other's verbal and non-verbal reactions.

Something that often got missed when newspapers were reporting on Grace Millane's murder was the fact that the examples brought up in the trial of her previous BDSM experiences had all included clear consent. An ex-partner of hers testified that they had practised choking together but also described in detail their consent arrangements.

'Grace and I would have a safe word most of the time, which we had discussed. [We] used a tapping practice too. If Grace tapped me three times then it would stop. Grace and I were careful to discuss not only the physical but the psychological aspects to practising BDSM,' he wrote in a statement, which was read to the jury.

When people play consensually they don't die.

I remember talking about this with another professional dominatrix who came on the podcast in 2019, and she was categorical about it. 'How does it go wrong? How?' she said. 'If you're connected to your partner, you're checking in with your partner, there's absolutely no way it could go wrong.' As a dominant herself she knows full well what it's like to dish out pain and humiliation while always making sure the person she's with is comfortable. 'Part of my job as a domme is to check in and really pay attention to my partner.'

For Jasmine, it's really important to start off playing with the psychological parts of kink before getting into the physical ones. 'People will see us flogging or choking and spanking or [doing] electro play or whatever – something physical – and they're like, "I want to do that." Great! But it's gonna take you a while to learn how to do this proficiently. So while you're learning this craft, learn how to give a command, learn how to negotiate boundaries, before you even touch a person,' she says. 'Learning about the responsibility of giving a command and helping someone see it through, and the rewards and punishment, without ever laying a hand on them, is incredibly powerful for both the dominant and the submissive.'

Starting with power dynamics rather than physical activities isn't about being scared, she says, it's about really getting to grips with what you enjoy about the kink and appreciating all the aspects of it. It also helps build trust and connection between partners.

'Of course, there are people who really do want the physical element of it, and I don't say you [should] deny people the experience that they want,' she says. 'But ... especially [for] those that are starting out, [I'd first ask] what does it feel like to take a command?'

One part of kinky sex that a lot of people have heard of is the concept of safe words. A safe word is a word you agree to use if you want to stop the play at any point. It's absolutely non-negotiable and saying it calls an immediate halt to any activity.

Some people like to choose safe words that are deliberately incongruous so that it breaks the mood. Words like 'pineapple' or 'mittens' or 'lawnmower'. You might remember that in *Fifty Shades of Grey*, Ana and Christian used the word 'yellow' as their safe word. Others recommend a traffic-light system where 'red' means stop, 'amber' or 'orange' means you're feeling unsure or you need a break, and 'green' of course means go. It's also totally OK to use regular words, although the reason people don't always opt for things like 'stop' and 'no' is because in the middle of a scene those might be words you automatically say but don't mean. For example, let's say you're enjoying an extended spanking session. The pleasure/pain boundary can be so delicate in that situation that it's just as likely you might moan 'noooooo' as it is that you'll moan 'yessssss'.

Of course, in those situations, a good partner should check in and make sure you mean what you're saying. And it should go without saying by now that those check-ins, that consent communication, can be a really sexy part of the scene in its own right. Here's an example:

Dominant: Naughty girl, I saw you flinch. You promised you were going to take your punishment without complaining. Are you going to be good for me?

Submissive: Yes, sir.

Dom: I think you're going to need ten more spanks with the paddle for that.

Sub: ∗*involuntary*∗ Nooooo ....

Dom: No??
Sub: Yes. I mean yes, sir.
Dom: Good girl. Now hold still for me.

I also remember the dominatrix who was on *Laid Bare* telling me she likes to ask her clients, 'How does that feel, baby?' which is such a sexy way of finding out if someone is still comfortable. It also actually adds to the power play by inviting them to affirm the dominant's actions or to express deference and gratitude.

If you've already discussed what you want to do beforehand, there isn't always a need to expressly ask, 'Can I do this?' or 'Is that OK?' You can usually start from the basis that the activity itself has been consented to, but you just need to make sure you're playing at the right level. So in the case of restraining someone, you might ask, 'Is that nice and tight?' as you pull the rope a tiny bit more.

There is also the option of using physical signals to let each other know how you're doing. This is especially helpful if one of you is restrained or positioned in such a way that they can't speak (for example, with a gag), or if you know that you struggle to articulate words when you're in the heat of the moment. The easiest thing is to agree a hand signal, gesture or tap that you can both clearly recognise and which can't be confused with anything else, although again, if your partner says something ambiguous or makes a sign you're not sure of, it is your responsibility to check in: 'Was that a signal, baby?' 'Can you do/say that again for me?'

Kink-shaming

It's OK to be intrigued by other people's kinks, to question them – heck, it's OK not to understand them at all. I still don't get many of the kinks people have, and I'd be lying if I said I've never pulled a face when a kink that included bodily waste is mentioned. I've even seen my followers say that some kinks deserved to be shamed, but what we must remember is that what *we* like might well be gross to someone else. And it's never black and white with kink either. One person's most shocking fantasy might be someone else's standard Saturday night. For example, I enjoy very light choking when having sex and having degrading words being whispered into my ear during each stroke. Now, depending where you are on the kink spectrum, that could either sound very fucked up or extremely vanilla.

The other thing about kink-shaming is that often it entirely misses the point. Most people who are into unusual or taboo activities know full well that they are niche interests. *That's part of the appeal!* As YouTuber Kat Blaque pointed out in a video last year, 'The BDSM community is like being in a roomful of nerds – nerds who are really passionate about paraphilias. The vast majority of kinksters do not want to [do] mainstream BDSM!'[10]

Plus, some people do get off on humiliation, so shaming them for it is absolutely not going to make any difference. If anything, you're playing into what they like anyway.

But imagine if people *didn't* judge others by what they like in the bedroom so that we could get to the point where we could actually have a conversation about it? Wouldn't there be room for a bigger and more explorative discussion?

It's not really surprising that a lot of people do judge kinks and fetishes in this way. As I said earlier, the idea that being kinky meant there was something wrong with you was actually backed up by scientific understanding for a really long time. It takes time to let go of these ideas, so in some ways I get why people struggle with it. But also, if you are finding yourself getting really hung up on what *other people* do in bed then maybe that says more about you than them ...

There's an expression in the kink community: 'Your kink is not my kink but your kink is OK' (sometimes shortened to 'YKINMKB-YKIOK'). Yeah, I know, it's not exactly catchy. But it does sum up the attitude we should be trying to adopt. Or maybe you know the expression 'Don't yuck my yum'? It's the same sort of thing. You don't have to be into everything that I'm into. You can even be disgusted by it (and as we already discussed, the fact that people are disgusted by it might even be part of the turn-on for me!) – that's OK. You're entitled to your feelings and nobody's saying you have to get involved in any nasty shit if it's not your cup of tea. But just because it's not for you, that doesn't mean you're entitled to police my consensual activities, or anyone else's for that matter.

I've had women tell me that I'm allowing myself to be degraded by men and that it isn't what healthy sex looks like. Well, if unhealthy sex is taking power over pleasure in a consensual way and communicating what makes my clit thump then I'll take it.

Vanilla doesn't mean boring

Sometimes when I talk about kinks or ask the guests on my show what's the nastiest thing they've ever done in bed (if you come on my show, you'd better know that I do love to ask that question!), I worry that some of my audience will think I'm suggesting that everyone has to be a freak or they're boring if they haven't done loads of crazy shit in bed. This is definitely not the case. Yes, I want to break down the stigma around BDSM so that people can feel confident to explore and not be slut-shamed for it. But that doesn't mean everyone has to be into it.

Being vanilla isn't a bad thing. Vanilla is universal, it's safe, it's pleasurable, it's fun. I've actually had people shame me for not being as adventurous as other sex educators before, and it was as if they felt the kinkier the sexual experiences, the better the sex content. But that type of thinking removes agency. Yes, experiences are very important, but do you know what is even more powerful? Knowing and feeling confident in your boundaries, educating yourself and speaking openly to other people about their bedroom stories.

You shouldn't force yourself to be who you're not. Don't let anyone ever pressure you or say you haven't lived. Sure, there's nothing wrong with light-hearted jokes about sexual preferences in the bedroom, but when it comes down to it, always stay true to your sexual boundaries and explore whenever *you're* ready to.

Sex isn't about ticking boxes or impressing your mates – although don't get me wrong, I love hearing those stories. But really, great sex is about doing what you enjoy. There's nothing wrong with experimenting if that feels exciting, but there's also a lot of pussy power to be had from knowing that something's not for you and having confidence in what you *do* like.

Ladies... it's time to share your kinks!

Kinks Twitter thread*

33, New Jersey, USA

I'm in an open relationship with my bf and we enjoy group sex. One of both our kinks is watching the other have sex with other people, he's watched 4 guys have sex with [me] together in one night. There was a lot of meat flying around, but I took it like a champ. My man was jacking off on the side as it was going on and then when they left had his turn with me. That's the kinkiest thing we've done and I'm watching him have sex with 3 other women next week.

---

*Not all the views expressed in the Twitter threads reflect my opinion as the author of this book, but it is important to me to share other perspectives and experiences of peoples' sexual expression and relationships.

25, Essex, UK

My ex used to beg me to peg him. It started with fingers and whatever and then he bought 2 different sized dildos and I started off thinking it was odd and then I got into it and now it's a fetish and I joke about pegging my current boyfriend and he's so against it but recently he let me eat ass and he LOVED it and now I wanna do it all the time (I love pleasing my man and he's just so shy with it all but he'll eat my ass for hours if I let him).

25, NYC, USA

Hello Oloni, I recently tried this act with my bf for the first time and I loved it. I tied him up in a chair in front of our bed, spread my legs gynaecologist style and forced him to watch me masturbate. He wasn't allowed to touch me at first but after some minutes I allowed him to use the toys on me. We finished it off with both of us masturbating across from each other. My favourite part was watching him restless when my moans kept getting louder and louder but he couldn't do anything aside from watching.

Anon

Hi Oloni, my friends will probably know this is me because I've been obsessed since Don-E came out but I really want to be handcuffed to a bed with a guy in the vendetta mask, fucking me aggressively. I don't know why but I'm just soooo turned on by that mask.

26, Buckinghamshire, UK

Please keep me anon, but I love my feet being touched – it turns me on so much. I love foot worshipping porn especially but too scared to ask my partner to do it to me. He openly knows I have a major foot fetish which is kind of taboo for a woman to have but I own it now. So now whenever we're chilling at home he'll just take my socks off and start gently tickling my feet and sliding his fingers in between my toes and my god it's orgasmic to me, gets me wetter than any other sexual act for sure. Plus any excuse to massage his feet and I'll be doing it. Damn I need all of that now.

31, Edinburgh, UK

The last guy I was with was into BDSM and was into orgasm torture, where he tied me up to the bed, used a separator to make sure I could not close my legs with a blind fold on my eyes, then he used a wand on my clit, it turned him on watching me cum till I could not take it any more to almost pain, I had to call him master. Never done that before, it was amazing! To be controlled like that! Phew, every woman should have that.

25, London, UK

Hi Oloni! This happened last year, I was the other woman with my now partner. Had been asking him to leave his then-girlfriend but we were in lockdown 3 and he didn't want to leave her over the phone (fair enough) so I was back on all the apps as I wasn't this man's girlfriend and could do what I want. I met a guy on FetLife, spoke for about a week. Went for a wholesome lockdown friendly walk with him and it was good, he wasn't a creep. The next night, [I] tell my now-partner I have a deadline the next day (which I did) so was busy doing uni work and couldn't talk. Instead, [I] had the guy from FetLife come over to scratch the submissive itch I had. I was absolutely destroyed, he was HUGE and had the girth to back it. I was spanked to my heart's desire and left with the prettiest bruises. He doesn't stay the night and goes. I'm instantly back in the routine of being on the phone to my love. Told him about 6 months later after we'd been together for a while and he still tenses up to this day when someone has the same name hahahahaha.

30, Birmingham, UK

Hey Oloni, I was dating this guy for a few weeks and one day he kept mentioning all the things he was into, then asked me. I jokingly said golden showers, which is piss play, and he said 'omg same'. When I realised he wasn't joking I asked if he wanted me to pee on him or the other way around. He didn't mind, but when we had a shower together asked if we could finally try it. I got on my knees and he released all over my chest. It felt very warm and he looked like he was having a lot of fun. 9/10 experience. I've never told my friends cus I think they'd laugh at me but I thought it was rather fun.

28, Miami, USA

Hi Oloni, plsssss make this anonymous. I really enjoy a lot of kink with my friends with benefits. We're both a switch so sometimes we change who the sub or dom is. We've done everything from spanking, kitten play, pretending to be a university student who's having sex with my professor. We change it up often and it's really fun. There's no judgment, just two people who live out their wildest sexual fantasies and we have a safe word.

30, London, UK

ANON! I had a man come over and be my foot stool for two hours while I caught up on *real housewives*. Then he cleaned my kitchen. Took his clothes off, laid in my bath and I had some girlfriends come over and we spent the evening drinking cocktails and using him as our toilet whenever we needed. Strictly water sports only. It was so sexy to have so many of us feel empowered by being so dominant. His penis was also caged so it wasn't about his arousal at all.

Conclusion

What should you take away from this book? I hope after joining me on this journey of sexual exploration you decide to be unapologetic about your sex life and how you choose to enjoy it. I want you to go forth and be truthful with yourself about the type of sexual experiences you want. This book was created with you in mind to make sure you're getting the most from your intimate experiences. Never apologise for basking in your sexuality.

The misinformation we've been given around sex has shaped how society sees sexuality. These myths are nothing more than fearmongering tactics to stop people, especially women, from engaging in something that's natural and pleasurable. Our sexual education system is flawed, and I don't even think it needs improvement – it needs a total rewrite.

Growing up as a Black woman who talks about sex has been a very scary journey; I know how judgemental my community can be. I'm met with criticism from men who start off sentences with, 'If she follows Oloni, she's [add insult here].' In translation, what they're saying is: 'If she doesn't want to be manipulated ...' 'If I can't disrespect her ...' Or 'If she's trying to make smarter choices ...' This is all because I discuss the many sides of women and sexuality for a living. Many struggle with this because of their assumption that women are naive beings and anyone who enjoys reading my content, whether it be educational or entertaining, will be influenced into using their sexuality how they want.

How dare we?

It's the idea of women having autonomy that scares some. If we have autonomy then they lose their historical power over us and with it their sense of self. Our sexual experiences should not be up for negotiation. Men have been able to benefit from a society that tells them that sex is only meant to be enjoyed by them and if we show an interest in it we aren't classy women, but sluts from the Madonna–whore dichotomy.

Each chapter in this book has been geared towards helping you understand the true reality of sex, not what's been subconsciously picked up in porn and added to your sex routine. We're cutting out the fake gasps when he slides it in, sis; we're not faking our moans or our orgasms to boost his ego. Instead, we're communicating and guiding our sexual partners towards a more pleasurable experience. Our intimate moments won't be with people who think they're in competition with our sex toys, but those who get that a suction toy and a vibrator are tools, not a replacement. With everything you've been taught in this book, the people you have sex with will have no choice but to step it up! You're not an inanimate object meant for masturbation, but a sexual being who is deserving of pleasure and who should only be engaging with partners who aim to centre it as well as their own.

In a dream world I'd love to receive fewer sex and relationship dilemmas from women, but instead testimonials about how they successfully and confidently spoke about their sexual health with their potential and current lover. This book answers most of the frequently asked questions and more, but reading is one thing. Anyone can read a book. Practising what you've read with your sexual partners and yourself? Now, *that's* where the real power lies. It's also a step in the right direction to understanding your body and your boundaries. *The Big O* wasn't made with the intention to encourage you to have more sex, but to improve the quality of the sex you're having and to have sex the way you wish to without the fear of being slut-shamed, judged or questioned. You can be sex-positive and have agency over your body whether you're celibate, or in an open or monogamous relationship. The message of *The Big O* is to shine a light and educate women on how to enjoy sex without feeling guilty for it and to tell the stories of how other women have had sex.

My single wish for anyone who has got this far in the book is to use some of the experiences and research, as well as my words, to push you into having better sex. A sexual glow-up that has you smiling all day; the type of sex that makes you daydream; the type of sex you can't wait to have again, that makes you want to tell anyone who will listen; the type that allows you to describe your orgasms in detail and tell your partner what helped get you there when they ask; the type that makes you confident in the bedroom because of all the new tips and tricks you've learned. Confidence is sexy, and knowing what you want and saying it out loud is even sexier.

If you were someone who didn't know how to ask your partner for oral sex, you should now! If you weren't sure how to experiment in the bedroom, well, you should now!

I want readers of *The Big O* not only to understand their bodies more, but to be honest about the type of sexual relationship set-up that makes them happy regardless of what society says, to practise safe sex in and out of commitments and to never feel any shame for what you choose to do with your body sexually. It is yours.

Oloni's 12 commandments

1. Always ask for consent.
2. Never settle for less in and outside of the bedroom.
3. Love who you want to love.
4. Touch thyself and experiment sexually.
5. Always slut-praise and celebrate your girls' sexual moments, unless you fear they're in a dangerous situation.
6. Make sexually smart choices.
7. Always have sex with someone who makes you feel good.
8. Never use sex to keep a man.
9. Only speak positive words about your body.
10. Never, ever fake an orgasm.
11. Never have sex for the approval of others.
12. Always discuss sexual health with your partners and get tested regularly.

Resources

Sexual assault and violence

Rape Crisis: rapecrisis.org.uk

RAINN: rainn.org

Refuge: refuge.org.uk

Galop: galop.org.uk

LGBTQ+ support and advice

Stonewall: stonewall.org.uk

LGBT Foundation: lgbt.foundation/

Gendered Intelligence: genderedintelligence.co.uk

MindOut: mindout.org.uk

Switchboard LGBQ+ Helpline: switchboard.lgbt

TransUnite directory of trans support groups: transunite.co.uk

The Asexual Visibility & Education Network: asexuality.org/

Inclusive sexual health

NAZ: naz.org.uk

Love Sex Life: lovesexlife.org.uk

Decolonising Contraception: decolonisingcontraception.com/

56 Dean Street: dean.st/

Terrence Higgins Trust: tht.org.uk/

Prepster: prepster.info

cliniQ: cliniq.org.uk

Sex worker rights

SWARM: swarmcollective.org

DecrimNow: decrimnow.org.uk/

Global Network of Sex Work Projects (NSWP): nswp.org

Quizzes and tests

Unofficial Kinsey Scale test: idrlabs.com/kinsey-scale/test.php

BDSM test: bdsmtest.org/select-mode

Emily Nagoski's accelerators/brakes worksheet: emilynagoski.com/come-as-you-are-worksheets

Shannon Boodram's relationship quiz: thegameofdesire.com/commitment

My fave podcasts (other than *Laid Bare*, of course!)

Two Twos Podcast (@twotwospodcast)

Two Black lesbians living in London speaking their unapologetic truth while creating a safe space for people like themselves and bridging the gap between LGBTQ+ people and cisgendered straight people!

Joy's World (@joysworldthepodcast)

A unique insight into the life of 'Fat, Black, Blind, SEXY single mother of one' Joy and all her juicy bits.

Lip Service Podcast (@aylipservice)

Syndicated radio star Angela Yee talks sex and relationships with the hottest stars in hip-hop and R&B. Join her and her friends each week as they coax stars into revealing their most intimate secrets from the bedroom. It's hip-hop like you've never heard before.

WHOREible Decisions (@whoreible_decisions)

Tune in for a new episode every Monday, where hosts Mandii B and WeezyWTF sit down with an array of guests and discuss topics such as: couples, doctors, pornstars, doms, subs, activists, celebs, and more about their sex lives and craziest kinks!

Multiamory (multiamory.com/podcast)

Multiamory offers support and advice for modern relationships. Whether you are monogamous, polyamorous, swinging, casually dating, or if you just do relationships differently, this podcast is there for you.

Monogamish Pod (monogamishpod.com)

A podcast about non-monogamy and polyamory through a Black Caribbean lens.

*F**ks Given by ComeCurious* (@comecurious)

Florence and Reed talk about sex, relationships and body positivity with no filter, no censor and absolutely no F**ks Given.

Educators, activists and influencers I love

Passport Cutty (@passport_cutty)

Shannon Boodram (@shanboody)

Jet Setting Jasmine (@jetsetjasmine); jsjlinks.com/

Angelica Lindsey-Ali (@villageauntie)

Yeside Olayinka-Agbola (@oloricoitus)

Dalychia Saah and Rafaella Fiallo aka Afrosexology (@afrosexology_)

Angela Yee (@angelayee); YouTube channel: youtube.com/c/AngelaYee

Mandii B and WeezyWTF from *WHOREible Decisions*; YouTube channel: youtube.com/c/WHOREibleDecisions

Yoni M (@yonitalkstv)

Yasmin Benoit (@theyasminbenoit)

Kat Blaque (@kat_blaque); YouTube channel: youtube.com/c/KatBlaque

Florence and Reed aka ComeCurious (@comecurious); YouTube channel: youtube.com/c/ComeCurious

Books I've learned from

Emily Nagoski, *Come As You Are: The Surprising New Science That Will Transform Your Sex Life* (Simon & Schuster, 2015)

Fern Riddell, *Sex: Lessons from History* (Hodder & Stoughton, 2021)

Habeeb Akande, *Kunyaza: The Secret to Female Pleasure* (Rabaah Publishers, 2018)

Dr Laurie Mintz, *Becoming Cliterate: Why Orgasm Equality Matters – And How to Get It* (HarperOne, 2017)

Alya Mooro, *The Greater Freedom: Life as a Middle Eastern Woman Outside the Stereotypes* (Little A, 2019)

Wednesday Martin, *Untrue: Why Nearly Everything We Believe About Women, Lust, and Infidelity Is Wrong and How the New Science Can Set Us Free* (Little Brown Spark, 2018)

Karen Gurney, *Mind the Gap: The Truth About Desire and How to Futureproof Your Sex Life* (Headline Home, 2020)

Gary Chapman, *The Five Love Languages: How to Express Heartfelt Commitment to Your Mate* (Northfield Publishing, 2022; 1992)

Justin Lehmiller, *Tell Me What You Want: The Science of Sexual Desire and How It Can Help You Improve Your Sex Life* (Robinson, 2018)

Other useful tools for sexual discovery

Sex menu template: sexmenus.wordpress.com/

Write a letter to your future self: futureme.org/

References

Chapter 1: My Sex Education

1. S. Mayor, 'Baby doll simulation scheme does not reduce teen pregnancies, study finds', *BMJ*, 354 (2016). DOI: 10.1136/bmj.i4666

2. S.A. Brinkman et al., 'Efficacy of infant simulator programmes to prevent teenage pregnancy: a school-based cluster randomised controlled trial in Western Australia', *The Lancet*, 388: 10057 (25 August 2016), pp. 2264–71.

3. J. Pin. 'The Nerves and Vasculature of the Clitoris Are Absent from OB/GYN Literature', *Medium* (23 March 2018). jessica86.medium.com/ob-gyns-dont-learn-the-nerves-and-vasculature-of-the-clitoris-ccc56e55ac90

4. H.E. O'Connell et al., 'Anatomy of the Clitoris', *The Journal of Urology*, 174: 4: 1 (2005), pp. 1189–95. DOI: https://doi.org/10.1097/01.ju.0000173639.38898.cd

5. Public Health England, 'Teenage Pregnancy Prevention Framework: Supporting young people to prevent unplanned pregnancy and develop healthy relationships', Local Government Association, London (May 2018).

6. Conor Stewart, 'Share of Births to Teenage Mothers in Europe 2017, by Country', Statista (24 August 2021). www.statista.com/statistics/921890/rate-of-births-to-teenage-mothers-in-europe-by-country

7. Sex Education Forum, 'Young People's Poll Reveals Gaps', Sex Education Forum (27 November 2018). www.sexeducationforum.org.uk/news/news/young-peoples-poll-reveals-gaps

8. Department for Education, 'Relationships and Sex Education (RSE) and Health Education: Statutory guidance for governing bodies, proprietors, head teachers, principals, senior leadership teams', UK Government (25 June 2019). https://www.gov.uk/government/publications/relationships-education-relationships-and-sex-education-rse-and-health-education

9. Natalie Morris, 'Sex Education in Schools Is "Failing Black and Minority Children"', *Metro* (23 September 2020). metro.co.uk/2020/09/23/sex-education-excludes-black-and-minority-children-leading-to-higher-rates-of-stis-13301426

10. 'The History of Porn', Pornhub Insights (6 October 2015). www.pornhub.com/insights/history-of-porn

11. Alexandra Topping, 'Black Girl Strip-Searched at London School to Sue Met Police', *Guardian* (18 March 2022). www.theguardian.com/uk-news/2022/mar/18/child-q-scandal-black-britons-letter-to-met-police

12. Hannah Giorgis, 'Many Women of Color Don't Go to the Police after Sexual Assault for a Reason', *Guardian* (7 October 2018). www.theguardian.com/commentisfree/2015/mar/25/women-of-color-police-sexual-assault-racist-criminal-justice

13. Justin Parkinson, 'The Significance of Sarah Baartman', BBC News (7 January 2016). www.bbc.co.uk/news/magazine-35240987

14. Clifton Crais and Pamela Scully, *Sara Baartman and the Hottentot Venus: A Ghost Story and a Biography* (Reprint: Princeton University Press, 2010).

Chapter 2: Society, Stigma and Slut-shaming

1. C.H. Mercer et al., 'Changes in sexual attitudes and lifestyles in Britain through the life course and over time: findings from the National Surveys of Sexual Attitudes and Lifestyles (Natsal)', *The Lancet*, 382: 9907 (2013), pp. 1781–94. DOI: https://doi.org/10.1016/s0140-6736(13)62035-8

2. Patrick Strudwick, 'This Man Spent 25 Years Fighting Newspapers Over Their Anti-Gay Reporting and Finally Won', BuzzFeed (18 June 2019). www.buzzfeed.com/patrickstrudwick/this-man-spent-25-years-fighting-newspapers-over-their

3. 'Life-Blood, or Death?' *The Times* (21 November 1984), p. 19. https://archive.org/details/NewsUK1984UKEnglish/Nov%2021%201984%2C%20The%20Times%2C%20%2361992%2C%20UK%20%28en%29/page/n17/mode/2up

4. K.F. Stanger-Hall and D. W. Hall, 'Abstinence-Only Education and Teen Pregnancy Rates: Why We Need Comprehensive Sex Education in the U.S.', *PLoS ONE*, ed. V.J. Vitzthum, 6: 10 (2011), p. e24658. DOI: https://doi.org/10.1371/journal.pone.0024658

5. Alya Mooro, *The Greater Freedom: Life as a Middle Eastern Woman Outside the Stereotypes* (Little A, 2019).

6. B. Montemurro and J.M. Siefken, 'MILFS and Matrons: Images and Realities of Mothers' Sexuality', *Sexuality and Culture*, 16: 4 (2012), pp. 366–88. DOI: https://doi.org/10.1007/s12119-012-9129-2

7. Wednesday Martin, *Untrue: Why Nearly Everything We Believe About Women, Lust, and Infidelity Is Wrong and How the New Science Can Set Us Free* (Little, Brown Spark, 2018).

8. B.A. Scelza et al., 'High Rate of Extrapair Paternity in a Human Population Demonstrates Diversity in Human Reproductive Strategies', *Science Advances*, 6: 8 (2020). DOI: https://doi.org/10.1126/sciadv.aay6195

9. Fern Riddell, *Sex: Lessons from History* (Hodder & Stoughton, 2021).

10. Ibid.

11. Lord Chancellor, Secretary of State for Justice and the Attorney General, *Limiting the use of complainants' sexual history in sex cases*, Ministry of Justice and Attorney General's Office (14 December 2017). https://www.gov.uk/government/publications/limiting-the-use-of-complainants-sexual-history-in-sexual-offence-cases (Accessed 6 March 2022.)

12. Steven Morris, 'Campaigners Fear Evans Case Will Stop Women Reporting Rape', *Guardian* (14 October 2016). www.theguardian.com/society/2016/oct/14/campaigners-fear-evans-case-will-stop-women-reporting

13. C.H. Mercer et al., 'Changes in sexual attitudes and lifestyles in Britain through the life course and over time: findings from the National Surveys of Sexual Attitudes and Lifestyles (Natsal)', *The Lancet*, 382: 9907 (2013), pp. 1781–94. DOI: https://doi.org/10.1016/s0140-6736(13)62035-8

14. 'Josh Cavallo: "I'm a Footballer and I'm Gay," Says Australian Player', BBC News (27 October 2021). www.bbc.co.uk/news/newsbeat-59060323

15. Paul MacInnes, 'Jake Daniels becomes first UK male footballer to come out as gay since 1990', *Guardian* (16 May 2022). https://www.theguardian.com/football/2022/may/16/jake-daniels-becomes-first-uk-male-footballer-to-come-out-as-gay-since-1990

16. 'Why Are More Female Professional Footballers Openly Gay or Bisexual than Male Players?' ITV News (7 July 2019). www.itv.com/news/2019-07-07/womens-world-cup-why-are-more-female-professional-footballers-gay-or-bisexual-than-their-male-counterparts

17. Gayle S. Rubin, 'Thinking Sex: Notes for a Radical Theory of the Politics of Sexuality' in Carole S. Vance (ed.), *Pleasure and Danger: Exploring Female Sexuality* (Routledge & Kegan Paul, 1984), pp. 267–319.

18. 'School Report (2017)', Stonewall (30 June 2020). www.stonewall.org.uk/school-report-2017

19. UK Government, 'National LGBT Survey: Summary Report', GOV.UK, Government Equalities Office (27 September 2018). https://bit.ly/3vfDYOk

20. Kaila Adia Story, 'Racing Sex – Sexing Race' in Carol E. Henderson (ed.), *Imagining the Black Female Body: Reconciling Image in Print and Visual Culture* (Palgrave Macmillan, 2010; 2015), pp. 23–43.

Chapter 3: Virginity

1. R. Mishori et al., 'The little tissue that couldn't – dispelling myths about the hymen's role in determining sexual history and assault', *Reproductive Health*, 16: 1 (2019). DOI: https://doi.org/10.1186/s12978-019-0731-8

2. Jen Gunter, 'A History of Hymens', *The Walrus* (4 June 2020). thewalrus.ca/a-history-of-hymens

3. 'Eliminating Virginity Testing: An Interagency Statement', World Health Organization Report (2018). https://www.who.int/publications/i/item/WHO-RHR-18.15

4. Hannah Summers, 'Exposed: UK Clinics Still Offering to "Restore Virginity" before Marriage', *Guardian* (31 October 2021). www.theguardian.com/society/2021/oct/31/exposed-uk-clinics-still-offering-to-restore-virginity-before-marriage

5. Lizzie Dearden, 'Yazidi sex slaves undergoing surgery to "restore virginity" after being raped by Isis militants', *Independent* (28 April 2015). www.independent.co.uk/news/world/middle-east/yazidi-sex-slaves-undergoing-surgery-to-restore-virginity-after-being-raped-by-isis-militants-10207352.html

6. Sam Hailes, 'Joshua Harris: Why I Regret Writing "I Kissed Dating Goodbye"', *Premier Christianity* (18 March 2019). www.premierchristianity.com/home/joshua-harris-why-i-regret-writing-i-kissed-dating-goodbye/275.article

7. Lyz Lenz, '"I Kissed Dating Goodbye" told me to stay pure until marriage. I still have a stain on my heart', *Washington Post* (27 July 2016). www.washingtonpost.com/news/acts-of-faith/wp/2016/07/27/as-a-young-evangelical-i-believed-a-bestselling-book-that-warned-me-to-stay-pure-until-marriage-i-still-have-a-stain-on-my-heart

8. D.A. Frederick et al., 'Differences in Orgasm Frequency Among Gay, Lesbian, Bisexual, and Heterosexual Men and Women in a U.S. National Sample', *Archives of Sexual Behavior*, 47: 1 (2017), pp. 273–88. DOI: https://doi.org/10.1007/s10508-017-0939-z

Chapter 4: Sexual Identity

1. Fern Riddell, Sex: Lessons from History (Hodder & Stoughton, 2021).

2. Ibid.

3. Sigmund Freud, *Three Essays on the Theory of Sexuality* (The Standard Edition of the Complete Psychological Works of Sigmund Freud, 7, 1901–05), pp. 123–246.

4. J. Drescher, 'Out of DSM: Depathologizing Homosexuality', *Behavioral Sciences*, 5: 4 (2015), pp. 565–75. DOI: https://doi.org/10.3390/bs5040565

5. Patrick Kelleher, 'How the Tories spent years promising a conversion therapy ban – only to betray LGBT+ people', PinkNews (31 March 2022). www.pinknews.co.uk/2022/03/31/conversion-therapy-uk-ban

6. 'A proposed bill on conversion therapy could do more harm than good', *Economist* (4 December 2021). www.economist.com/britain/2021/12/04/a-proposed-bill-on-conversion-therapy-could-do-more-harm-than-good

7. Chaka L. Bachmann and Becca Gooch, 'LGBT IN BRITAIN: Health Report', YouGov, Stonewall, London (7 November 2018).

8. D. Bhugra, and G. Colombini, 'Sexual Dysfunction: Classification and Assessment', *Advances in Psychiatric Treatment*, 19: 1 (2013), pp. 48–55. DOI: https://doi.org/10.1192/apt.bp.112.010884

9. Karen Gurney, *Mind the Gap: The Truth About Desire and How to Futureproof Your Sex Life* (Headline Home, 2020).

10. T.M. Brown and E. Fee, 'Alfred C. Kinsey: A Pioneer of Sex Research', *American Journal of Public Health*, 93: 6 (2003), pp. 896–7. DOI: https://doi.org/10.2105/ajph.93.6.896

11. 'The Kinsey Scale', Kinsey Institute. kinseyinstitute.org/research/publications/kinsey-scale.php (Accessed 25 March 2022.)

12. J. Bancroft et al., 'The Dual Control Model: Current Status and Future Directions', *The Journal of Sex Research*, 46: 2–3 (2009), pp. 121–42. DOI: https://doi.org/10.1080/00224490902747222

13. Emily Nagoski, *Come As You Are: The Surprising New Science That Will Transform Your Sex Life* (Simon & Schuster, 2015).

14. https://www.emilynagoski.com/come-as-you-are-worksheets

15. C.H. Mercer et al., 'Changes in sexual attitudes and lifestyles in Britain through the life course and over time: findings from the National Surveys of Sexual Attitudes and Lifestyles (Natsal)', *The Lancet*, 382: 9907 (2013), pp. 1781–94. DOI: https://doi.org/10.1016/s0140-6736(13)62035-8

16. A.M. Johnson et al., 'Sexual Behaviour in Britain: Partnerships, Practices, and HIV Risk Behaviours', *The Lancet*, 358: 9296 (2001), pp. 1835–42. DOI: https://doi.org/10.1016/S0140-6736(01)06883-0

17. LGBT+ Pride 2021 Global Survey, Ipsos (June 2021). https://www.ipsos.com/en/-lgbt-pride-2021-global-survey

18. D.A. Frederick et al., 'Differences in Orgasm Frequency Among Gay, Lesbian, Bisexual, and Heterosexual Men and Women in a U.S. National Sample', *Archives of Sexual Behavior*, 47: 1 (2017), pp. 273–88. DOI: https://doi.org/10.1007/s10508-017-0939-z

19. E.W. Corty and J.M. Guardiani, 'Canadian and American Sex Therapists' Perceptions of Normal and Abnormal Ejaculatory Latencies: How Long Should Intercourse Last?' *The Journal of Sexual Medicine*, 5: 5 (2008), pp. 1251–6. DOI: https://doi.org/10.1111/j.1743-6109.2008.00797.x

Chapter 5: Getting to Know Your Body

1. W. Driemeyer et al., 'Masturbation Experiences of Swedish Senior High School Students: Gender Differences and Similarities', *The Journal of Sex Research*, 54: 4–5 (2016), pp. 631–41. DOI: https://doi.org/10.1080/00224499.2016.1167814

2. 'TENGA Global Self-Pleasure Study: 2018 Report: United States', TENGA, (30 April 2018). www.tenga.co/press/TENGA_2018_US_Full_Report.pdf

3. Eric Suni, 'The Relationship Between Sex and Sleep', Sleep Foundation (11 March 2022). www.sleepfoundation.org/physical-health/sex-sleep

4. G.A. Coria-Avila et al., 'The Role of Orgasm in the Development and Shaping of Partner Preferences', *Socioaffective Neuroscience & Psychology*, 6: 1 (2016), p. 31815. DOI: https://doi.org/10.3402/snp.v6.31815

5. Douglas Jehl, 'Surgeon General forced to resign by Whitehouse', *New York Times*, (10 December 1994), pp. 1–30.

6. Claudia Dreifus, 'Jocelyn Elders', *New York Times* (30 January 1994), p. 16.

7. 'Groundbreaking Research into What Feels Good and Why', OMGYES. www.omgyes.com/en/?hv=1 (Accessed 22 April 2022.)

8. Elisabeth A. Lloyd, *The Case of the Female Orgasm: Bias in the Science of Evolution* (Harvard University Press, 2005), p. X.

9. B. Whipple, 'Female Ejaculation, G Spot, A Spot, and Should We Be Looking for Spots?' *Current Sexual Health Reports*, 7: 2 (2015), pp. 59–62. DOI: https://doi.org/10.1007/s11930-015-0041-2

10. C. Ann, 'A proposal for a radical new sex therapy technique for the management of vasocongestive and orgasmic dysfunction in women: The AFE Zone stimulation technique', *Sexual and Marital Therapy*, 12: 4 (1997), pp. 357–70. DOI: https://doi.org/10.1080/02674659708408179

11. Kate Sloan, 'How Finding My A-Spot Unlocked the Best Orgasm of My Life', *Glamour* (20 April 2017). www.glamour.com/story/finding-my-anterior-fornix-unlocked-best-orgasm-of-my-life

12. Caroline Hire, 'A Timeline of Tantra', British Museum. www.britishmuseum.org/exhibitions/tantra-enlightenment-revolution/timeline (Accessed 4 May 2022.)

13. T.L. Woodard and M.P. Diamond, 'Physiologic Measures of Sexual Function in Women: A Review', *Fertility and Sterility*, 92: 1 (2009), pp. 19–34. DOI: https://doi.org/10.1016/j.fertnstert.2008.04.041

14. Catarina Quaresma and Paul B. Sparzak, *Anatomy, Abdomen and Pelvis, Bartholin Gland* (StatPearls Publishing, 24 January 2022).

15. R. Sabatini and R. Cagiano, 'Comparison profiles of cycle control, side effects and sexual satisfaction of three hormonal contraceptives', *Contraception*, 74: 3 (2006), pp.220–23. DOI: https://doi.org/10.1016/j.contraception.2006.03.022

16. 'Vaginal Dryness', NHS.uk, (10 January 2022). www.nhs.uk/conditions/vaginal-dryness/

17. J.B. Korda et al., 'SEXUAL MEDICINE HISTORY: The History of Female Ejaculation', *The Journal of Sexual Medicine*, 7: 5 (2010), pp. 1965–75. https://doi.org/10.1111/j.1743-6109.2010.01720.x

18. S. Salama et al., 'Nature and origin of "squirting" in female sexuality', *The Journal of Sexual Medicine*, 12: 3 (2015), pp. 661–6. DOI: https://doi.org/10.1111/jsm.12799

19. B. Whipple, 'Ejaculation, Female', *The International Encyclopedia of Human Sexuality* (17 November 2014), pp. 1–4. DOI: https://doi.org/10.1002/9781118896877.wbiehs125

20. John D. Nguyen and Hieu Duong, *Anatomy, Abdomen and Pelvis, Female External Genitalia* (StatPearls Publishing, 2022). https://www.ncbi.nlm.nih.gov/books/NBK547703/

21. Z. Pastor and R. Chmel, 'Differential diagnostics of female "sexual" fluids: a narrative review', *International Urogynecology Journal*, 29: 5 (2018), pp. 621–9. DOI: https://doi.org/10.1007/s00192-017-3527-9

22. F. Wimpissinger et al., 'The Female Prostate Revisited: Perineal Ultrasound and Biochemical Studies of Female Ejaculate', *The Journal of Sexual Medicine*, 4: 5 (2007), pp. 1388–93. DOI: https://doi.org/10.1111/j.1743-6109.2007.00542.x

23. Helen Thomson, 'Female Ejaculation Comes in Two Forms, Scientists Find', *New Scientist* (25 May 2018). www.newscientist.com/article/dn26772-female-ejaculation-comes-in-two-forms-scientists-find

24. Habeeb Akande, *Kunyaza: The Secret to Female Pleasure* (Rabaah Publishers, 2018).

25. Jonathan Amos, 'Ancient Phallus Unearthed in Cave', BBC News (25 July 2005). news.bbc.co.uk/2/hi/science/nature/4713323.stm

26. Fern Riddell, *Sex: Lessons from History* (Hodder & Stoughton, 2021).

27. Rachel P. Maines, *The Technology of the Orgasm: 'Hysteria,' the Vibrator, and Women's Sexual Satisfaction* (Johns Hopkins University Press, 1998).

28. H. Lieberman and E. Schatzberg, 'A Failure of Academic Quality Control: The Technology of Orgasm', *Journal of Positive Sexuality*, 4: 2 (2018), pp. 24–47. DOI: https://doi.org/10.51681/1.421

29. Robinson Meyer and Ashley Fetters, 'Victorian Doctors Didn't Treat Women with Orgasms, Say Historians', *The Atlantic*, (7 September 2018). www.theatlantic.com/health/archive/2018/09/victorian-vibrators-orgasms-doctors/569446

30. Jim Waterson, 'Half of Adults in UK Watched Porn during Pandemic, Says Ofcom', *Guardian* (8 September 2021). www.theguardian.com/media/2021/jun/09/half-british-adults-watched-porn-pandemic-ofcom

31. A.M. Maddox et al., 'Viewing Sexually-Explicit Materials Alone or Together: Associations with Relationship Quality', *Archives of Sexual Behavior*, 40: 2 (2009), pp. 441–8. DOI: https://doi.org/10.1007/s10508-009-9585-4

32. Estrella Jaramillo, 'Audio Porn? Women Are Leading In The Multi-Million Dollar Category of Erotic Tech', *Forbes* (14 August 2019). www.forbes.com/sites/estrellajaramillo/2019/08/14/audio-erotica-multi-million-dollar-opportunity-women-disrupting/?sh=c71dea26f489

33. Silva Neves, 'Compulsive Sexual Behaviour: A Paradigm Shift', *New Psychotherapist* (October 2021), pp. 42–7.

Chapter 6: What Kind of Sex Should We Be Having?

1. Sigmund Freud, *Three Essays on the Theory of Sexuality* (The Standard Edition of the Complete Psychological Works of Sigmund Freud, 7, 1901–05), pp. 123–246. https://icpla.edu/wp-content/uploads/2017/11/Freud-S-Three-Essays-on-the-Theory-of-Sexuality.pdf

2. Elisabeth A. Lloyd, *The Case of the Female Orgasm: Bias in the Science of Evolution* (Harvard University Press, 2005).

3. K.L. Blair et al., 'Not All Orgasms Were Created Equal: Differences in Frequency and Satisfaction of Orgasm Experiences by Sexual Activity in Same-Sex Versus Mixed-Sex Relationships', *The Journal of Sex Research*, 55: 6 (2017), pp. 719–33. DOI: https://doi.org/10.1080/00224499.2017.1303437

4. H.E. O'Connell et al., 'Anatomy of the Clitoris', *The Journal of Urology*, 174: 4: 1 (2005), pp. 1189–95. DOI: https://doi.org/10.1097/01.ju.0000173639.38898.cd

5. R.N. Pauls, 'Anatomy of the Clitoris and the Female Sexual Response', *Clinical Anatomy*, 28: 3 (2015), pp. 376–84. DOI: https://doi.org/10.1002/ca.22524

6. A. Carvalheira and I. Leal, 'Masturbation Among Women: Associated Factors and Sexual Response in a Portuguese Community Sample', *Journal of Sex & Marital Therapy*, 39: 4 (2013), pp. 347–67. DOI: https://doi.org/10.1080/0092623x.2011.628440

7. L.D. Wade et al., 'The Incidental Orgasm: The Presence of Clitoral Knowledge and the Absence of Orgasm for Women', *Women & Health*, 42: 1 (2005), pp. 117–38. DOI: https://doi.org/10.1300/J013v42n01_07

8. D.A. Frederick et al., 'Differences in Orgasm Frequency Among Gay, Lesbian, Bisexual, and Heterosexual Men and Women in a U.S. National Sample', *Archives of Sexual Behavior*, 47: 1 (2017), pp. 273–88. DOI: https://doi.org/10.1007/s10508-017-0939-z

9. E.A. Armstrong et al., 'Accounting for Women's Orgasm and Sexual Enjoyment in College Hookups and Relationships', *American Sociological Review*, 77: 3 (2012), pp. 435–62. DOI: https://doi.org/10.1177/0003122412445802

10. Laurie Mintz, *Becoming Cliterate: Why Orgasm Equality Matters – And How to Get It* (HarperOne, 2017).

11. Porn Categories, Pornhub. www.pornhub.com/categories (Accessed 18 March 2022.)

12. A. B. Mallory et al., 'Couples' Sexual Communication and Dimensions of Sexual Function: A Meta-Analysis', *The Journal of Sex Research*, 56: 7 (2019), pp. 882–98. DOI: https://doi.org/10.1080/00224499.2019.1568375

13. R. Roels and E. Janssen, 'Sexual and Relationship Satisfaction in Young, Heterosexual Couples: The Role of Sexual Frequency and Sexual Communication', *The Journal of Sexual Medicine*, 17: 9 (2020), pp. 1643–52. DOI: https://doi.org/10.1016/j.jsxm.2020.06.013.

14. D.A. Frederick et al., 'Differences in Orgasm Frequency Among Gay, Lesbian, Bisexual, and Heterosexual Men and Women in a U.S. National Sample', *Archives of Sexual Behavior*, 47: 1 (2017), pp. 273–88. DOI: https://doi.org/10.1007/s10508-017-0939-z

15. B. Voeller et al., 'Mineral Oil Lubricants Cause Rapid Deterioration of Latex Condoms', *Contraception*, 39: 1 (1989), pp. 95–102. DOI: https://doi.org/10.1016/0010-7824(89)90018-8

16. J.M. Brown et al., 'Intravaginal Practices and Risk of Bacterial Vaginosis and Candidiasis Infection Among a Cohort of Women in the United States', *Obstetrics & Gynecology*, 121: 4 (2013), pp. 773–80. DOI: https://doi.org/10.1097/aog.0b013e31828786f8

17. D. Veale et al., 'Am I Normal? A Systematic Review and Construction of Nomograms for Flaccid and Erect Penis Length and Circumference in up to 15 521 Men', *BJU International*, 115: 6 (2015), pp. 978–86. DOI: https://doi.org/10.1111/bju.13010

18. H.Ü. Sayin and C.H. Schenck, 'Neuroanatomy and Neurochemistry of Sexual Desire, Pleasure, Love and Orgasm', *SexuS Journal* 4: 11 (2019), pp. 907–946.

19. Carolyn Farnsworth, 'What to know about nipple orgasms', Medical News Today (27 February 2022). https://www.medicalnewstoday.com/articles/nipple-orgasm#who-can-have-it

20. The laws on revenge porn: https://www.lawtonslaw.co.uk/resources/what-is-the-revenge-porn-law-in-england/

21. T. Xue-rui, et al., 'Changes of Blood Pressure and Heart Rate during Sexual Activity in Healthy Adults', *Blood Pressure Monitoring*, 13: 4 (2008), pp. 211–17. DOI: https://doi.org/10.1097/mbp.0b013e3283057a71

22. B.R. Komisaruk et al., 'Orgasm', *The Psychologist*, 21 (February 2008), pp. 100–03.

23. P. de Sutter et al., 'Who Are the Orgasmic Women? Exploratory Study among a Community Sample of French-Speaking Women', *Sexologies*, 23: 3 (2014), pp. e51–7. DOI: https://doi.org/10.1016/j.sexol.2014.05.003

24. Amanda Chatel, 'This is how women are really getting off', *Bustle* (18 October 2019). www.bustle.com/p/12-techniques-women-use-to-have-orgasm-according-to-omgyes-6803697

25. E.A. Armstrong et al., 'Accounting for Women's Orgasm and Sexual Enjoyment in College Hookups and Relationships', *American Sociological Review*, 77: 3 (2012), pp. 435–62. DOI: https://doi.org/10.1177/0003122412445802

26. R.D. Schweitzer et al., 'Postcoital Dysphoria: Prevalence and Psychological Correlates', *Sexual Medicine*, 3: 4 (2015), pp. 235–43. DOI: https://doi.org/10.1002/sm2.74

Chapter 7: Consent

1. 'Rape and Sexual Consent – Chapter 6: Consent', Crown Prosecution Service (21 May 2021). https://www.cps.gov.uk/legal-guidance/rape-and-sexual-offences-chapter-6-consent

2. Thames Valley Police, 'Tea and Consent', YouTube. https://www.youtube.com/watch?v=pZwvrxVavnQ&t=109s

3. 'Gender Based Violence', Canadian Federation of Students – Ontario/Fédération Canadienne Des Étudiantes et Étudiants – Ontario. cfsontario.ca/campaigns/gender-based-violence (Accessed 4 April 2022.)

4. 'Sexual offences victim characteristics, England and Wales: year ending March 2020', Office for National Statistics (18 March 2021). www.ons.gov.uk/peoplepopulationandcommunity/crimeandjustice/articles/sexualoffencesvictimcharacteristicsenglandandwales/march2020

5. 'Nature of sexual assault by rape or penetration, England and Wales: year ending March 2020', Office for National Statistics (18 March 2021). www.ons.gov.uk/peoplepopulationandcommunity/crimeandjustice/articles/natureofsexualassaultbyrapeorpenetrationenglandandwales/yearendingmarch2020

6. Mariel Padilla, 'North Carolina Lawmakers Pass Bill to Close Sexual Assault Loopholes', *New York Times* (2 November 2019). www.nytimes.com/2019/11/01/us/north-carolina-sexual-assault-loophole.html

Chapter 8: Letting Go of Sexual Hang-ups

1. Katie Forster, 'Labiaplasty: Vaginal Surgery "World's Fastest-Growing Cosmetic Procedure," Say Plastic Surgeons', *Independent* (12 July 2017). www.independent.co.uk/news/health/labiaplasty-vagina-surgery-cosmetic-procedure-plastic-study-international-society-aesthetic-plastic-surgeons-usa-a7837181.html

2. L. Liao et al., 'An Analysis of the Content and Clinical Implications of Online Advertisements for Female Genital Cosmetic Surgery', *BMJ Open*, 2: 6 (2012), p. e001908. DOI: https://doi.org/10.1136/bmjopen-2012-001908

3. 'The Global Prevalence of Erectile Dysfunction', King's College London (3 July 2019). www.kcl.ac.uk/news/the-global-prevalence-of-erectile-dysfunction

4. 'Erectile Dysfunction (Impotence)', NHS.uk, (18 November 2021). www.nhs.uk/conditions/erection-problems-erectile-dysfunction

5. Suzannah Weiss, 'Why It's Never Mattered How Long You Could Last in Bed', *Playboy* (31 May 2013). www.playboy.com/read/it-doesn-t-matter-how-long-you-last-in-bed

6. C.H. Mercer et al., 'Changes in sexual attitudes and lifestyles in Britain through the life course and over time: findings from the National Surveys of Sexual Attitudes and Lifestyles (Natsal)', *The Lancet*, 382: 9907 (2013), pp. 1781–94. DOI: https://doi.org/10.1016/s0140-6736(13)62035-8

7. 'Female Genital Mutilation (FGM)', NHS.uk (18 November 2021). www.nhs.uk/conditions/female-genital-mutilation-fgm

8. 'Female Genital Mutilation', World Health Organization (4 September 2019). www.who.int/health-topics/female-genital-mutilation

9. 'Sudan Criminalises Female Genital Mutilation (FGM)', BBC News (1 May 2020). www.bbc.co.uk/news/world-africa-52502489

10. K. West, 'Naked and Unashamed: Investigations and Applications of the Effects of Naturist Activities on Body Image, Self-Esteem, and Life Satisfaction', *Journal of Happiness Studies*, 19: 3 (2017), pp. 677–97. DOI: https://doi.org/10.1007/s10902-017-9846-1

11. K. West, 'I Feel Better Naked: Communal Naked Activity Increases Body Appreciation by Reducing Social Physique Anxiety', *The Journal of Sex Research*, 58: 8 (2020), pp. 958–66. DOI: https://doi.org/10.1080/00224499.2020.1764470

Chapter 9: Relationships and Heartbreak

1. D.H. Baucom et al., 'Assessing Relationship Standards: The Inventory of Specific Relationship Standards', *Journal of Family Psychology*, 10: 1 (1996), pp. 72–88. DOI: https://doi.org/10.1037/0893-3200.10.1.72

2. Eir Nolsoe, 'How Do People Find Love?' YouGov (12 February 2020). https://yougov.co.uk/topics/lifestyle/articles-reports/2020/02/13/how-do-brits-find-love

3. 'Over 50% of Couples Will Meet Online by 2031', eharmony (24 January 2014). www.eharmony.co.uk/dating-advice/dating/over-50-of-couples-will-meet-online-by-2031

4. Mia Levitin, *The Future of Seduction* (Unbound, 2020).

5. A. Muise et al., 'Broadening Your Horizons: Self-Expanding Activities Promote Desire and Satisfaction in Established Romantic Relationships', *Journal of Personality and Social Psychology*, 116: 2 (2019), pp. 237–58. DOI: https://doi.org/10.1037/pspi0000148

6. Karen Gurney, *Mind the Gap: The Truth About Desire and How to Futureproof Your Sex Life* (Headline Home, 2020).

7. Gary Chapman, *The Five Love Languages: How to Express Heartfelt Commitment to Your Mate* (Northfield Publishing, 2022).

8. L. Firestone, 'Staying Compatible by Staying Yourself', *Psychology Today* (21 February 2011). www.psychologytoday.com/us/blog/compassion-matters/201102/staying-compatible-staying-yourself

9. Esther Perel, *Mating in Captivity: Unlocking Erotic Intelligence* (Harper Paperbacks, 2017).

10. K.P. Mark, et al., 'Infidelity in Heterosexual Couples: Demographic, Interpersonal, and Personality-Related Predictors of Extradyadic Sex', *Archives of Sexual Behavior*, 40: 5 (2011), pp. 971–82. DOI: https://doi.org/10.1007/s10508-011-9771-z

11. Justin Lehmiller, *Tell Me What You Want: The Science of Sexual Desire and How It Can Help You Improve Your Sex Life* (Robinson, 2018).

12. M.L. Haupert et al., 'Prevalence of Experiences With Consensual Nonmonogamous Relationships: Findings From Two National Samples of Single

Americans', *Journal of Sex & Marital Therapy*, 43: 5 (2016), pp. 424–40. DOI: https://doi.org/10.1080/0092623x.2016.1178675

13. Livvy, 'On Monogamous Non-Monogamy ...' The Other Livvy (16 May 2019). theotherlivvy.com/2019/05/16/on-monogamous-non-monogamy

14. From Shannon Boodram's website and book, *The Game of Desire*: https://www.thegameofdesire.com/commitment

15. E.M. Jackson, 'STRESS RELIEF: The Role of Exercise in Stress Management', *ACSM'S Health & Fitness Journal*, 17: 3 (2013), pp. 14–19. DOI: https://doi.org/10.1249/fit.0b013e31828cb1c9

16. M. Ridge et al., 'The fourth National Survey of Sexual Attitudes and Lifestyles (Natsal-4): Responses to the Consultation on Questionnaire Content', Natsal (20 October 2020). www.natsal.ac.uk/natsal-survey/natsal-4

Chapter 10: Sexual Compatibility

1. A. B. Mallory et al., 'Couples' Sexual Communication and Dimensions of Sexual Function: A Meta-Analysis.' *The Journal of Sex Research*, 56: 7 (2019), pp. 882–98. DOI: https://doi.org/10.1080/00224499.2019.1568375

2. Sigmund Freud, *Three Essays on the Theory of Sexuality* (The Standard Edition of the Complete Psychological Works of Sigmund Freud, 7, 1901–05), pp. 123–246.

3. Jessica Klein, 'How the Pandemic Has Changed Our Sex Lives', *BBC Worklife*, (23 April 2021). www.bbc.com/worklife/article/20210419-how-the-pandemic-has-changed-our-sex-lives

4. H. Woolhouse et al., 'Women's Experiences of Sex and Intimacy after Childbirth: Making the Adjustment to Motherhood', *Journal of Psychosomatic Obstetrics & Gynecology*, 33: 4 (2012), pp. 185–90. DOI: https://doi.org/10.3109/0167482x.2012.720314.

5. Beth Ashley, 'How a Digital Detox Could Transform Your Sex Life', *Red Online* (14 January 2022). www.redonline.co.uk/health-self/self/a27238848/digital-detox

6. A. Sansone et al., 'Relationship Between Use of Videogames and Sexual Health in Adult Males', *The Journal of Sexual Medicine*, 14: 7 (2017), pp. 898–903. DOI: https://doi.org/10.1016/j.jsxm.2017.05.001

7. R. Basson, 'The Female Sexual Response: A Different Model', *Journal of Sex & Marital Therapy*, 26: 1 (2000), pp. 51–65. DOI: https://doi.org/10.1080/009262300278641

8. N. Bunzeck and E. Düzel., 'Absolute Coding of Stimulus Novelty in the Human Substantia Nigra/VTA', *Neuron*, 51: 3 (2006), pp. 369–79. DOI: https://doi.org/10.1016/j.neuron.2006.06.021

9. Y. Wang et al., 'Novelty Seeking Is Related to Individual Risk Preference and Brain Activation Associated with Risk Prediction during Decision Making', *Scientific Reports*, 5: 1 (2015). DOI: https://doi.org/10.1038/srep10534

10. T. Wingo et al., 'Novelty Seeking and Drug Addiction in Humans and Animals: From Behavior to Molecules', *Journal of Neuroimmune Pharmacology*, 11: 3 (2015), pp. 456–70. DOI: https://doi.org/10.1007/s11481-015-9636-7

11. Ibid.

12. C. H. Mercer et al., 'Changes in sexual attitudes and lifestyles in Britain through the life course and over time: findings from the National Surveys of Sexual

Attitudes and Lifestyles (Natsal)', *The Lancet*, 382: 9907 (2013), pp. 1781–94. DOI: https://doi.org/10.1016/s0140-6736(13)62035-8

13. S.K. Gonzalez-Rivas and Z.D. Peterson, 'Women's Sexual Initiation in Same- and Mixed-Sex Relationships: How Often and How?' *The Journal of Sex Research*, 57: 3 (2020), pp. 335–50. DOI: https://doi.org/10.1080/00224499.2018.1489489

14. B.C. Leigh et al., 'Drinking and Condom Use: Results from an Event-Based Daily Diary', *AIDS and Behavior*, 12: 1 (2007), pp. 104–12. DOI: https://doi.org/10.1007/s10461-007-9216-9

Chapter 11: Casual Sex

1. Karen Gurney, *Mind the Gap: The Truth about Desire and How to Futureproof Your Sex Life* (Headline Home, 2020).

2. D.P. Schmitt, 'Universal Sex Differences in the Desire for Sexual Variety: Tests from 52 Nations, 6 Continents, and 13 Islands', *Journal of Personality and Social Psychology*, 85: 1 (2003), pp. 85–104. DOI: https://doi.org/10.1037/0022-3514.85.1.85

3. Wednesday Martin, *Untrue: Why Nearly Everything We Believe About Women, Lust, and Infidelity Is Wrong and How the New Science Can Set Us Free* (Little, Brown Spark, 2018).

4. J. R. Wood et al., 'Was It Good for You Too?: An Analysis of Gender Differences in Oral Sex Practices and Pleasure Ratings among Heterosexual Canadian University Students', *The Canadian Journal of Human Sexuality*, 25: 1 (2016), pp. 21–29. DOI: https://doi.org/10.3138/cjhs.251-a2

5. Peggy Orenstein, *Girls & Sex: Navigating the Complicated New Landscape* (Harper, 2016).

6. K.L. Blair et al., 'Not All Orgasms Were Created Equal: Differences in Frequency and Satisfaction of Orgasm Experiences by Sexual Activity in Same-Sex Versus Mixed-Sex Relationships', *The Journal of Sex Research*, 55: 6 (2017), pp. 719–33. DOI: https://doi.org/10.1080/00224499.2017.1303437

7. E.A. Armstrong et al., 'Accounting for Women's Orgasm and Sexual Enjoyment in College Hookups and Relationships', *American Sociological Review*, 77: 3 (2012), pp. 435–62. DOI: https://doi.org/10.1177/0003122412445802

Chapter 12: Sexual Health

1. Fern Riddell, *Sex: Lessons from History* (Hodder & Stoughton, 2021).

2. P.V. Liao and J. Dollin, 'Half a century of the oral contraceptive pill: historical review and view to the future', *Canadian Family Physician/Medecin de famille canadien*, 58: 12 (2012): e757–60.

3. 'National Health Service (Family Planning) Act 1967', UK Parliament. www.parliament.uk/about/living-heritage/transformingsociety/private-lives/relationships/collections1/parliament-and-the-1960s/national-health-service-family-planning-act (Accessed 29 March 2022.)

4. Kimberly Daniels and Joyce C. Abma, 'Current Contraceptive Status Among Women Aged 15–49: United States, 2015–2017', *Centers for Disease Control and Prevention*, NCHS Data Brief No. 327 (December 2017). www.cdc.gov/nchs/products/databriefs/db327.htm

5. THT Press Office, 'Heterosexual HIV Diagnoses Overtake Those in Gay Men for First Time in a Decade', Terrence Higgins Trust (7 February 2022). www.tht.org.uk/news/heterosexual-hiv-diagnoses-overtake-those-gay-men-first-time-decade

6. L.M. Lopez et al., 'Progestin-Only Contraceptives: Effects on Weight', *Cochrane Database of Systematic Reviews*, 7: CD008815 (2013). DOI: https://doi.org/10.1002/14651858.cd008815.pub3

7. 'Combined Pill', NHS.uk (11 March 2022). www.nhs.uk/conditions/contraception/combined-contraceptive-pill

8. Rachel Schraer, 'Are Women Turning Their Back on the Pill?' BBC News (7 August 2018). www.bbc.co.uk/news/health-44885503

9. Ibid.

10. J. Bull et al., 'Typical Use Effectiveness of Natural Cycles: Postmarket Surveillance Study Investigating the Impact of Previous Contraceptive Choice on the Risk of Unintended Pregnancy', *BMJ Open*, 9: 3 (2019), p. e026474. DOI: https://doi.org/10.1136/bmjopen-2018-026474

11. J.J. Reynolds-Wright and R.A. Anderson, 'Male Contraception: Where Are We Going and Where Have We Been?' *BMJ Sexual & Reproductive Health*, 45: 4 (2019), pp. 236–42. DOI: https://doi.org/10.1136/bmjsrh-2019-200395

12. Department of Health and Social Care, 'Abortion Statistics, England and Wales: 2020', GOV.UK (29 December 2021). www.gov.uk/government/statistics/abortion-statistics-for-england-and-wales-2020/abortion-statistics-england-and-wales-2020

13. T. Gondwe et al., 'Novel Bacterial Vaginosis-Associated Organisms Mediate the Relationship between Vaginal Douching and Pelvic Inflammatory Disease', *Sexually Transmitted Infections*, 96: 6 (2019), pp. 439–44. DOI: https://doi.org/10.1136/sextrans-2019-054191

14. J.J. Lehmiller, 'A Comparison of Sexual Health History and Practices among Monogamous and Consensually Nonmonogamous Sexual Partners', *The Journal of Sexual Medicine*, 12: 10 (2015), pp. 2022–8. DOI: https://doi.org/10.1111/jsm.12987

15. T.D. Conley et al., 'Unfaithful Individuals Are Less Likely to Practice Safer Sex Than Openly Nonmonogamous Individuals', *The Journal of Sexual Medicine*, 9: 6 (2012), pp. 1559–65. DOI: https://doi.org/10.1111/j.1743-6109.2012.02712.x

16. 'Gonorrhoea', NHS.uk (18 November 2021). www.nhs.uk/conditions/gonorrhoea

17. 'How HIV Is Transmitted', Terrence Higgins Trust. https://www.tht.org.uk/hiv-and-sexual-health/about-hiv/how-hiv-transmitted (Accessed 11 April 2022.)

18. The WHO Department of Global HIV, Hepatitis and Sexually Transmitted Infections Programmes, 'HIV/AIDS', World Health Organization (30 November 2021). www.who.int/data/gho/data/themes/hiv-aids

19. WHO Press Office, 'Globally, an Estimated Two-Thirds of the Population under 50 Are Infected with Herpes Simplex Virus Type 1', World Health Organization (28 October 2015). www.who.int/news/item/28-10-2015-globally-an-estimated-two-thirds-of-the-population-under-50-are-infected-with-herpes-simplex-virus-type-1

20. 'Genital Herpes? It's Not What You Think', Herpes Viruses Association. https://herpes.org.uk (Accessed 29 March 2022.)

21. C. Johnston et al., 'O11.1 Decline in Genital Shedding in the Year after First Clinical Episode Genital Herpes Simplex Virus Type 1', *Oral Presentation Session 11* (2017). DOI: https://doi.org/10.1136/sextrans-2017-053264.61

Chapter 13: Kinks, Fetishes and BDSM

1. L. Holvoet et al., 'Fifty Shades of Belgian Gray: The Prevalence of BDSM-Related Fantasies and Activities in the General Population', *The Journal of Sexual Medicine*, 14: 9 (2017), pp. 1152–9. DOI: https://doi.org/10.1016/j.jsxm.2017.07.003

2. Justin Lehmiller, '3 Sex Fantasies That Are More Common Than You Think', Sex & Psychology, (7 October 2021). www.sexandpsychology.com/blog/2019/2/1/three-sexual-fantasies-that-are-more-common-than-you-think-2

3. Justin Lehmiller, *Tell Me What You Want: The Science of Sexual Desire and How It Can Help You Improve Your Sex Life* (Robinson, 2018).

4. Franki Cookney, 'Most "Coronavirus Porn" Isn't What You Think It Is', *Forbes* (26 May 2020). www.forbes.com/sites/frankicookney/2020/04/30/in-a-global-pandemic-the-surge-in-coronavirus-porn-is-no-surprise/?sh=653c20012734

5. Melanie Curry, 'Here's Everything to Know About Adult Breastfeeding and Erotic Lactation', *Men's Health* (16 August 2021). www.menshealth.com/sex-women/a37105749/adult-breastfeeding-erotic-lactation

6. Hannah Price, 'Domestic Abuse Bill: For These Victims, a New Law Is Long Overdue', BBC News, (1 May 2021). www.bbc.co.uk/news/uk-56945169

7. Stephen D'Antal, 'Grace Millane Was a Member of BDSM Dating Sites, Jury Hears', *Mail Online* (19 November 2019). www.dailymail.co.uk/news/article-7699457/Grace-Millane-member-BDSM-dating-sites-jury-hears.html

8. Lizzie Dearden, 'Millionaire Who Claimed Girlfriend Died after "Rough Sex" Loses Appeal', *Independent* (15 November 2019). www.independent.co.uk/news/uk/crime/rough-sex-murder-john-broadhurst-natalie-connolly-death-defence-appeal-latest-a9203421.html

9. UK Government, 'Domestic Abuse Act 2021: Overarching Factsheet', GOV.UK, UK Home Office (25 January 2022). www.gov.uk/government/publications/domestic-abuse-bill-2020-factsheets/domestic-abuse-bill-2020-overarching-factsheet

10. 'Should BDSM Be Mainstream? | Kat Blaque', YouTube, uploaded by Kat Blaque, (10 March 2021). https://www.youtube.com/c/KatBlaque/featured

Acknowledgements

I'd like to thank my mum who has always been a supporter of my dreams even if she didn't quite get it at first. Without your love, prayers and wisdom I wouldn't be here. My sister, Temi, my world, my soulmate thank you for continuously letting me disturb you with all my random ideas, for encouraging me to drown out the noise and to always focus on my goals. To my partner who spent many late nights listening to me reread over chapters. I love you and thank you. I'd also like to show my gratitude to my amazing co-writer Franki Cookney who helped me along this journey. I appreciate the time we spent together whispering about sex hoping no one could hear our conversations at the RSA House. I'm also extremely grateful to all my contributors for being so generous with their experiences and allowing me to include many different lived experiences within this book. Thanks also to Olivia Cassano and Jeffrey Ingold for their invaluable and thoughtful advice. To my agents at WME and publisher, HarperCollins, thank you for giving me the encouragement to finally create the book of my dreams, *The Big O.*

Index